INTO THE PAST

Buildings of the
Mennonite Commonwealth

by Rudy P. Friesen
with Sergey Shmakin

INTO THE PAST, BUILDINGS OF THE MENNONITE COMMONWEALTH
Copyright ©1996 Rudy P. Friesen

Published by Raduga Publications,
a division of R.F.P. Holdings Ltd.
200-2033 Portage Avenue
Winnipeg, Canada R3J 0K8
Fax No.: (204) 885-1504
E-Mail: Raduga@FriesenTokar.mb.ca

Canadian Cataloguing in Publication Data

    Friesen, Rudy P., 1942-

      Into the past, buildings of the Mennonite
    Commonwealth

      Includes index.
      ISBN 0-921258-05-4

    1. Architecture, Mennonite - Ukraine. 2. Historic
    buildings - Ukraine. 3. Mennonites - Ukraine -
    History. I. Shmakin, Sergey, 1951-   II. Title.

    NA1455.U47F74 1996   720'.947'71   C96-920112-5

Printed in Canada by Christian Press, Winnipeg, Manitoba
Layout and cover design by Gerald Loewen, Winnipeg, Manitoba

International Standard Book Number: 0-921258-05-4

To my mother and father
who lived their youth
during the last days of the
Mennonite Commonwealth
and who instilled in me
a deep respect for my heritage.

CONTENTS

FOREWORD

When my son, born in Australia and raised in New Zealand, visited England aged eleven, he was eager to see the signs of a history in a land whose past he had only seen in books and heard his parents talk about. In particular he wanted to see old buildings, especially medieval castles. But when his grandmother took him to see a castle he was greatly disappointed. "It is all broken" he announced. *The Lord has thrown down the high defences ..., has levelled them to the earth and brought them down to the dust* (Isaiah 25:12).

The reaction of many North American Mennonite visitors to Ukraine on seeing the villages and remaining buildings of their former colonies is sometimes similar. Often the villages have disappeared, the remaining farm houses have nearly always lost their wooden barns and outhouses and, bedecked in Ukrainian whitewash, seem stunted and forlorn. Most of the walls and grand gateways of properties have been demolished for their bricks and the general sense of order and prosperity of streets, yards and farms has given way to a feeling of disorder and decay. Yet standing proudly among this apparent desolation are a number of impressive buildings, some stark and neglected like the sad walls of the Landeskrone church, but others still noble and functioning, occasionally even in their originally intended role. Factories still produce goods. Schools in villages and towns conjure up a time when Mennonite and not Ukrainian children once filled their classrooms. Municipal buildings, grand private town houses and even estates serve as hospitals, children's homes or government offices. The churches though have never echoed to the sound of music or prayer for over half a century although since the end of the Soviet era at least one has become an Orthodox church.

But if a visitor stops and reflects for a moment, it is truly remarkable what has survived from the period when Mennonites first settled in New Russia until nearly all had been forced to leave by the 1940's. More importantly the buildings clearly reflect in a stark material sense the immense achievements of Mennonites in Imperial Russia. From early earth huts to wooden buildings and then to structures of stone and steel, the built landscape bears mute witness to the development of a complex Mennonite world in 125 years. This included social and occupational diversity, an economy based on farming and industry with factories and mills, the increasing wealth of sections of the population, the complex construction of community welfare institutions beyond the local congregation and their meeting houses, and cultural pretensions with the establishment of centres of higher education. These cultural interests also are revealed in other aspects of the built environment. The impressive buildings the Mennonites constructed, especially in the late Imperial era, move beyond mere function and in their form and decoration reveal a new sophistication and aesthetic as well as a remarkable understanding of the wider world of architectural design and decoration developing in contemporary Russia and other parts of Europe.

It is clear that these buildings were places constructed to impress and to instruct not just a new generation of Mennonites, but also non-Mennonites. Far from signifying that Mennonites were the "quiet in the land" who owed allegiance neither to place nor princes and only to God, these new buildings often spoke loudly with the language of pride,

FOREWORD

progress and achievement. And the message they conveyed was clear. These Mennonites had arrived and intended to stay. But while buildings were built to outlive the generation which constructed them, all in the end will be broken, levelled and brought to dust.

Even so, it is perhaps ironic that while so much of Mennonite social and cultural life was suddenly brought to halt and weakened in revolution and war, and then brutally destroyed under Stalin, much of its built environment has survived because of the perversity of a Soviet regime which nationalized the buildings, but then lacked the wealth or skill to replace or upgrade them. And while we might welcome the fall of a regime which had long outlived its own rhetoric of righteousness, in the new environment of commercial growth and private ownership in Russia and Ukraine much of what remains of the Mennonite built past is at risk not from neglect, but from redevelopment. So this book is not only important, but also timely.

The book is also an immense achievement combining special skills with a particular understanding. Rudy, trained as a professional architect, brings his own skill and knowledge to understanding the complex world of the surviving and lost built environment of the Russian Mennonites who lived in what is today Ukraine. But, with the assistance of his Ukrainian co-workers and the fading memories of those who once inhabited this region, Rudy has built on his own ancestral roots to the area to contextualize the buildings in a wider historical framework of architectural and Mennonite history. At the same time this is not a dry work of scholarship, overburdened by footnotes and large chunks of text. While the text concisely informs, the eye and mind is fascinated with pictures of past and present, focused on form and detail, while understanding is amplified with plans and maps and contemporary advertisements. General readers will find much to inform, delight and surprise while scholars will have to rethink many of their assumptions about the complexity of Mennonite life in Russia and Ukraine.

James Urry
Department of Anthropology
Victoria University of Wellington
New Zealand

PREFACE

Much has been written in recent years about the Russian Mennonite experience, that is, the period of time that began in 1789 when the first Mennonites from Prussia settled along the Dnieper River in what became the Chortitza Colony, to 1943, when the last Mennonites left the Mennonite villages and embarked on the Great Trek to Germany.

Occasional references are made in these writings to the various buildings that were erected during this time, that is, until 1917. But they are usually made in the context of what the buildings were used for. Very little has been written about how the buildings came about, why they were designed the way they were, what influenced their design, and what they tell us about Mennonite life in Russia.

My interest in the Russian Mennonite experience began when I was a child. My parents often recalled with fondness their early years in Russia. Of course, they also talked about the very difficult years following the Revolution, and until 1926 when they were able to emigrate. In the summer of 1978, I had the opportunity to tour the former Mennonite Colonies of Chortitza and Molotschna, together with my parents. This included a visit to Rudnerweide, in the Molotschna, the village where my father was born and spent his youth, as well as Gnadenfeld where he had attended Zentralschule. This experience intensified my interest in the Russian Mennonite experience. Many of the buildings that I had seen photographs of in publications such as **Heritage Remembered** by Gerhard Lohrenz and **In the Fullness of Time** by Walter Quiring, I was able to experience in real life, and in their physical context. Although they were no longer in their original condition and although their surroundings had likely changed over the years, it seemed to me that to physically experience these buildings was the closest one could come to reliving that Russian Mennonite experience.

When the political climate in the former U.S.S.R. began to change several years ago, it seemed an opportune time to take detailed stock of what was left of the Russian Mennonite built environment, to document this heritage, and to make more people aware of it.

Although there had been many tours over the years that included the former Mennonite Colonies of Chortitza and Molotschna in their itinerary, usually only a few days were devoted to these areas. As well, there were many people who were very interested in their heritage, but had been hesitant to travel there. With the changes that were taking place, however, it occurred to me that the former Mennonite Colonies could become a significant tourist destination. I could visualize the restoration of some of the former Mennonite buildings and grounds. I thought about utilizing these buildings for such things as: providing accommodation for visitors; having our Mennonite colleges hold summer courses in former Mennonite schools with "graduation ceremonies" held in a restored Mennonite church; and developing interpretive facilities that would explain the Russian Mennonite story.

I was therefore delighted to read in the September 1990 issue of the **Mennonite Historian** that a certain Mr. Sergey N. Shmakin of Zaporoshye, Ukraine had taken it upon himself to restore the well-known Mädchenschule in Rosental, Chortitza Colony (now part of Zaporoshye) and to establish a small museum that would acquaint visitors with the

PREFACE

history of the Mennonite colonies in the region.

   The January 23, 1991 issue of **Der Bote** then carried an article taken from a Zaporoshye newspaper which described in some detail, the restoration work at the Mädchenschule and the beauty of its exterior. It referred to Sergey Shmakin as a native Zaporoshye, concerned about his city and committed to improving and beautifying it. When he discovered the deteriorating Mädchenschule it awoke in him a desire to restore it to its original beauty. I immediately made contact with Sergey. We determined that our interests and objectives were similar and agreed that there was a need to document and describe the former Mennonite buildings that still remain in order to increase interest in this heritage. The result was the decision to publish this book together.

   In October 1991, I was invited to Zaporoshye to begin the process of documentation. Sergey, Olga Shmakina and I toured the former Chortitza and Molotschna Colonies and inspected many buildings. Olga, a professional tour guide, has over the years accompanied many Mennonite tours and, as a result, has become very knowledgeable about the Russian Mennonite story. Her assistance in locating former Mennonite buildings was invaluable. After my departure, the documentation process continued. Sergey also took it upon himself to carry out an inventory of remaining Mennonite graveyards.

   As I began to research each of the buildings in order to prepare descriptions of them, I found information was somewhat limited. A series of articles were then published in **Der Bote** in order to solicit information from those who might still remember the buildings. Many readers responded with both information and photos. As much as possible, this feedback has been incorporated into this book. Since 1991, I have had the opportunity to visit the former Mennonite Colonies a number of times, each time discovering more Mennonite buildings and more information about them. But, there is still much research to be done. I view this book as only the beginning of the story about the Russian Mennonite "built environment", and hope that the feedback from readers will continue.

   There are numerous people who have assisted in making this book possible and who deserve sincere thanks. My co-author, Sergey Shmakin and Olga Shmakina, have shown their sincere interest in things Mennonite and have made a tangible effort to save a part of our heritage. Many of the fine photographs included in this book have been taken by P. Reitsin, a local photographer, and many of the building plans have been prepared by P. Turkovsky, a local architect. James Urry generously shared his knowledge, photos and thoughts. The late David G. Rempel indicated his willingness to share information, but unfortunately passed away shortly thereafter. Erwin Strempler, the former Editor of Der Bote, so capably translated my articles that were laced with architectural jargon. Lawrence Klippenstein of the Mennonite Heritage Centre provided valuable assistance. Alexander Tedeev, of the Zaporoshye State Archives provided valuable information about existing documents. William Schroeder graciously consented to the use of his colony maps in this book. Gerald Loewen applied both his talents and his patience to the book's graphics. Then there were those who provided additional

PREFACE

information and photographs, both current and historical, those who responded to the articles in Der Bote, either by letter, by telephone, or in person, and those who acted as couriers between Zaporoshye and Winnipeg.

Finally, I wish to thank my wife, Irene, and my family, for their support while working on this project.

Rudy P. Friesen
Winnipeg, Canada
July 1996

EXPLANATORY NOTES

- This book has been published by Raduga Publications, named, with respect, after the Verlagsgesellschaft Raduga that was established in Halbstadt, Molotschna Colony, in 1909. Raduga (the Russian word for rainbow) published, printed and distributed various Mennonite books, hymnals, and periodicals. Since it provided the opportunity for Mennonite books to be published, it seemed appropriate to resurrect the Raduga name for the purpose of publishing this book.

- This book contains information about the two original Mennonite Colonies, Chortitza and Molotschna, as well as several daughter settlements. Not all villages in each settlement have been included, nor have all settlements been included. Only those villages and settlements where adequate information has been found are included. A chapter has been devoted to each settlement. Within each chapter the villages are in alphabetical order.

- Within each village, only those buildings have been described for which adequate information was available. In some cases this includes buildings that no longer exist, where those buildings contribute to a fuller insight into Mennonite life at that time. Information for each building has been taken from a variety of reliable sources. However, complete historical accuracy cannot be assured.

- Numerous village plans have been included. They have been prepared on Autocad (software program by Autodesk, Inc.) and are based on plans obtained from a variety of sources. They appear with north toward the top of the page. They, however, are not always at the same scale since they have been reduced varying amounts to suit the format of the book. The buildings that are described for a given village are numbered. Those numbers appear on the village maps indicating their location. Buildings that still exist are shown as solid blocks and buildings that no longer exist are shown as hollow blocks. In some cases other significant former landmarks are also identified.

- The village plans also provide an indication of the layout and development of the villages. When the villages were initially settled, they were first measured and surveyed (abgemessen). The building sites, i.e. farmyards, were then defined by a plow furrow (abgepflügt). The farms were then drawn by lot (verlost). Each farm was usually 65 dessiatine in area and was referred to as a full farm (Vollwirte). These farms were not to be subdivided, according to the original Charter of Privileges awarded to the Mennonites. However, after the land reforms of the 1860's, they were sometimes subdivided into two, thereby creating two half-farms (Halbwirte), and occcassionally they were subdivided further into quarter-farms. Each village plan also made provision for smaller building lots for craftsmen and tradespeople (Anwohner). After the land reforms, some of these people were able to acquire small plots of land for farming purposes. These were

EXPLANATORY NOTES

referred to as small farms (Kleinwirte). In each village there were also renters (Einwohner), who worked as servants or labourers for others and who could not afford to own land.

- The Mennonite Colonies were required by the Russian government to implement a form of self-government. Each village had an assembly consisting of all adult male farm owners. This assembly elected a village mayor (Schultze) and two assistants (Beisitzer) for two-year terms. It was responsible for all local affairs including elections, public order, use of lands (including the planting of crops), fire regulations, and the communal maintenance of roads, bridges, and public buildings. Each colony formed a separate governmental unit or district (after 1870 the Molotschna Colony was separated into two districts). District meetings were held in the district office (Gebietsamt, after 1877 known as the Volost), attended by the village mayors, at which a district mayor (Oberschultze) was elected as chairman of the district, along with his assistants (Beisitzer). The district mayor represented the district at meetings with government officials and was responsible for affairs in his district, for community funds, and for passing on government orders to local officials for implementation.

- At one time the individual villages were referred to as colonies, i.e. the colony of Halbstadt. This included the village itself as well as the farmland that belonged to the farmers in that village. It followed then that the settlement as a whole was referred to as the Molotschna Colonies. To avoid confusion, however, this book uses the more common terminology, i.e. the village of Halbstadt and the Molotschna Colony.

- Mennonite names have been spelled in a variety of ways. In this book, an attempt has been made to spell Mennonite names the way they would have been spelled (in German) at the time of their use, i.e. prior to 1917.

- The use of building names in this book may appear to be inconsistent. Where the names of individual buildings are easily translated, this has been done, e.g. "Dorfschule" is referred to as the village school. However, where they are difficult to translate accurately, they have been left in the original German, e.g. "Zentralschule" is used rather than central school or secondary school. Buildings for worship were officially referred to as "prayerhouse" (Bethaus). They, however, were commonly referred to as "church" (Kirche). The term "church" is therefore used throughout the book.

- The various references in this book to measurements may appear to be inconsistent. References to land measurement are expressed in dessiatine, a measurement used since the first Mennonite settlers arrived. For comparison purposes this term has

EXPLANATORY NOTES

been used throughout. Distance measurements, however, are expressed in kilometres (km) rather than in verst, the measurement used at the time, since most references to distances may be of benefit to present-day readers and travellers. For similar reasons, building dimensions have been indicated in metres (m).

1 dessiatine = 1.092 hectares = 2.7 acres
1 verst   = 1.0668 km   = 0.663 miles
1 arskin   = 0.71 m   = 28 inches

• Considerable amount of white space has been provided in the layout of this book. Readers are encouraged to use this space to make notes, especially where new information has been found or where corrections are required to existing information, and forward copies of same to the author at:

200-2033 Portage Avenue
Winnipeg, Canada
R3J 0K8
or: Fax No.: (204) 885-1504
or: E-Mail: Friesen@FriesenTokar.mb.ca

1. HISTORICAL BACKGROUND

1. HISTORICAL BACKGROUND

The Mennonite story began during the time of the Reformation with the emergence of the Anabaptist movement. Followers of this movement were referred to as Anabaptists because they rejected infant baptism and rebaptized those who committed themselves to this new life of faith, seeking to live according to the teachings of Christ. The Anabaptists were considered the "left wing of the Reformation" and even Martin Luther considered them to be dangerous radicals that should not be tolerated. The central principles of the Anabaptist movement included adult baptism as a sign of faith, the formation of separate communities, peaceful non-resistance, and rejection of the oath.

Anabaptism emerged in the early 1520's, first in Zurich, Switzerland and then in southern Germany. Despite severe persecution by Protestant and Catholic authorities, Anabaptism spread rapidly across Europe.

In the early 1530's the Anabaptist movement also began in The Netherlands and northern Germany. There was an initial period of violence during which time some of its members attacked the City of Muenster in order to establish the Kingdom of God there. But soon thereafter, the Dutch Anabaptists moved in a peaceful direction.

In 1536, a young Catholic priest, Menno Simons, decided to reject the teachings of the Church and joined the pacifist wing of the Dutch Anabaptist movement. He soon became a leader amongst this group and by the 1540's his followers were being referred to as "Menniste" or Mennonites. He worked tirelessly for 25 years in The Netherlands

and north German states, with the authorities continuously on his trail. His motto, which he inscribed on all his letters and articles, was 1. Corinthians 3:11,

"For other foundation can no man lay than that is laid, which is Jesus Christ".

While much of Europe continued with religious intolerance and non-conformists continued to be burned at the stake, there was one area of Europe where authorities chose to permit religious differences. The tolerance of the Polish crown tended to attract many religious minorities, particularly to the Vistula River basin including the City of Danzig. Many Mennonite communities developed in this area, with the large majority of the people coming from The Netherlands and north German states (Lowlands), seeking both religious freedom and economic opportunities especially for their expertise in draining and farming marshlands. Others came from various other German states, from Switzerland, and from Hutterite communities in Moravia. The Mennonite communities in Poland therefore became a kind of "melting pot" of various Anabaptist groups.

However, there was one division that continued. In The Netherlands a division between Frisian and Flemish Mennonites had occurred, based on regional differences in customs and interpretations of congregational practices. These differences carried over to Poland, where the terms no longer had any regional meanings, but referred to differences in congregational matters. The Flemish were very strict, used the ban to maintain

1. HISTORICAL BACKGROUND

discipline, admitted few outsiders, and did not allow marriages to members of other Mennonite congregations unless they were re-baptized. The Frisians were more lenient and open, admitted outsiders, and allowed marriages to Mennonites from other congregations.

However, it was in the Vistula Delta area that the Mennonites developed their ethnic identity. Low German (Plautdietsch) became their everyday working language, although Dutch was the language used in church services. This changed to High German in the late 1700's.

They also found economic success in this area. Through hard work they turned the swampy marshes into fertile farmland. They created flourishing communities and became involved in the business and cultural life of the cities. By the mid-1700's there were Mennonites involved in most occupations including merchants, bankers, craftsmen, manufacturers, and brewers.

Although the religious tolerance generally continued, there were local regulations that placed limitations on the Mennonites. In some areas they were not allowed to have citizenship and in others they were not allowed to build churches. In 1772, with the first partition of Poland, most of the areas where Mennonites lived came under Prussian rule. Religious freedoms continued and exemption from military service was extended in exchange for annual payments to the crown. However, economic restrictions followed and by 1786 Mennonites were no longer allowed to purchase additional land.

With these restrictions on economic

development, the Mennonites began to look elsewhere for expansion. In the meantime Catherine the Great, the Tsarina of Russia, had issued a manifesto in 1763 inviting European colonists to settle land in southern Russia that she had recently won back from the Turks. She became aware of the dissatisfaction among the Mennonites in Prussia and in 1786 she sent a special envoy, Georg von Trappe, to persuade them to take up her offer of free land.

The Mennonites sent two delegates, Jakob Hoeppner and Johann Bartsch to southern Russia to investigate. They recommended emigration and selected a site for the first settlement, on the lower Dnieper River, near the City of Kherson. This area had good soil and excellent pasture, and was accessible to nearby markets. They also negotiated the terms and conditions of Mennonite emigration with the Russian authorities. These included religious freedom and exemption from both military service and swearing of oaths. Also each family was to be provided with 65 dessiatine of arable land, access to certain hay lands and woodlands, as well as fishing rights. Funding for food and transportation was to be provided, along with ten years of exemption from taxes. In 1787 Catherine the Great signed a decree outlining these terms.

That same year, the first group of six families left the Vistula Delta area for southern Russia. By the fall of 1788, 228 families had left. When they arrived in souther Russia in the spring of 1789, they were advised by Potempkin, then Governor General of the area, that they would not be able to settle on the land

1. HISTORICAL BACKGROUND

that Hoeppner and Bartsch had selected, because it was too close to the ongoing hostilities with the Turks. He directed them to an alternate site, along the Chortitza River near where it flows into the Dnieper River. Some of this land happened to be owned by Potempkin. The Mennonites were unhappy about this change, since the land was not nearly as good as what had been selected. This discontent continued for some time with Hoeppner and Bartsch being accused of deception. Hoeppner eventually even spent some time in jail as a result.

When these first settlers arrived at the new location they set up tents for temporary shelter. They then moved out to their respective villages as each village became established. It was a difficult beginning since many of the settlers' belongings had been looted during the journey. Upon arrival, the Russian government had not only located them on poorer land, but it also did not live up to its obligations in terms of finances and lumber for building. Also many of the first settlers were poor artisans with limited farming experience. Since there were no ministers among them, there was also a lack of spiritual leadership.

Initially most settlers became involved in sheep raising, silk production and spinning and weaving. But over time significant advancements in agriculture occurred and eventually the growing of grain became significant. Flour mills and factories producing agricultural machinery were subsequently established.

By 1824, the development of the Chortitza Colony was complete. Because it was the first Mennonite settlement in Russia, it also became known as the Old Colony.

In the meantime an even larger tract of land had been designated for further Mennonite settlement. It was located east of the Molochnaia River. In 1803, 193 families left Prussia to settle in the new Molotschna Colony. They spent the first winter with the Mennonites in the Chortitza Colony. Then, together with another 162 families that arrived that spring, they moved onto the designated land. These settlers were better prepared than those that had settled the Chortitza Colony. Most were experienced farmers who had sold their farms and were able to bring capital with them. They also brought wagons, farm animals, and furniture.

By 1836, 42 villages had been established by settlers from Prussia. By 1863 another 13 villages had been established, but they were all the result of internal Colony expansion.

The Molotschna Colony became the most successful Mennonite agricultural settlement in Russia and, up until 1860, was considered by the government authorities to be the showpiece of all European settlements. Much of its success was attributable to the efforts of one man, Johann Cornies. Cornies lived and worked in the Molotschna Colony. In 1830 he was appointed chairman of the Agricultural Society, an organization that was given extensive powers in the running of the Colony. He used this position to carry out reforms in agriculture, horticulture, and most significantly the education system. Some of the programs he implemented included crop rotation (summerfallow) and the

1. HISTORICAL BACKGROUND

establishment of small forests in each village. His authority also extended to the Chortitza Colony. Although his achievements were significant his authoritarian methods were controversial.

While the Molotschna Colony continued to prosper financially, various disputes developed including theological ones. The Kleine Gemeinde (small church) had already broken away from the Gross Gemeinde (large church) in 1812. Then in 1860 the Mennonite Brethren Church was formed by those who felt that the Grosse Gemeinde's spiritual life was lacking.

An even greater dispute that subsequently developed focused on land ownership. The original conditions of settlement did not permit the 65 dessiatine land holdings to be subdivided. Since most Mennonite families were large and only one son could inherit the farm, a large landless group emerged. Not only were they economically disadvantaged, but without owning land, they also did not have the right to vote and thereby influence municipal issues. The result was a long and bitter dispute between the landless and the landowners. It did not reach resolution until after the government stepped in and issued an imperial decree in 1866 giving the landless access to various reserve lands.

Eventually a land tax was implemented, whereby all landowners contributed to a fund that was used to carry out land reforms and to purchase new land. Money was also raised through a head tax and through renting public land to farmers. This led to the establishment of daughter colonies by both the Molotschna and the Chortitza

Colonies, throughout Russia.

In the meantime changes outside the Mennonite colonies began to develop. After its defeat in the Crimean War, the Russian government initiated a variety of major reforms. The ones that impacted the Mennonites most were the educational reforms which included compulsory teaching of the Russian language, and military reforms including the introduction of universal compulsory conscription. This, in part, led to the emigration in the 1870's of approximately 15,000, many of whom were conservative Mennonites, to North America (mostly to Manitoba and Kansas).

Those that remained behind accepted many of the changes and negotiated a new arrangement with regard to military service. The government insisted on young Mennonites serving their country, but agreed to allow forms of alternate service. The Mennonites chose to have their young men work at planting trees in southern Russia as part of an afforestation program. This became known as the Forstei and led to the establishment of several forestry camps in 1880. The cost of building and maintaining these Forstei facilities was fully the responsibility of the Mennonite community.

However, the Russification process continued and the Mennonites made every effort to maintain their separate identity. This led to the establishment of numerous secondary and higher institutions of learning, as well as hospitals and facilities for the aged, the orphans, and the mentally handicapped. The many institutions were financially supported primarily through taxation. Economic prosperity made it possible to

1. HISTORICAL BACKGROUND

meet these obligations as well as to pay the other necessary local and national taxes.

The nationalistic and revolutionary trends continued to develop in Russia, resulting in strong anti-"German" colonist feelings. During World War I, with Germany and Russia at war, a series of laws and decrees, referred to as the "Liquidation Laws" were passed by the Tsarist government, for purposes of expropriating the colonists' properties.

However, in 1917 revolution broke out, the Tsar was deposed and political chaos followed. Civil war broke out mainly between the Bolshevik Red Army and the White Army led by officers of the Tsarist army. The Mennonites also suffered from the attacks of bandit bands such as that led by the anarchist Nestor Makhno. With the victory of the Red Army in 1919/20 the Bolsheviks abolished private land ownership and all major industries were nationalized. With the end of economic independence and the loss of local political control the Mennonite Commonwealth, almost a state within a state in Tsarist times, came to end.

The Mennonite settlements suffered tremendously from the ravages of war including murder, rape and plundering. Drought, famine, and epidemics followed in the early 1920's. Soon after, the opportunity for emigration was created when Canada opened its doors. Approximately 20% of the 100,000 Mennonites in the Soviet Union at that time found their way to Canada.

For those who remained, life remained uncertain in spite of improved economic conditions. Many Mennonite teachers were dismissed and communist curricula were introduced to the schools. Young men faced increasing problems avoiding military service. Then in 1929 emigration was ended and collectivization of the land began. So-called rich Mennonites or "kulaks" were arrested and deported. Churches were closed and turned into club houses, nurseries, schools, and granaries. Ministers were arrested and exiled as were other leaders of the Mennonite community.

In 1937-38 the Stalin purges took place. Many hundreds of Mennonite men were taken at night and thought to be exiled. It is now known that most were shot the same night. In 1941 when war broke out between the Soviet Union and Germany, many Mennonite men were evacuated and sent east. During the German occupation that followed, life in the Mennonite settlements returned to relative normality for those that remained. Schools and churches reopened and some Mennonites returned to private farming. However, this only lasted until 1943, when the German Army began its retreat. Virtually all remaining Mennonites in Russia and Ukraine, totalling approximately 35,000, then left on the trek westward to Germany, some by train and some by wagons. Of these, some 12,000 found their way to Canada and South America. The others were sent back to the Soviet Union where they were forced to locate in the eastern regions of the country.

This brought an end to the Mennonite villages in southern Russia. Today one can only find the occasional individual of Mennonite background living in these villages.

2: MENNONITE BUILDINGS

2. MENNONITE BUILDINGS

"Architecture is the will of the age conceived in spatial terms", Ludwig Mies van der Rohe, 1923.

Buildings are an expression of the people who built them. They can tell us a great deal about the society that was responsible for their creation. Today little is left of the Mennonite Commonwealth in Russia, but many buildings still remain. They tell us about a people that went from modest agrarian beginnings, relatively isolated from the society around them, to considerable wealth, pride and significant involvement in society. It is quite conceivable that if life before the Revolution had continued on, the Mennonites in Russia would have assimilated into Russian society to the same extent that they have today in other societies. The purpose of this book is not to judge Mennonite society of pre-Revolutionary Russia, but rather to simply present the information that is still available through the buildings that remain.

When the Mennonites settled in Russia they brought with them certain building traditions from Prussia. Buildings were modest and utilitarian. As economic conditions improved, they became more substantial both in terms of materials and ornamentation. Yet little outside influence was evident. This was not only due to the fact that there was little contact with the surrounding society, but there was also little in the way of buildings that could cause influence.

In 1860, the Russian government began to carry out major social reforms which resulted in Russian society experiencing significant change. Rapid urbanization occurred and building technology advanced. But no dominant architectural style evolved. Rather, it was a period of eclecticism, where a variety of classical revival styles would often be combined on a given facade. Most buildings were constructed with brick walls covered with stucco, which could easily be adapted to create architectural ornamentation of various styles. It was suggested by one writer at the time to be "a disorderly mess, entirely appropriate to the disorder of the day".

This was followed in the early 1900's by the beginning of the modern movement or the "style moderne", which parallelled and was influenced by the developments in western Europe at the time. Those who recognized the need for modern architecture saw western Europe as a model and many Russian architects toured and studied in western Europe after their formal studies in Russia. The influence, therefore, of the early modern movements, such as Art Nouveau (France), Jugendstil (Germany), and Arts and Crafts (Scotland/England), is not surprising, although some of the early Russian modernists tended to take an eclectic approach, incorporating decorative elements from the various movements into their design.

The influence of what was happening in Russian society as well as in western European society can be seen in many Mennonite buildings of the latter part of the 19th Century and early 20th Century. They clearly indicate that the Mennonites were becoming acculturated to the society around them. Factors contributing to the design of Mennonite buildings that reflect

2. MENNONITE BUILDINGS

this process, include: 1. pressure by the authorities to Russianize the Mennonite people, especially through changes to their educational system; 2. a broad awareness by the Mennonites of what was happening culturally in other parts of Russia and in western Europe, through travel and the reading of various publications, particularly by those who were influential in and provided financial support for the many Mennonite institutions; 3. the training of Mennonite architects and engineers in Russian and western European universities; and 4. the possibility that non-Mennonite architects, engineers, or builders may have been responsible for some of the building designs.

Following is a brief outline of the development of various building types that took place in the Mennonite settlements.

HOUSING

When the Mennonites arrived in southern Russia, the first shelters that many of them erected were partially below grade sod huts with thatched roofs (semlins). Some also built small wood huts if lumber was available to them. However, they soon began to construct more permanent homes, based on a model or design that they had used in the Vistula Delta area.

The layout of this longhouse model was quite simple — the house, located near the front street, had rooms grouped around a central oven, referred to as the black kitchen (schwartze Küche) with its large chimney. The house was then connected to the barn (Stall), which in turn, was connected to the shed (Scheune), with all three usually being in a row, or in some cases the shed being at a 90° angle (Querscheune).

This model was actually brought by the Mennonites to the Vistula Delta from Holland, although the Dutch model did not have the central black kitchen but instead had a centrally located open hearth. They then adopted the idea of the black kitchen from their neighbours in the Vistula Delta. It was this model then that they brought with them to Russia. It is also interesting to note that, although they brought this particular model to the Vistula Delta area from Holland, they did adopt other existing forms of buildings from their Vistula Delta neighbours, for example, the square yard layout, where the house, barn and shed were laid out in a U-shape, but were not connected; another example was the arcaded farm house. But for some reason they brought only the longhouse model to Russia.

Most of the first permanent homes built in the Chortitza Colony were two room houses with walls of clay and straw, and thatched roofs. After approximately 1815 more substantial homes began to be built. The houses were constructed of square logs with dove-tailed jointing, while the stable and barn were of timber frame (Fachwerk), covered with vertical wood siding.

The first homes in the Molotschna Colony were similar except that the houses did not use log construction, but rather a form of timber frame construction (Fachwerk). The walls of the houses were plastered with a mixture of clay and straw and then whitewashed. Again the roofs were thatched.

2. MENNONITE BUILDINGS

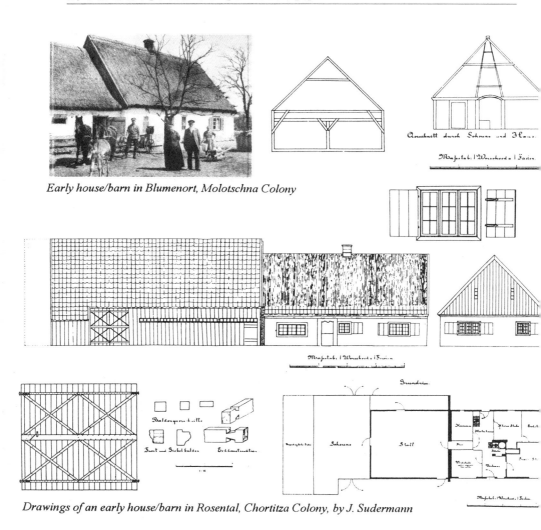

Early house/barn in Blumenort, Molotschna Colony

Drawings of an early house/barn in Rosental, Chortitza Colony, by J. Sudermann

Drawings of a country home designed by J. Sudermann in 1920

2. MENNONITE BUILDINGS

Over time the layout and design became quite standardized throughout the Chortitza and Molotschna Colonies. This is likely the result of the establishment of the Agricultural Society (Landwirtschafts Verein) in 1830 and its leader Johann Cornies. This Society controlled many aspects of Mennonite life in Russia including that of building construction. It prescribed the layouts for the houses and how they should be appointed, and specified safety requirements such as firewalls between house and stable, fire retardant-treated roofing materials (straw thatch and wood shingles) and spacing between buildings. Because of these rigid standards and because the Mennonite community tended to have little contact with its neighbours, there was very little outside influence on the design of its buildings.

By 1870 most of the first homes in the colonies had been replaced with structures of burned clay brick walls and clay tile roofs. However, even though new building materials and techniques were adopted, the house form was still virtually the same as that found in the Vistula Delta at the end of the 18th Century.

By the end of the 19th Century, however, the style had begun to change. Houses became larger and both houses and barns were built with highly decorative brick walls. Large decorative gates were located at the street entrances to the farm yards. Outside influences became evident and often non-Mennonites were hired to carry out the construction.

The large estate owners and industrialists generally abandoned the old traditional style and many constructed large, ostentatious homes in styles popular at the time in Russia and western Europe. These large estate homes present a major contrast to the modest homes that the first Mennonite pioneers built in Russia approximately 100 years earlier.

CHURCHES

The first meeting house was built in 1798 in the village of Chortitza, Chortitza Colony, not long after the first Mennonites arrived in Russia. In 1835 it was replaced by a newer, larger church building. This new Chortitza church building resembled a large farm house and was very plain in appearance. In 1822 a similar large church building was constructed in Rudnerweide, Molotschna Colony. It too resembled a large farm house and was very plain in appearance.

These early church buildings had their roots in the Vistula Delta area where the Mennonites emigrated from, and their design was based on the unique church design developed in that area. This unique design resulted from the distinctive concepts of the congregation and of worship, which their theology professed, as well as, from the fact that they were not allowed to build their own worship facilities up until the middle of the 18th Century. Until that time they worshipped in homes and barns.

But after 1750, when they were allowed to built their own worship facilities, at least five prayer houses, as they were called, were constructed in the Vistula Delta area. However, this approval was based on certain conditions.

2. MENNONITE BUILDINGS

In accordance with the restriction placed on Mennonites to not proselytize for their faith, their prayer houses were not permitted to resemble "churches".

These first five prayer houses that were built, therefore, were all very similar. They were built of wooden log construction, with steep roofs and plain windows and proportions similar to the houses. The main entrances were not emphasized and the sanctuary spaces were only subtly expressed on the exterior with somewhat larger windows. Generally the exterior appearance was plain, almost severe, in keeping with the Mennonite ethos of plainness. Inside, the seating was arranged in a U-shape around the slightly raised chancel which was located along the long wall. The men's and women's seating was separated. There was a balcony across the back of the sanctuary.

These early Prussian church buildings, then, became the models for the first church buildings in Russia, even though in Russia there were no similar restrictions. Although the Chortitza and Rudnerweide church buildings were built with thick brick walls instead of wooden log construction, their overall appearance and layout were very similar. In fact, the Chortitza church building was even more plain with all windows, for example, being equal in size. However, both were located parallel to the village street, thereby contrasting the houses in the villages, and therefore standing out from them.

The design of the church buildings in Russia, however, changed over time, at first subtly and later quite substantially. The church building in Ohrloff,

Molotschna Colony, shows similar proportions, roof line, and interior layout to the earlier buildings, but the window treatment shows a higher level of sophistication, both in terms of size variations and decorative treatment around them.

The design of the church building in Gnadenfeld, Molotschna Colony, constructed in 1854, was based on that of the Mennonite church in Danzig, and parallels the development happening there at the time. The windows were arched and the roof changed to a hip roof. The building was still located parallel to the street and, in fact, was given considerable prominence in terms of the village layout. The interior layout was still quite traditional, except for the two side balconies.

A similar church building was constructed in Neuhalbstadt, Molotschna Colony, i.e. large baroque-like arched windows. However, it had appendages to it, one for the main entrance on the long side, and at the ends for side entrances.

The arched windows soon gave way to Gothic shaped windows, in accordance with the trend in church architecture generally in Europe at the time to the neo-Gothic style. Along with the Gothic shaped windows, came other manifestations of the Gothic style including the most significant change to what had been a unique Mennonite feature, and that was the interior layout. To truly reflect the neo-Gothic style, the front platform was placed at one end of the rectangular sanctuary space, main entrance at the other end, and a centre aisle between the two. The axis had shifted 90° and the character of the

2. MENNONITE BUILDINGS

Chortitza Mennonite Church building

Melitopol Mennonite Church Building

2. MENNONITE BUILDINGS

church building was no longer uniquely Mennonite. Examples of this type of design include the church building at Nikolaipol, Yazykovo Colony, built in 1888, and the church buildings in Kronsweide and Neuendorf, Chortitza Colony. It should be noted, however, that these church buildings retained the cottage style roof, had minimal ornamentation on the exterior, and were located parallel to the village street.

But the neo-Gothic style continued to develop and church buildings constructed in Petershagen, Landskrone, and Schönsee in the Molotschna Colony, showed this development clearly. The roof shapes were changed to create gable ends, side walls had buttresses between the windows, and the exteriors had extensive ornamentation. They, in fact, resembled mini-Gothic cathedrals. The church in Einlage, Chortitza Colony, built in 1900 in this neo-Gothic style even had a "rose window" in the gable end, albeit of brick rather than of stained glass like the original Gothic cathedrals.

Similar to the development of the Mennonite homes, these church buildings with their style, ornamentation and layout, present a major contrast to the first prayer houses built in Russia.

SCHOOLS

One of the rights that was granted to the Mennonites when they first immigrated to Russia was the management of their own school system. In Prussia and the Vistula Delta they had already developed a commitment toward the education of their children, and this commitment they brought with them.

However, it seems that they built few schools in Prussia and therefore brought no real tradition of school construction with them to Russia. Yet soon after their arrival they began to build schools. Virtually every village, within a year or two after it was established, had its own school. The first schools were rather primitive and sometimes doubled as workshops so that the teachers could also carry on their regular work.

Although they brought no tradition of school construction with them, they did bring with them a rich heritage of building construction in the form of the house-barns and the prayer houses, which resembled the houses. The early schools were therefore very similar in terms of proportions and outward expressions such as windows and doors. Their appearance was plain and austere, with their steep thatched roofs and gable ends with vertical wood siding. Like the churches, the schools were placed parallel to the village streets, presumably to contrast with the houses.

In 1808, soon after the Molotschna Colony was established, a school regulation (Schulverordnung) was issued, which was to regulate school conditions and their construction in the villages.

Things began to change substantially in 1843 when the Agricultural Society (Landwirtschaftsverein) led by Johann Cornies was given authority over schools, first in the Molotschna and then in the Chortitza Colony. It introduced sweeping changes to the educational system, including school facilities. One of its many new regulations called for the old, narrow schools to be replaced by proper school buildings that would be spacious

First village school in Margenau, Molotschna Colony

Village school in Margenau, Molotschna Colony, built after 1843 with "Cornies" roof style

Village school in Rosenort, Molotschna Colony, built in 1895

2. MENNONITE BUILDINGS

and bright, thereby enhancing the learning process. Under Cornies' influence a new school building style evolved, identified by a hip gable roof. This roof became known as the "Cornies style" roof. It is said that Cornies preferred this roof shape because it reminded him of the buildings in his native Prussia. This roof style was also occasionally used on church and school buildings.

In 1870 the administration of the educational system changed again and school boards (Schulrat) were established in each of the colonies. However, Mennonite control over its schools gradually gave way to the Russian Ministry of Education and in 1881 all schools were placed under its control, and a period of strong Russianization began.

Despite this, Mennonite education expanded and many new learning institutions were established including Zentralschulen (secondary schools for boys), Mädchenschulen (secondary schools for girls), and Lehrerseminaren (teacher training institutes). There was a flurry of school construction during the latter part of the 19th Century and the beginning of this Century, up to 1914. Almost as many styles are evident from this period as there were schools built and generally they reflected the eclectic approach to architectural design at the time, in particular the incorporation of classical revival styles, e.g. the Greek revival style of the Halbstadt Zentralschule, Molotschna Colony, the neo-Gothic style of the Nikolaifeld Zentralschule, Yazykovo Colony, and the various styles of the Chortitza

Mädchenschule in Rosental, Chortitza Colony. But there was also some evidence of the influence of the Jugendstil and subsequent early modern movement, e.g. the Lehrerseminar, Chortitza Colony, and the Ohrloff Zentralschule, Molotschna Colony. These individualistic designs came from the individual architects or engineers retained for these projects. The designs may have also been influenced by the wealthy estate owners or industrialists who often were instrumental in the establishment and ongoing operations of these schools and were major contributors to the cost of their construction.

As with church buildings, these many Mennonite school buildings present a major contrast to the first schools built in Russia.

INSTITUTIONS

There is reference in historical documents dealing with Mennonites in Prussia to hospices. They were usually located adjacent to the churches and the services they provided for the homeless and the less fortunate were considered to be part of the church's responsibility. However, it is doubtful that they would have served as a model for the institutions that were eventually built by the Mennonites in Russia. It is likely that the first hospital built in a Mennonite village was in about 1870, in the village of Chortitza. However, it was not actually built by the Mennonite community but rather by the Zemstvo, which was a rural administration established by the local government. It was a small, very primitively equipped facility with two

2. MENNONITE BUILDINGS

beds that were maintained by the Chortitza factory owners since they were obligated to provide medical services for their workers.

In 1909 the Zemstvo constructed a new community hospital in Chortitza. Soon thereafter, in 1910, the factory owners built their own hospital next to the community hospital.

Around the same time a number of other institutional facilities were built in the Colonies. Between 1900 and 1914, three hospitals (Muntau, Waldheim, and Ohrloff) two homes for the elderly (Rückenau and Kuruschan), an orphanage (Grossweide), a school for the deaf (Tiege), and a school of nursing (Muntau) were built in the Molotschna Colony. During the same time a mental institution (Bethania), a TB facility (Insel Chortitza), and a privately owned Sanatorium (Alexandrabad) were built in the Chortitza Colony.

Since most of these institutions were supported by major donations from wealthy Mennonite estate owners and factory owners, their designs were probably influenced by these individuals, who were well travelled and knowledgeable about trends in other parts of Russia and western Europe. These facilities show a broad range of styles similar to non-Mennonite buildings of the day.

INDUSTRIAL BUILDINGS

When the Mennonites immigrated to Russia, many brought a trade or a craft with them and soon began to ply their trade. Many but not all of them, farmed as their main occupation, and carried out their trade or craft as a sideline. At first they worked out of their houses, e.g. weaving, clock making, etc., and in many cases they soon constructed small buildings on their yards for these purposes, e.g. blacksmith shops, bakeries, etc. Likely these first industrial facilities were very utilitarian in nature and sparse in terms of equipment, and it does not seem that they would have been necessarily based on any models from Prussia, with the exception of the windmills. The early windmills in Russia were very similar to those built by the Mennonites in Prussia.

Initially the production of Mennonite industry was mostly for local consumption. This did not change much until the mid-1800's, at which time it began to revitalize itself and changed to manufacturing for a larger market. New shops began to open throughout the Colonies. The most important industry seemed to be the manufacture of heavy duty farm wagons, referred to as Podwoden. The Crimean War of 1854-56 was a particular boon to this industry and after the war these wagons became particularly popular and the demand for them grew very rapidly.

This demand caused the manufacturers to streamline their production methods and to eventually diversify into production of other kinds of farm machinery. After 1860 there were a number of workshops that were producing a variety of farm machinery. These small workshops, which were still very utilitarian, soon expanded into factories. Between 1860 and 1914 this industry expanded tremendously and many large factories were built.

2. MENNONITE BUILDINGS

Early windmill

Pharmacy in Tiege, Molotschna Cole

Johann Epp Mill in Petrowka, Omsk Settlement

2. MENNONITE BUILDINGS

Another industry that grew rapidly after the Crimean War was flour milling. Although there were still windmills in many villages, many Mennonite entrepreneurs built large new steam driven mills during that time.

The construction of these large factories and mills was generally similar, usually built of brick with considerable amount of decorative brick work. The arc motif was particularly common in the brick work and often the windows were also arched. Some of the later industrial buildings became very decorative in their outward appearance, especially the mills.

Generally these Mennonite industrial buildings were similar in appearance to industrial buildings in other parts of Russia and western Europe. It seems that factory and mill owners travelled extensively, especially to industrial expositions in western Europe and sometimes even to America. They were likely influenced by what they learned and what they saw, and since there were few precedents for these types of buildings, this probably had a direct impact on their design. It is interesting to note, however, that although these industrial buildings usually used the most modern equipment and materials available, this was not expressed in their building design. Light steel structures were used and metal components such as stairs, e.g. the Chortitza Mädchenschule, Rosental, were manufactured. But the buildings were clad with decorative brick.

There were also a variety of other small industrial buildings in the Mennonite Colonies (brick factories, breweries, etc.). These, too, were usually constructed of brick and varied in their elaborateness of brick detailing. Generally they were not unlike similar non-Mennonite buildings.

OTHER BUILDING TYPES

Numerous other building types were constructed in the Mennonite Colonies in Russia, during the late 1800's and early 1900's. These included banks and credit unions, Volost buildings, pharmacies, various shops, and Forstei buildings. They, too, show a variety of building styles generally similar to non-Mennonite buildings of the day.

GATEPOSTS & FENCES

When the villages were first settled, very basic wood picket fences were constructed around the farmyards. Over time, however, this changed, particularly in the Molotschna Colony. It seems that when the Mennonites started constructing their houses with bricks they soon began to construct large gateposts and decorative fences, also using bricks. The fences were used to define the properties at the street and the gateposts were used to emphasize the entrances to the individual yards. Over time they became more decorative and ostentatious, one seemingly trying to outdo the next. The gateposts were much larger than was necessary, considering the scale of the farmyard buildings and the village street, and appear to have become a way of expressing the status of the farmyard's inhabitants.

The large gateposts were usually a mirror image of each other, except that

2. MENNONITE BUILDINGS

the one nearest to the house would have an opening that one could walk through whereas the opposite gatepost would have the lower portion of the opening closed in. The gateposts themselves were often not symmetrical in themselves with two columns carved into the brick on one side of the opening and a one column on the other side.

Schools and churches were also built with decorative fences and gateposts, for the same reasons. Usually they were designed in an architectural style that complemented the buildings themselves.

Gateposts in Ohrloff, Molotschna Colony

Gateposts in Alexanderkrone, Molotschna Colony

3. CHORTITZA COLONY

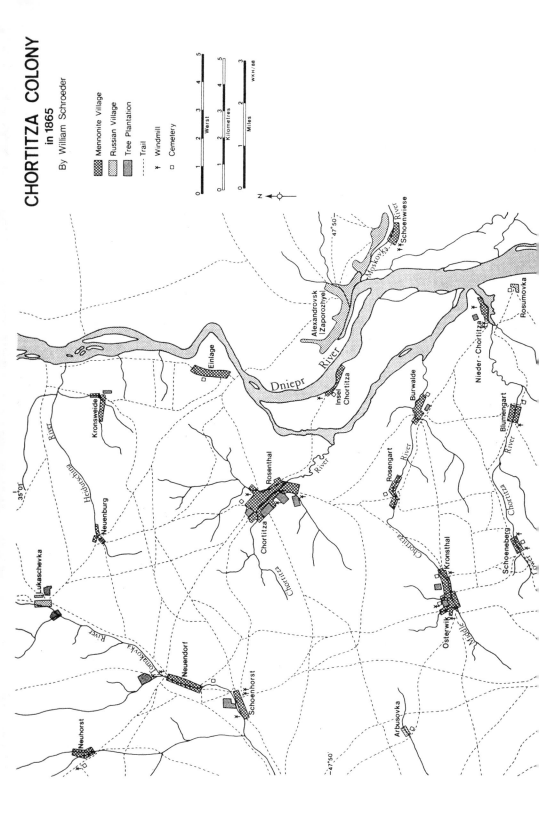

CHORTITZA COLONY
in 1865
By William Schroeder

Mennonite Village
Russian Village
Tree Plantation
---- Trail
⚹ Windmill
▫ Cemetery

Werst
1 2 3 4 5

Kilometres
1 2 3 4 5

Miles
1 2 3

WKH/88

N

Dniepr River

35°0′

47°50′

47°50′

Lukaschevka
Neuhorst
Neuendorf
Schoenhorst
Kronsweide
Neuenburg
Einlage
Rosenthal
Chortitza
Rosengart
Burwalde
Insel Chortitza
Alexandrovsk (Zaporozhye)
Schoenwiese
Rosumovka
Nieder-Chortitza
Blumengart
Kronsthal
Schoeneberg
Osterwik
Arbusovka

Tomakovka River
Chortitza River
Moskovka River
Chortitza River
Chortitza River
Mühle
Hertschune River

The former Chortitza Colony is located along the Dnieper River, with most former villages located on the west side of the river opposite the former City of Alexandrovsk, now Zaporoshye. It was the first Mennonite colony to be established in what was then New Russia. The first group of settlers consisting of 288 families, arrived from the Danzig area in July, 1789. Each family received 65 dessiatine of land. They established temporary shelters near a large oak tree in what became the village of Chortitza. Some of the settlers began to construct their houses on individual plots of land, similar to what they had done in the Danzig area. However, they soon recognized the security that villages could provide and relocated to the villages that had been established for them. By 1790, eight villages had been established.

In 1797 the villages of Schönwiese and Kronsgarten were established. Founded by Frisian Mennonites, they were the only villages of the Chortitza Colony to be located east of the Dnieper River. Schönwiese was located immediately south of Alexandrovsk. Kronsgarten was located northwest of Ekaterinoslav (Dnepropetrovsk), a considerable distance from the rest of the Chortitza Colony.

By 1824 another eight villages had been established, completing the development of the Chortitza Colony. The administration office (Volost) was located in the village of Chortitza. Although the beginning was very difficult, the settlement grew. From 1820 to 1850 the population doubled from 4,000 to 8,000 people. Grain-growing became significant replacing sheep farming. Eventually large mills and factories developed. By 1917, the Chortitza Colony had increased in size to 150,000 dessiatine, from an initial 33,000 dessiatine. With its significant industry, the Chortitza Colony eventually became the wealthiest and most important Mennonite settlement in Russia.

Eventually the original houses were replaced with more substantial brick houses. Although the early buildings were quite austere, the later buildings became quite decorative. The common village house was built of brick and had several windows, usually arched, in the gable facing the street. Many of the wealthy factory owners built elaborate and grand houses. The industrial buildings, too, were generally quite decorative. After the civil war the land was collectivized and the factories were nationalized.

Following are the present Russian names of the Chortitza villages:

Blumengart . . . . no longer exists
Burwalde . . . . Baburka
Chortitza . . . . . . Verkhnyaya Khortitsa
Einlage . . . . no longer exists
Insel Chortitza . . . . . Ostrov Khortitsa
Kronsgarten . . . . Polovitsa
Kronstal . . . . Dolinskoye
Kronsweide . . . . Vladimirovka
Neuenburg . . . . Malashovka
Neuendorf . . . . Shirokoye
Neuhorst . . . . no longer exists
Nieder Chortitza   Nizhnyaya Khortitsa
Neuosterwick . . . . Dolinskoye
Rosengart . . . . Novoslobodka
Rosental . . . . . . Verkhnyaya Khortitsa
Schöneberg . . . . Smolyanoye
Schönhorst . . . . Vod
Schönwiese . . . . Shenvize

BURWALDE

Chortitza Colony

The village of Burwalde was settled in 1803 by 27 families that cáme from various existing Chortitza Colony villages. It was probably named after Bärwalde in Prussia, modified slightly through the use of Low German. In addition to the 65 dessiatine that each family received, 325 dessiatine of surplus land was given to the village as compensation for its difficult to settle site. Also support in the amount of 1,040 Rubles was provided by the government. The village was located along a small river by the name of Ritsch, also referred to as the Middle Chortitza River, a tributary of the Dnieper River. The main street of the village was placed generally parallel to the river with farmyards on the north side backing onto it.

Burwalde had a village school as well as a church building that was constructed in 1864. There was also a store and a windmill. By 1918 the population was over 500 and there were 51 farms with a total of approximately 3,000 dessiatine. Today the village, known as Baburka, along with the surrounding land, is part of a collective farm. Very few Mennonite buildings remain, but a number of gravestones can be found in the cemetery.

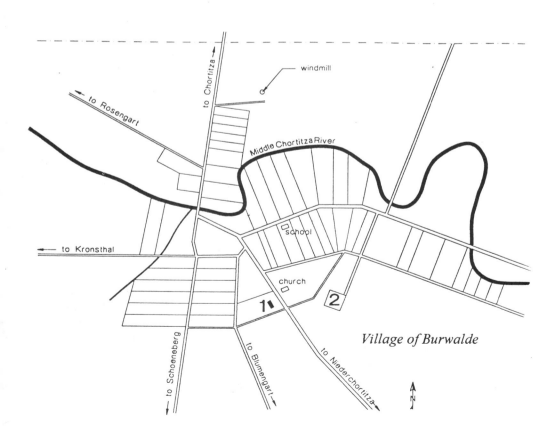

Village of Burwalde

BURWALDE

Chortitza Colony

1. STORE

This store was located on a side street, directly across from the church. It was similar in appearance to the houses of the village. The walls were constructed of brick, the gable ends were covered with vertical wood siding, and the windows had modestly decorated wood frames. This would suggest that the building was of fairly early vintage.

Today the building is still in fairly good condition. The walls have been covered with stucco and the original roof has been replaced with corrugated cement- asbestos. It is now used as a post office.

Detail of front wall

Former store in Burwalde

BURWALDE

2. CEMETERY

The following gravestones have been identified:

●Helena Tiessen
geb. Loewen
December 18, 1834 - April 30, 1864

●Helena Thiessen
geb. ...
... 1854 - ... 1872

●Johann Ens
August 19, 1853 - May 15, 1911

●Dietrich Hildebrand
March 18, 1824 - November 12, 1902

Aganetha geb. Klassen
February 10, 1828 - October 23, 1900

●Johan Patkau
March 6, 1837 - May 21, 1911

●Julius Ens
January 5, 1829 - June 2, 1905

Elisabeth ...
geb. Rempel
May 4, 1844 - November 15, 1909

●Katarina Töws
geb. Löwen
August 20, 1839 - March 24, 1910

Wilhelm J. Töws
September 19, 1840 - March 17, 1919

●Anna Pathkau
geb. Hildebrandt
October 27, 1838 - February 8, 1909

●Heinrich Hamm
October 6, 1825 - February 27, 1890

●Julius Pathkau
September 11, 1819 - October 9, 1891

Margareta geb. Hildebrand
January 25, 1820 - August 10, 1901

●Johann Klasen
August 8, ... - January ...

●Heinrich Klassen
June 19, 1832 - September 4, 1904

●Heinrich Klassen
April 5, 1900 - September 21, 1908

Abraham ...
January 8, 1908 - October 10, 1908

●G... E...
... 1849 - ... 1867

●F... K...
... 1791 - ...

●Be...
... 1854 - ... 1872

War damaged gravestone

BURWALDE

Chortitza Colony

Helena Thiessen, 1854-1872

Anna Pathkau, 1838-1909

Johann Ens, 1853-1911

Johann Klasen

CHORTITZA-ROSENTAL

CHORTITZA

The village of Chortitza was established in 1789, the first Mennonite village in Russia. It was located along a branch of the Chortitza River which flows into the Dnieper River, hence the village name. Initially, 34 families settled in Chortitza.

The first village street was placed parallel to the river, on its east side. Another village street was soon added on the west side of the river and parallel to it. This became known as the New Row (Neue Reihe) whereas the first street became known as the Old Row (Alte Reihe). These streets were then connected near the south end of the village with a cross street, to what became known as Main Street (Hauptstrasse). This street was a continuation of the Main Street of the adjacent village of Rosental.

ROSENTAL

The village of Rosental was also established in 1789 and was located immediately south of the village of Chortitza. It had one main street which ran parallel to the Chortitza River, although some distance away. The village was named after this river valley which was to one day have a large community garden filled with roses. Initially 20 families settled in Rosental.

CHORTITZA-ROSENTAL

Because of their location, the villages of Chortitza and Rosental became the most important centre of the Chortitza Colony. The Volost office, the administrative centre for the colony, was located in Chortitza. The largest church in the colony, the Chortitza Mennonite Church, had its main church building in Chortitza. There were numerous educational facilities, a general hospital and a hospital for the factory workers. There were as many as 131 businesses in Chortitza-Rosental, ranging from small stores to very large factories.

Today the two villages are a suburb of the City of Zaporoshye known as Verkhnyaya Khortitsa. Numerous former Mennonite buildings still exist. However the cemeteries of both villages are gone, many of the gravestones having been used in the construction of building foundations·over the years.

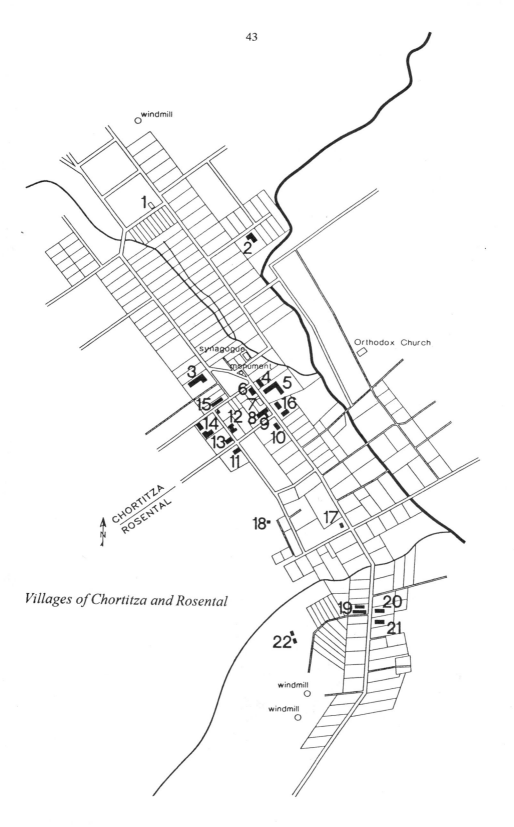

windmill

1

2

synagogue
monument

Orthodox Church

3

15

14

13

11

6 4 5

7

12 8 9 16

10

CHORTITZA
ROSENTAL

N

18

17

Villages of Chortitza and Rosental

19 20

21

22

windmill

windmill

CHORTITZA-ROSENTAL

1. CHORTITZA VILLAGE SCHOOL

The village school in Chortitza was built in 1912, replacing a very old school building. The new facility had two large bright classrooms with high ceilings, that could accommodate 40 to 50 pupils each. It also had a spacious recreation hall, a wide corridor, and two teacher's residences, one of which was in a separate building. There was a hot water heating system and a ventilation system.

The exterior masonry walls were plastered creating decorative features around the windows and at the corners. The hip roof was covered with metal sheeting and two steep gable facades faced the street.

At the time of the official opening on December 23, 1912, it was considered to be the finest facility of its kind in the Chortitza Colony and an appropriate monument to the importance of education. The building no longer exists.

Chortitza village school in 1914

CHORTITZA-ROSENTAL

Chortitza Colony

2. A.J. KOOP FACTORY

Abraham J. Koop first started as an apprentice under Pieter Lepp (Lepp & Wallman Factory). In 1864 he opened a small blacksmith shop in Chortitza. He built his own foundry in 1874 and substantially expanded it in 1877. The same year he set up his first steam engine. His factory manufactured seeder plows (bukkers), fanning mills, binders, and other farm machinery. In 1888 he started building a subsidiary factory in Schönwiese and transferred a large portion of his manufacturing activity there. Eventually the Koop factory, known as Gesellschaft A.J. Koop, Fabriken Landwirtschaftlicher Maschinen, became one of the largest Mennonite factories in Russia.

A.J. Koop Factory in Chortitza

CHORTITZA-ROSENTAL   *Chortitza Colony*

The buildings of the Koop factory in Chortitza still exist today, including the administration building which measures approximately 12 m by 22 m, and the factory building which measures 14 m by 22m.   They are not in very good condition.   The brick walls have been whitewashed and the roofs have been replaced with corrugated cement-asbestos.

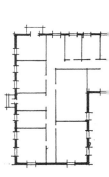

Administration building

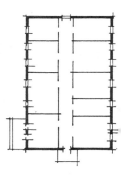

Factory building

CHORTITZA-ROSENTAL

Chortitza Colony

3. HILDEBRAND & PRIESS FACTORY

This factory was established in Chortitza by Kornelius Hildebrand who started out as a watchmaker. He soon got involved in the machine industry through the help of his mentor, Pieter Lepp. He built a small steel foundry and started producing plows and fanning mills. Gradually this small workshop expanded into the K. Hildebrand's Söhne & Priess factory which eventually employed close to 200 people. In 1890 it expanded to Schönwiese to be nearer to the main railroad. The factory specialized in manufacturing plows, mowers, threshing machines, and seeders.

Today the buildings of the Chortitza facility are still being used including the former administration building and factory building. The buildings were constructed of brick and although the walls have been whitewashed, the fine detailing is still evident.

Advertisement from 1913

Administration building

Factory building

CHORTITZA-ROSENTAL *Chortitza Colony*

4. NIEBUHR BANK

This bank was established in 1904 by the firm of H.A. Niebuhr u. Ko. which was owned by Herman Niebuhr and Jakob Dueck.

The building is of brick construction, with slightly arched windows, and fine brick detailing, particularly around the windows and at the base and top of the walls. It is a low scale building, set back a few feet from the street. The original roof has been replaced with corrugated cement-asbestos. The small entrance at the front may have been added at a later date.

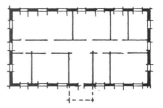

Niebuhr Bank building

Advertisement from 1913

CHORTITZA-ROSENTAL _Chortitza Colony_

5. LEPP & WALLMANN FACTORY

The Lepp & Wallmann factory was founded in the 1880's when Andreas Wallmann joined forces with his father-in-law, Pieter Lepp. Pieter Lepp had trained as a clockmaker in Prussia and had started making typical Mennonite clocks in Chortitza. In 1853 he produced his first threshing machine and in 1860 opened the first steel foundry in Chortitza. Andreas Wallmann was one of the largest estate owners of the Chortitza Colony and provided the capital to expand the enterprise. This factory, known as Gesellschaft Lepp u. Wallmann, manufactured various agricultural implements and became the largest of all Mennonite factories in Russia. In 1885 it expanded to

Advertisement from 1913

Administration building

CHORTITZA-ROSENTAL

Chortitza Colony

Schönwiese and by 1889 produced 1200 reapers, 220 threshing machines and 500 winnowers per year, as well as steam engines, boilers and hydraulic presses.

Today several buildings of the Chortitza facility still exist including the former administration building which measures 18 m by 26 m, and factory building which measures 10 m by 52 m. Both buildings were constructed of brick and had large windows. Although the walls have been painted, the fine brick detailing is still evident.

Factory building

CHORTITZA-ROSENTAL *Chortitza Colony*

6. VOLOST

This building was the administrative centre for the Chortitza Colony which included 18 villages. The administration's responsibilities included dealing with the elected village councils, schools, justice, orphan's fund, alternative forestry services, fire insurance, land purchases for new settlements and the construction of roads and bridges. The centrally located building included a large meeting room, a court room, archive, a safe, a room for the crown's representative, and three offices. The main entrance was originally located on the north side of the building and led directly to the meeting room in which district meetings were held. The building was described as "beautiful, functional, and roomy". In 1930 it was turned into a community club.

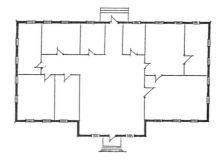

Volost building in 1900

CHORTITZA-ROSENTAL

Chortitza Colony

The building appears much the way it originally did. The front parapet has an arched section at the centre of the front projection. This design detail occurs on several buildings in the Chortitza Colony. The ornamental treatment around the windows creates a strong contrast. The sills of the tall vertical windows are quite low to the ground, reducing the scale, or apparent height of the building.

The original metal roof has been replaced with corrugated cement-asbestos and a small canopy has been added over the relocated main entrance door. The exterior brick walls are covered with plaster and painted. The brick fence at the street no longer exists.

Detail of side wall

Volost building today

CHORTITZA-ROSENTAL   *Chortitza Colony*

7. CHORTITZA MENNONITE CHURCH

The Chortitza Mennonite Church building was built in 1835 after the first church building, which had become too small, was taken down and reconstructed in the village of Neuendorf. The new church building was a large two storey structure with very thick exterior walls made of clay and then plastered. It was a very plain looking building resembling a large farm house with its clay tile roof and vertical wood gables. It was based on the design of the Mennonite church at Heubuden, Prussia, but was even more plain both inside and outside. The small shuttered windows were all the same size, whereas the Heubuden church and most churches like it, had two larger windows behind the pulpit. The main entrance was directly opposite the pulpit, whereas the Heubuden church and others like it often had the entrance on the end wall.

Generally the interior of this church was in the tradition of Mennonite churches in Prussia and Holland, with the pulpit/platform along the long side. This provided for shorter distances and more

View from balcony

Chortitza Church building from yard

CHORTITZA-ROSENTAL

intimacy between the speaker and the listeners. In this church the song leaders sat in a small balcony to the left of the pulpit. The women and children sat on the main floor and the men in the balcony. The choir loft was also in the balcony, at the south end of the building.

The church building was located parallel to the street with the pulpit/platform side facing the street and the main entrance facing the church yard at the rear. There was a brick fence along the street which also surrounded the Volost building next door.

This was one of the largest Mennonite congregations in Russia. In 1907 it had 3,570 baptized members and 18 ministers. The church was closed in 1935 and converted to a movie theatre. In the early 1940's it was reopened for a short time, but then later was demolished. A community theatre (Dom Kultur) is now situated where the church once stood. Although this building bears no resemblance to the original church building, it is possible that some of its walls have been incorporated into the theatre's construction. The walls around the main theatre space are very thick, as the original walls of the church were, and the proportions of this space are similar to what the church sanctuary would have been.

Chortitza Church interior in 1930

CHORTITZA-ROSENTAL
Chortitza Colony

8. CHORTITZA ZENTRALSCHULE

The Chortitza secondary school was established in 1842. The first building was constructed in 1870 and was located parallel to the main village street. With its arched gable windows, it is typical of buildings in the Chortitza Colony. In 1890 a 2 year pedagogical course was introduced and a model school was constructed on the same school yard. In approximately 1891 an addition was built perpendicular to the original building complete with a clock and a small bell tower over it. The clock was donated by the Kroeger factory. For many years this clock was the focal point for the Chortitza-Rosental community.

Today the building is still used as a school. But the famous clock tower is gone, the roof is now covered with corrugated cement-asbestos and the brick walls have been painted.

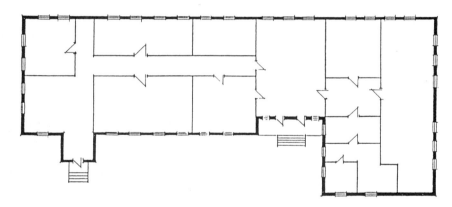

Chortitza Zentralschule in the 1940's

CHORTITZA-ROSENTAL

Chortitza Colony

Chortitza Zentralschule today

Main entrance

Window detail

Typical classroom

CHORTITZA-ROSENTAL

Chortitza Colony

9. MUSTERSCHULE

Located on the same grounds as the secondary school, the model school was built in 1890 when a 2 year pedagogical course was introduced at the secondary school. The model school was built as an elementary school, to provide teaching experience for those enrolled in this course. It also had a full-time teacher and approximately 35 students in five grades. The building cost approximately 10,000 Rubles to build. It was used for this purpose until 1913 when the teacher training facility opened next door.

Today it is a private residence. The roof has been altered and a small addition has changed its appearance somewhat. Its brick walls are painted, but the fine brick detailing, particularly at the top of the wall and at the building corners, is still visible.

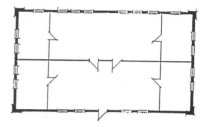

Musterschule

CHORTITZA-ROSENTAL *Chortitza Colony*

10. CHORTITZA MÄDCHENSCHULE

The Chortitza girls' school was founded on September 11, 1895 to provide a high school education for Mennonite girls. Tuition was 20 Rubles per year. By 1903 there were 71 students and so in 1904 this new facility was built in the village of Rosental. The cost of construction including the renovation of another building on the site into two teacher's residences, amounted to 39,000 Rubles. Mrs. Katharina Wallman, one of the founders of the school, donated 10,000 Rubles toward its construction.

On the main floor there were 4 classrooms with large windows, a spacious vestibule, a teacher's room and a teacher's residence. There was also a residence for the school caretaker on the lower level. A wide metal stair with decorative cast iron railings manufactured by the Lepp & Wallmann factory, led to the second floor where a large auditorium was located. Three large arched doors led into this auditorium where the girls assembled each day for the morning sermon. Since it was equipped with a stage, it was also used frequently by the community for concerts and literary events.

The front entrance, which was only used by the students on special occasions, had two large wood doors with a decorative motif consisting of circles with three vertical lines below. The arched window above the entrance shows the influence of the Jugendstil style with its pattern based on flowers, stems, and large leaves. The spacious front vestibule had enough coat hooks on both side walls for all the girls' coats and hats.

The exterior walls were primarily red brick with carved off-white brick used for various decorative elements, creating a rich and colourful facade with a mixture of styles. The front facade has considerable depth to it, and appears as a series of facades resembling north European canal houses.

This building is still in fairly good condition today and has been partially restored. The original black and sand-coloured tile floor can still be seen in the corridors. It still functions as a school.

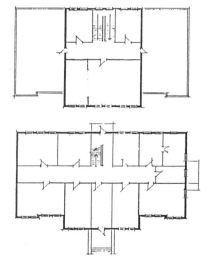

Mädchenschule in 1904

59

dchenschule today

Facade detail

Main entrance doors

Metal stair with "Lepp & Wallman" imprint

ond floor auditorium

Main floor corridor

CHORTITZA-ROSENTAL   *Chortitza Colony*

11. WALLMAN HOUSE

The construction of this castle-like building which became known as "Die Burg", was undertaken by Mrs. Wallman, the widow of the factory owner. She had received Kindergarten training in Germany and intended to include a Kindergarten facility in this building. Construction was not yet complete when the civil war began and was finally completed in 1930 at which time it was made into teacher's apartments. Today it is used as an administration building for the local educational authority.

The three storey building has walls of brick and stone with a variety of arched and bay windows. Some of the roof forms indicate a Jugendstil influence. However the original roof has been replaced with corrugated cement-asbestos.

Wallman House today

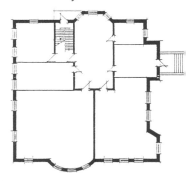

Wallman House after completion

CHORTITZA-ROSENTAL

Chortitza Colony

12. LEHRERSEMINAR

Constructed in 1912 and officially opened October 20, 1913, this teacher training facility was spacious with three large classrooms and a very large auditorium which was used not only for school theatre productions but also for community functions. It also included a model school for practice teaching elementary students. The walls were made of dark brown brick with vertical pilasters between the windows and an unusual Jugendstil influenced main entrance design. The roof appears to have been metal sheeting.

Today the building exterior is much like it was originally, except that the roof is now corrugated cement-asbestos and a third wing has been added at the rear. It is still being used as a school.

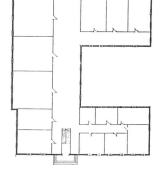

...hrerseminar after completion

Lehrerseminar today

CHORTITZA-ROSENTAL

Chortitza Colony

Lehrerseminar before the Revolution

Window detail

Entrance facade

Main entrance

CHORTITZA-ROSENTAL
Chortitza Colony

13. FACTORY HOSPITAL

This hospital was built for factory workers in about 1910. It was primarily funded by the Lepp & Wallmann factory. Today it is still used as a hospital and is part of the large adjacent hospital complex. Its brown brick construction and detailing compliment the other hospital buildings.

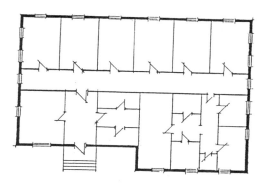

Factory Hospital

CHORTITZA-ROSENTAL

14. HOSPITAL

Until approximately 1880, the village of Chortitza had a very small and primitive hospital that served the whole Colony. Around that time the first doctor, Dr. Jacob Esau, began to serve the hospital and so it was expanded with the construction of a small operating room. By 1904 it had 12 hospital beds. Then in 1909, a new hospital was built in Chortitza by the regional government (Zemstvo) to serve the surrounding area. The buildings that still exist today were built between 1909 and 1912, but have been subsequently modified.

Around the same time, the factory owners, who were responsible for providing medical services for their workers, constructed a separate factory hospital adjacent to the regional hospital facilities.

Today these buildings are all part of a complex that still functions as a hospital. The buildings are of various shapes and sizes but are built of the same brown brick with similarities in detailing that create an overall consistency.

Doctor's Residence in 1912

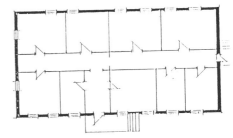

Former Doctor's Residence, now Maternity House

CHORTITZA-ROSENTAL

Chortitza Colony

15. HOUSING FOR FACTORY WORKERS

This rowhousing was provided for the factory workers of Chortitza. Housing was provided for many of the workers of the various factories. These houses were probably for the workers at the Lepp & Wallmann factory. Each was approximately 83 m² in area. The walls were brick and the roofs were clay tile.

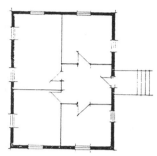

Factory worker's house

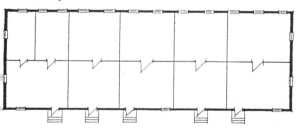

Row housing for factory workers

16. H. DYCK HOUSE AND MILL

This house and adjacent mill belonged to the H. Dyck family. Located on the border between the two villages, the house was in Chortitza and the mill in Rosental.

The 1½ storey house was constructed of brick. It was located parallel to the street. An intersecting roof created a gable facade facing the street which emphasized the front entrance. A second floor balcony extended over the entrance.

The elaborate brickwork is still evident. The gables all have small circular windows and the end gables have larger arched windows similar to other houses of the area. The building is not in very good condition. The exterior walls have been painted and various additions and modifications have been made to it. The original roof has been replaced with corrugated cement-asbestos.

The flour mill was also built of brick. It has been changed substantially. The height has been reduced, the roof structure has been replaced, and the exterior walls have been painted. However, the suggestion of vertical columns is still evident in the brickwork. Both buildings are still used today for industrial purposes.

H. Dyck House

H. Dyck Mill

CHORTITZA-ROSENTAL   *Chortitza Colony*

17. ROSENTAL VILLAGE SCHOOL

The village school in Rosental was located near the centre of the village. Built around 1900, the one storey structure was placed parallel to the street. The exterior walls were brick and included a variety of window openings including three fully arched windows facing the street. The roof was covered with clay tiles.

Today the building is painted a dull green, with the brickwork around the windows and at the building corners painted white to emphasize these details. The roof structures and gables have been changed and the roofs are now covered with corrugated cement-asbestos. The building is no longer used as a school. Today it is a factory producing precast

concrete floor slabs. It is likely that the second wing was built at a much later date. Although the brick detailing complements the original building, it is much narrower in width.

Window detail

Rosental village school building today

Rosental village school in 1913

18. PHOTO ATELIER

The photographer, Peter Gerhard Rempel, built this studio behind his house in Rosental in 1908, after his return from Germany, where he had trained to become a photographer. Its design is very interesting in that it seems to have been ahead of its time. It is similar to a painting by Mondrian, the Dutch abstractionist painter. Yet abstract art did not really begin until several years later. Actually, at the time, Classical Revival styles were still common in architecture and the Jugendstil movement had become popular in western Europe. There were very few buildings at the time where the structure was so clearly expressed on the exterior, where there was a total absence of ornament, and where the windows were no longer "holes in the wall", but rather large curtains of glass. The Deutscher Werkbund, which advocated this kind of design philosophy, was established in 1907, and may have influenced the design of this studio. The Deutscher Werkbund eventually lead to the International Style and the establishment of the Bauhaus in the 1920's.

This studio had a simple wood post and beam structure with brick infill and a large curtain of windows. There was no ornamentation other than the structure itself. It was a simple utilitarian building.

The large window wall provided natural light for taking photos inside. The glass was white-washed to filter the light. The amount of light was controlled with curtains hung along the inside of the window wall. A portion of the roof was also glass and the light through it was controlled by moveable slats along the ceiling.

It is not known whether Peter Rempel designed this building himself. Since his brother Gerhard was an architect and his brother Johann an engineer, he may have had some assistance. Unfortunately the building no longer exists today.

Peter Rempel's Photo Atelier in 1910

CHORTITZA-ROSENTAL
Chortitza Colony

19. KROEGER FACTORY

The Kroeger Clock factory had its beginnings when Johann Kroeger came from West Prussia to Chortitza in 1804 bringing with him his skills as a clockmaker and some basic tools and materials to make clocks. From modest beginnings in a small cottage, the business grew to the point where in approximately 1900 a new 2 storey workshop and office building was built with provision for future expansion. It included a blacksmith shop and a foundry, as well as an adjacent residence and stable for horses.

The workshop measured 9 m wide by 13 m long, with the narrower gable end facing the street. The building was constructed of locally made red bricks and a red clay tile roof. The brick walls had pilasters at each corner, a projected brick cornice, and decorative peaked brick lintels over the windows. The front entrance projected out slightly and had a DAVID KRÖGER sign (in Russian) over it which included a clock. The gable had vertical wood siding and two arched windows. The overall appearance was relatively austere and simple.

In approximately 1910, the workshop was expanded with a 8.5 m long addition to the rear and a small addition to the north side which included a stair to the upper floor. A further addition to the rear, 9 m in length, was subsequently built to house the foundry.

The ground floor of the building was used as office and showroom, with the casting cleaning room at the back. On the upper floor were the machine shop and fitting and assembly shops. The attic was used as the pattern/paint shop as well as for storage. The cast iron and brass foundries were at the rear. On the same property was a small brick building which was used as a blacksmith's shop and core shop.

Adjacent to the workshop was the residence of David D. Kroeger, the owner and great grandson of Johann Kroeger. It was also made of local red brick walls and red tile roof. It was built like a typical Mennonite farmer's house, similar to the others in the villages, with the dwelling toward the street, a summer kitchen to the side, and a barn and shed to the rear, the latter built of wood.

In addition to the pendulum wall clocks found in most Mennonite homes, the factory also produced large clocks for factories, mills, and schools as well as steeple clocks for churches. The secondary school in Chortitza had a steeple clock from this factory, as did a church in Moscow.

Eventually the production of clocks was replaced by such items as Kroeger stationary engines (manufactured under license from Germany), plow-shares and other agricultural machinery parts.

Advertisement from 1904

CHORTITZA-ROSENTAL   *Chortitza Colony*

Soon after the sons, David Kroeger and Johann Kroeger took over the business, it was separated, with David taking ownership of this factory and Johann taking the clock manufacturing to another location in Rosental.

In 1923 this factory was expropriated. It continued to produce motors, metal parts for farm machines, and metal lathes up until 1930. There were approximately 40 employees at that time. From 1927 to 1930 it also became a teaching facility for a local technical school. But after 1930 all the machinery was removed and relocated to a technical teaching facility in Chortitza. In 1931 the buildings were all transferred to the local collective farm, "Rote Fahne", the workshop being converted to a clubhouse and the family house to an office. Today the former workshop is a cinema and the former house a grocery store. They have been altered considerably. A non-descript addition has been constructed at the front of the workshop and the windows along the side walls have been filled in with brick. However, the cornice and the details over the windows are still visible.

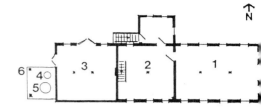

1.   MACHINE SHOP
2.   FIT-UP AND SHEET METAL SHOP
3.   FOUNDRY
4.   CAST IRON SMELTER
5.   BRASS SMELTER
6.   FUEL AND RAW MATERIALS SHED

Kroeger Factory building in 1902

Kroeger Factory building today

CHORTITZA-ROSENTAL   *Chortitza Colony*

20. JOHANN D. KROEGER HOUSE

Located across the street from the Kroeger factory, this house at one time belonged to Johann D. Kroeger, great-grandson of founder Johann Kroeger. When Johann relocated the clock factory to another site in Rosental, he also relocated his residence to that site.

This house was typical of the older houses in the village, with the connected barn and shed to the rear. The front gable was covered with vertical wood siding. The house appears to have the original clay tile roof and decorative wood frames and shutters around the windows.

Johann Kroeger House

CHORTITZA-ROSENTAL

Chortitza Colony

21. DAVID KROEGER HOUSE

Located immediately south of the Johann D. Kroeger House, this house once belonged to David Kroeger, grandson of founder Johann Kroeger. Built sometime after 1859, this house was typical of the older houses in the village, with the connected barn and shed to the rear. The rooms of the house were grouped around the central kitchen and chimney. The front gable was covered with vertical wood siding. The house appears to have the original clay tile roof and decorative wood frames around the windows.

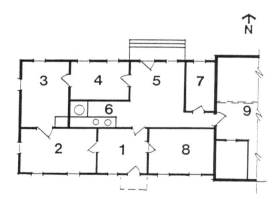

1. FRONT ENTRANCE
2. PARLOR
3. BEDROOM
4. BEDROOM
5. REAR ENTRY AND EATING AREA
6. KITCHEN
7. PANTRY
8. SUMMER ROOM
9. BARN & STABLE

CHORTITZA-ROSENTAL

Chortitza Colony

22. PENNER BRICK FACTORY

This brick factory owned by Johannes Penner, was one of two such factories in Chortitza-Rosental. There are two remaining buildings. They are built of brick, but the original tile roofs have been replaced with corrugated cement-asbestos. They are no longer used as a brick factory.

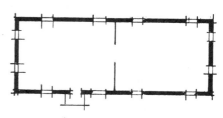

Penner Brick Factory buildings

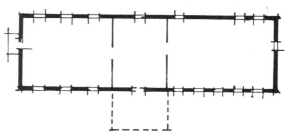

EINLAGE

The village of Einlage was established in 1789 by 41 families from Prussia. It was named after a village in Prussia by the same name, which was located in a low area at a bend in the Nogat River, a location very similar to that of this new village along the Dnieper River. Soon after the village was settled, it experienced serious flooding. It was then moved to slightly higher ground.

The location of Einlage was quite favourable for agriculture, industry and business. Early industries included the first Mennonite wagon factory (H. Unger) and a factory (J. Friesen) that produced the first grain reaper in 1879. This factory was later taken over by Koop & Co. and expanded to produce motors, steel rollers for rolling mills and other agriculture related products. There were also several large flour mills (including H. Unger and K. Martens), lumber yards, carpenter shops and numerous other businesses. Between 1902 and 1907 a railroad was built through Einlage which contributed to further development of business and industry. This railroad crossed the Dnieper River on one of the largest arch-span supported bridges in the world at that time.

Soon after the settlement began, a village school was constructed. It was replaced several times. The last replacement was constructed in 1900. It had four large classrooms and a library. A private school also operated for a period of time. There were two churches, including a Mennonite Brethren church constructed in 1904.

Einlage became one of the largest villages in the Chortitza Colony. By 1914 it had a population of 1,500 and approximately 3,000 dessiatine of land. However, during the civil war it suffered the same consequences as the rest of the Colony. Then during the 1920's a large hydro-electric power dam, Dnjeprostroj, was constructed on the Dnieper River, and the village of Einlage disappeared under water. A new settlement was subsequently established on higher land nearby. The dedication of this new settlement occurred on October 23, 1927. It was again named Einlage, but was later changed to Kitchkas.

EINLAGE

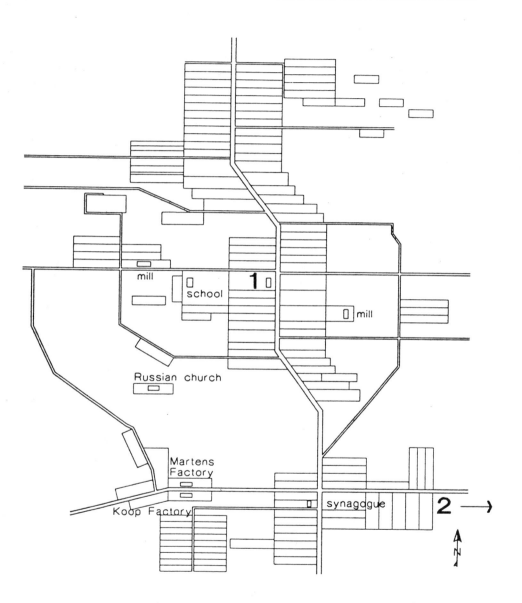

Village of Einlage

EINLAGE

1. MENNONITE CHURCH

The Einlage Mennonite Church building was completed December 27, 1900 at a cost of almost 17,000 Rubles. Prior to this, church services were held in the village school. Responsible for its construction were Peter Reimer, Jakob Fröse, and Abraham Unger.

The church building was built in a neo-Gothic style complete with large Gothic shaped windows and large circular brick patterns on the end walls that gave the appearance of "rose" windows such as those found on the large Gothic cathedrals of Western Europe. It is said that the design was actually based on the Heubudener Mennonite Church in Marburg, West Prussia, and that consideration had been given to building a bell tower similar to the Mennonite Church in Melitopol.

The layout of the church building was similar to other Mennonite churches built at that time, with a long rectangular sanctuary having the pulpit/platform at one end, and a balcony with a harmonium organ at the other end. However, the rectangular plan of approximately 12m by 24m, was placed at right angles to the street. The sanctuary had a seating capacity of over 400. There were

extensions off either side of the sanctuary which contained separate entrances for men and women. The men's entrance also included a room for the song leaders (Vorsänger) with direct access to the sanctuary. A high brick fence separated the church grounds from the main street. A very ornate brick entrance gate provided access to the churchyard.

The building no longer exists today. It is said that it was dismantled prior to Einlage being flooded by the power dam.

Interior view, pulpit/platform

Interior view, balcony

Street facade of Einlage Church building

EINLAGE

2. ALEXANDRABAD

Alexandrabad, a private sanitorium, was constructed directly across the Dnieper River from Einlage by Wieler brothers. It was modelled after a sanitorium in Dresden, Germany. In approximately 1910, the industrialist, Jakob Niebuhr, purchased the facility and then expanded and modernized it. He eventually passed ownership of the facility on to his son-in-law, Böttcher.

The main building housed a variety of facilities including individual guest rooms, a large dining room, a large kitchen, an X-ray department and a bathing and massage area. The bathing area included steambaths, carbonic acid baths and other special baths. Up to four doctors were available to provide treatment for a variety of health problems. Special diets were offered including vegetarian meals.

Surrounding the building was a park area in which numerous buildings were located as well as small cottages for those guests who wished to live in privacy. A dock on the bank of the river provided boat access to the facility. In the evenings an orchestra would often play in the park area, entertaining the guests.

This facility provided both health and recreational services. At the beginning of World War I it was confiscated by the government and turned over to the City of Alexandrovsk. During the civil war it ceased to operate. Then, after the construction of the power dam, it disappeared under water.

Sanatorium

Alexandrabad

am Dnjepr bei Alexandrowsk.

Ausgerüstet nach Dr. Lahmanns System mit den neuesten Naturheilmitteln:

Licht-, Luft- und Sonnenbäder, Wasserheilverfahren, Dampfbäder, kohlensaure Bäder u. drgl.

Elektrische Heilmittel:

Faradisation, Galvanisation, Franklinische Kopfdusche, Vierzellenbad, Vibration und Röntgenapparat, Massage, allgemeine und spezielle bei Frauenkrankheiten. Behandelt werden: Nervenkranke, Erholungsbedürftige, müde, abgespannte Chroniker, Gelähmte, Herz-, Magen- und Nierenkranke; ferner: Frauenkrankheiten, Stoffwechselerkrankungen: Gicht, Rheumatismus aller Art, Zuckerkrankheiten, Blutarmut, Bleichsucht u. drgl.

Spezieller Magenkrankentisch!
================ Vegetarischer Tisch!

Prospekte auf Wunsch gratis und franko.

Adresse für Briefe und Depeschen: Alexandrowsk, Gouv. Jekaterin., Alexandrabad.

Advertisement from 1912

Alexandrabad main building

INSEL CHORTITZA   *Chortitza Colony*

The village of Insel Chortitza was one of the original eight Mennonite villages founded in 1789. The original settlers, 12 families in total, came from Prussia and included the family of Jakob Hoeppner, one of the original delegates that came to Russia to look for suitable land.

The village was named after the island on which it was situated. Eventually it was informally referred to as Insel Kamp. It's layout was somewhat different from the other Mennonite villages, in that the majority of the farmyards were on one side of the village street. On the other side of the street was the Dnieper River with a beach along its bank. The rear areas of the farmyards sloped up from the river and incorporated orchards and vineyards. Behind the farmyards was a field road, beyond which were the farmers' individual fields.

Insel Chortitza had a village school but there was no church. The village was served by the Chortitza Mennonite Church. Since travel to Chortitza was usually difficult in the early years, the school was often used for church services.

In 1889, a monument was erected in honour of Jakob Hoeppner. It was located on his land where his gravestone was also located. This was done as part of the centennial observance of Mennonite settlement in Russia. Today this monument is located at the Mennonite Heritage Village in Steinbach, Canada.

In 1916, as a result of a government initiative to liquidate all lands owned by Germans, the City of Alexandrovsk (which later became Zaporoshye) purchased the entire island of Chortitza. This was done with the promise that the villagers would be able to purchase back their farmyards and buildings. This promise, however, was not kept, and the islanders soon scattered, buying farms in other Mennonite villages. Insel Chortitza ceased to exist as a Mennonite village in 1917.

Today there is only one original Mennonite building left, a house-barn at the south end of the village. There are numerous gravestones in the cemetery, although they are somewhat difficult to find, since the cemetery has been expanded substantially in recent years.

The Chortitza Island, referred to as Ostrov Khortitsa, is now a recreational zone, with no building development permitted. There is a museum that depicts the history of the region. It includes a minimal display representing the Mennonite period.

INSEL CHORTITZA

Chortitza Colony

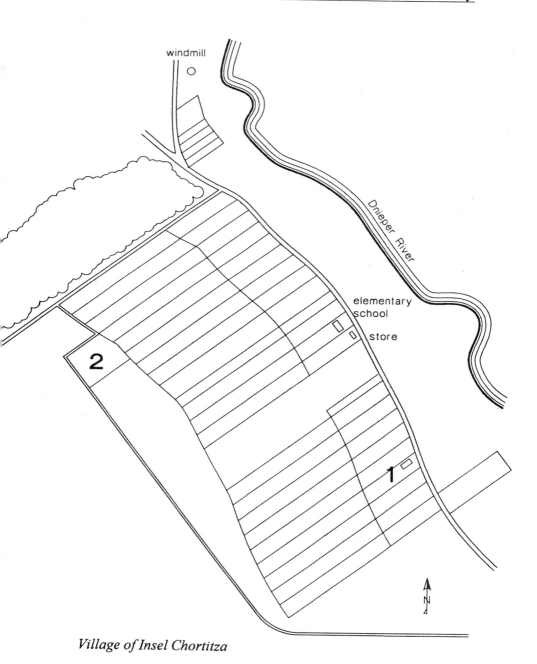

windmill

Dnieper River

elementary
school

store

2

1

N

Village of Insel Chortitza

INSEL CHORTITZA

Chortitza Colony

1. HOUSE/BARN

The one house/barn left in the former village of Insel Chortitza is representative of the Chortitza Colony, with its brick walls and arched gable windows. The original roof, however, has been replaced with corrugated cement-asbestos. The house is still in use today.

House/barn, Insel Chortitza

2. CEMETERY

The following gravestones have been identified:

● Katarina Peters
geb. Schellenberg
November 3, 1796 - September 14, 1866

● Maria ...
... Schellenberg
... January - ...

● Katharina Hildebrand
geb. Friesen
(Wife of Jakob Hildebrand 3.09.1795-5.10.1867)
... 1806 - August 23, 1860
(A monument in the shape of a book)

● J. Hildebrand
October ... - ...

● Johann Hildebrand
... - ...

● Maria Hildebrand
March 15, 1883 - July 2, 1900

● Katharina Hildebrand
geb. Schellenberg
August 18, 1830 - November 19, 1888

● Bernhard Hildebrand
June 11, 1840 - December 31, 1910

● Sara Hildebrand
geb. Peters
August 6, 1834 - January ..., 1872

INSEL CHORTITZA

Chortitza Colony

●Wilhelm Hildebrand
December 26, 1894 - November 23, 1905

●Elizabeth Klassen
geb. Hildebrand
May 15, 1809 - March 5, 1895

●Elis. Friesen
January 10, 1819 - ... 31, 1886

Korn. Friesen
December 15, 1820 - January 14, 1889
(on opposite sides of the same gravestone)

●Jakob Wiebe
February ..., 1867 - May ..., 1870

●David Janzen
February 12, 1842 - February 10, 1901

●Abraham Pathkau
September 7, 1823 - November 12, 1906

●Abraham Pathkau
September 3, 1855 - April 1, 1903

●Anna Wiebe
January 10, 1874 - February 3, 1898

●Peter Klassen
... - ...

●Anton Berg
March 8, 1822 - December 17, 1902

Abraham Hoeppner, 1801-1855

Jakob Hildebrand

Katharina Hildebrand, 1806-1860

INSEL CHORTITZA

- Katharina Klassen
  geb. Pet...
  ... 1832 - ...

- Agata Letkemann
  geb. Kasdorf
  February 28, 1891 - February 21, 1907

- Helena Hildebrandt
  geb. Hepner
  May 11, 1775 - June 18, 1833

- Abraham Hoeppner
  December 18, 1801 - November 23,
  1855
  (This monument has been restored and
  is located at the Mädchenschule in
  Rosental)

- Katharina Wiebe
  geb. Hildebrand
  January 4, 1814 - September 30, 1896

- Jakob Wiebe
  February 29, 1836 - November 23,
  1914

- Anna Friesen
  ... 1817 - ... 1856

- Jakob Hildebrand
  September 3, 1795 - October 5, 1867

- Peter Hildebrand
  March 3, 1754 - March 27, 1849
  (Alt 95 Jahre 25 Tage)

- Peter Wiens
  September 17, 1800 - September 9,
  1888
  Katharina Wiens
  geb. Penner
  October 10, 1809 - August 25, 1870

- Isaak Driedger
  December 27, 1833 - March 6, 1898

  Helena Driedger
  geb. Klassen
  May 24, 1839 - October 24, 1906

- David Kazdorf
  October 2, 1874 - May 28, 1909

Katharina Peters, 1796-1866

Katharina Hildebrand, 1830-1888

KRONSWEIDE

Chortitza Colony

The village of Kronsweide was established in 1789 by 35 families from Prussia. The name of the village was likely chosen by these settlers as being appropriate for the location.

It was established on a rocky flat area along the bank of the Dnieper River. Due to a shortage of water, it was relocated in 1833 approximately 5 km. away. The new location was in the valley of a tributary of the Heidutschina River.

Six families stayed behind in what became known as Alt-Kronsweide. In 1910 the rest of the old village was purchased for the site of the Bethania Mental Institute.

The new Kronsweide grew to become a thriving community. It had a village school and a church building. This was the centre of the Kronsweide Mennonite Church, one of the larger congregations in the Chortitza Colony.

In October 1919, during the civil war, Kronsweide was destroyed and many of its residents were murdered. The rebuilding of the village slowly began in 1925 and continued unti 1943. Today the village is known as Vladimirovka.

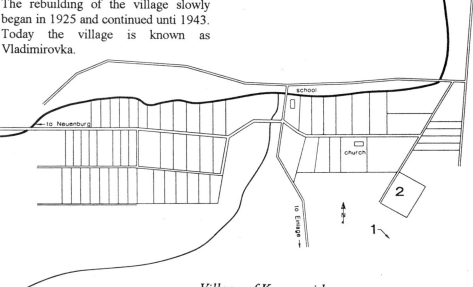

Village of Kronsweide

KRONSWEIDE

1. BETHANIA HEILANSTALT

The Bethania Mental Institute was founded in 1910 and was located between Einlage and Kronsweide in what was known as Alt-Kronsweide. It was supported by all Mennonite settlements in Russia and provided care for the mentally handicapped, epileptics, and those with nervous disorders.

The facility was modelled after the Bodelschwingh Institute in Bielefeld, Germany. An architect from Germany, Baumeister Siebold, who had experience in designing facilities of this type, was hired to design the new facility and prepare the necessary drawings. A building committee was then appointed and construction began. Peter Schellenberg, who became the facility's first house father, was appointed to oversee the construction.

Initially two separate buildings were constructed, each with 16 beds. Bethel, the women's ward, was completed March 16, 1911, and Salem, the men's ward, was completed August 20, 1911. Cost of these buildings was 122,000 Rubles. Construction was then started on the main building. It was completed in March, 1913 and included an additional men's and women's ward, each with a capacity of 22 beds.

The facility included a farm where some of the patients were able to participate in farm work, and a bakery where several patients assisted. There was also a large commercial kitchen and dining room, as well as a large hall which could accommodate gatherings of up to 300 people.

40,000 Rubles were donated by Wilhelm Schröder, as an endowment, with the request that two rooms be funded for the use of anyone regardless of religion. Whereas the cost of maintaining a patient was set at 300 Rubles a year, there were a total of 15 "free" beds funded by individuals or churches for those who could not afford it. All rooms were single rooms and patients could come and go freely, similar to the facility in Bielefeld. The slowness of construction was partially blamed on the plans being from an out-of-country architect. Changes had to be made continually since not everything suited local conditions and since Bethania was to be a more advanced facility.

After the civil war, Bethania was taken over by the government. It operated until May 9, 1917, when it was evacuated in anticipation of the flooding resulting from the construction of the Dneprostroy power dam on the Dnieper River. It, therefore, no longer exists today.

KRONSWEIDE

Salem men's ward

Kitchen

Bethania main building

KRONSWEIDE

2. CEMETERY

The following gravestones have been identified:

●Kornelius Friesen
July 20, 1842 - August 4, 1904

●W... J...
1844

●Susanna Funk
geb. Telitzky
February 28, 1872 - June 27, 1912

●Jakob Krahn
February 19, 1845 - November 23, 1905

Anna Krahn
August 4, 1830 - February 7, 1904

●A... K...
1854

●Aganetha Dyck
geb. Bergman
February 16, 1814 - May 15, 1889

●Anna Krahn
September 25, 18.. - May 18, 1911(?)

Jakob Krahn
May 20, 1898 - June 25, 1910

Kornelius Krahn
May 22, 1903 - September 15, 1906

●La(r)a Penner
May 8, 1860 - July 28, 1864

●Heinrich Peters
August 1, 1832 - April 12, 1898

Jakob Krahn, 1845-1905

Kornelius Friesen, 1842-1904

NEUENBURG

The village of Neuenburg was established in 1789 by 16 families from Prussia. The name of the village was likely chosen by these settlers as being appropriate for the location. It was located along the Heidutschina River with a wide main street located along side the river. Farmyards were located on only one side of the main street, the river side.

Neuenburg was one of the smallest villages of the Chortitza Colony. It had a village school, a windmill, two stores, and a village granary.

After the civil war the land was confiscated and incorporated into a collective farm. Today the village is known as Malashovka. In the cemetery, there is one gravestone that has been identified: David Warkentin - September 27, 1825-October 23, 1910

David Warkentin, 1825-1910

cemetery

to Neuendorf

windmill
○

old cemetery

Heidutschine River

school

to Kronsweide →

to Einlage

N

Village of Neuenburg

NEUENDORF

Chortitza Colony

The village of Neuendorf was established in 1789 by 38 families. The settlers came from Prussia and may have named the village after Neuendorf in West Prussia, although none of the settlers came from that village. It eventually became one of the largest villages of the Chortitza Colony.

The first church building was built in approximately 1835 and was actually the reconstruction of the first wooden church building from the village of Chortitza which had been dismantled to make way for a new church building. This first church building was eventually replaced with a new larger and finer church building in 1873. It served the villages of Neuendorf, Schönhorst and Neuhorst. The building was demolished in the 1950's and the material used for the

construction of a hospital in the village of Chortitza.

Neuendorf had a village school. In 1934 a nearby flour mill was expanded and converted to an intermediate school. Both buildings still exist today. There were numerous commercial and industrial establishments including a general store, a lumber yard, and a grain merchant, as well as several flour mills. The Orphans' Administration (Waisenamt) for the Chortitza settlement was located in Neuendorf.

In 1910 the village name was changed to Shirokoye. After the civil war the land was confiscated and incorporated into a collective farm. Today there are still a number of the original Mennonite buildings left. There are also several gravestones to be found in the cemetery.

House built in 1910, Neuendorf

NEUENDORF

Chortitza Colony

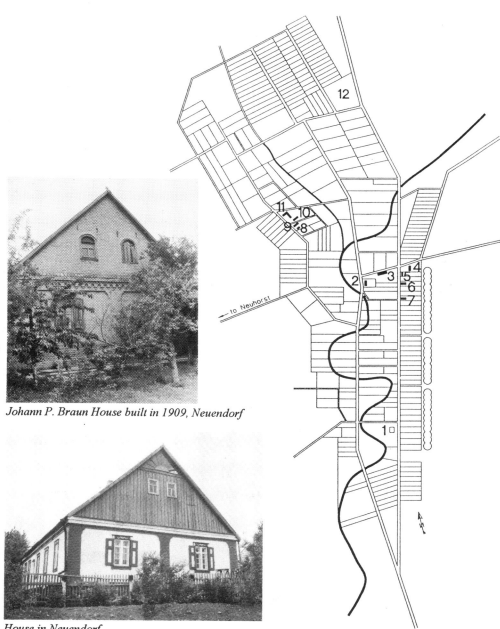

Johann P. Braun House built in 1909, Neuendorf

House in Neuendorf

Village of Neuendorf

NEUENDORF

1. NEUENDORF MENNONITE CHURCH

The Neuendorf Mennonite Church building was built in 1873, replacing the old church building which had been constructed in the 1830's. The new church building was a large two storey structure generally based on the traditional Mennonite church design. Located parallel to the street, the building's exterior masonry walls were plastered and had minimal decoration. The only variations from the early churches were slightly arched windows and a hip roof instead of the traditional gable roof.

The pulpit/platform was located along the long side facing the street and the main entrance was directly opposite, facing the church yard to the rear. The building was demolished in the 1950's and the material used for the construction of a hospital project in Chortitza.

Neuendorf Church building from yard

NEUENDORF

2. VILLAGE SCHOOL

This former village school is situated parallel to the former main street of the village. It is a long building with a small addition toward the school yard. The walls are typically of brick construction with fine detailing at the eaves. The windows have decorative wood framing around them. The upper level windows in the gable ends are not arched, but flat, which is unusual for buildings in the Chortitza Colony.

The building has recently been converted to teachers' residences. The exterior walls are painted white and the window shutters are no longer there. The roof has been replaced with corrugated cement-asbestos.

Window detail

Village school building

NEUENDORF

Chortitza Colony

3. MILL

This building was constructed in 1903/04 as a steam powered flour mill by Salomon Bergen and Jakob Martens from the village of Schönhorst. It was subsequently sold to Peter and Jakob Heinrichs. After the Revolution it was confiscated.

In 1934 it was substantially changed in order to be utilized as an intermediate school. A second floor was added including a new roof structure. The exterior walls were covered with plaster, including the original brick walls. However, the outline of the original brick detailing can still be seen on portions of the lower facade. The roof is covered with clay roof tiles. It is still used as a school today.

Building converted to school

Original mill building

NEUENDORF

4. GRANARY

This village granary was built of brick. The brick treatment of the walls suggests structural columns. An unusually wide column at the centre of the long wall contains the entrance door. The brick buttresses at the end wall appear to have been added at a later date.

The vertical wood siding on the gables is still in place. However, the brick walls have been painted and the roof has been replaced with corrugated cement-asbestos. The building is still used for grain storage.

Village granary

NEUENDORF

Chortitza Colony

5. TIESSEN HOUSE

This brick house, with its arched gable windows, is fairly typical of the houses of the Chortitza Colony. The lower windows have decorative wood frames. The house, however, has been placed parallel to the street rather than perpendicular the way most houses were.

At one time this house belonged to a Tiessen family. After the civil war it was converted and used as the village council building. The front addition which is now the entrance to the building, was likely added at that time. The exterior walls have been painted and the roof has been replaced with corrugated cement-asbestos.

Tiessen House

NEUENDORF

6. PENNER HOUSE

This house at one time belonged to the "Waisen" Penner family. It's fairly plain brick detailing and wood frame windows suggest that it was one of the older houses in the village. It has been expanded and modified and the roof has been changed to corrugated cement-asbestos. It is still in use today.

Penner House

NEUENDORF

Chortitza Colony

7. H. BRAUN HOUSE

This house once belonged to the Hans Braun family. Its brick detailing and clay tile roof were fairly typical for the area. It is still in use today.

H. Braun House

NEUENDORF

Chortitza Colony

8. HOUSE

This house was built in 1913. It measured 11 m by 18 m and was located perpendicular to the street. It is typical for the area in terms of its brick detailing and clay tile roof. It is still in use today.

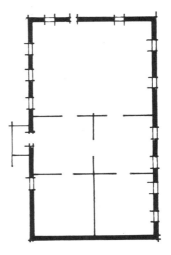

House built in 1913

NEUENDORF

Chortitza Colony

9. HOUSE/BARN

This house and barn were located perpendicular to the main street. They were built of brick with typical arched gable windows facing the street. The rear gable has vertical wood siding. The roof is covered with original clay roof tiles and has an unusual dormer window. The building has been substantially modified over the years and is now used as a storage shed.

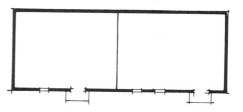

House/barn from yard

House/barn from street

NEUENDORF

10. P. HILDEBRAND HOUSE

This house is fairly representative of the earlier houses in the Chortitza Colony, with decorative wood framing around the windows and vertical wood siding on the gables. It measured 9m by 21 m and was placed perpendicular to the main street. The walls have been painted and the roof has been replaced with corrugated cement-asbestos. After the civil war it was converted to a maternity house.

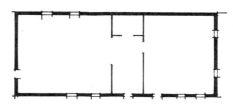

P. Hildebrand House

NEUENDORF

11. BARN/SHED

This barn and shed are fairly representative of the buildings of the area and are similar to the later houses in terms of their brick detailing and arched gable windows. The roof has been replaced with corrugated cement-asbestos. The brick buttresses at one end of the building were likely added at a later date.

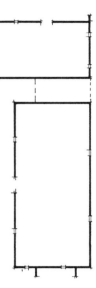

Barn/shed

NEUENDORF

Chortitza Colony

12. CEMETERY

The following gravestones have been identified:

- Franz Thiessen
  February 20, 1832 - January 30, 1892

  Anna Thiessen geb. Hildebrand
  April 11, 1834 - August 13, 1905

- David Hildebrand
  March 20, 1822 - January 1, 1904

- Maria Ens
  geb. Penner
  January 31, 1862 - April 12, 1902

- Heinrich Hildebrand
  June 1, 1843 - January 30, 1902

- Heinrich Janzen
  July 18, 1851 - November 10, 1908

  Helena Janzen
  geb. Schröder
  July 26, 1853 - April 12, 1908

- Margaret Klassen
  geb. Regier (or Kröger)
  ... 1820 - ... 1902

- Peter Ennz
  October 23, 1877 - June 5, 1908

- Anna Dyck
  April 10, 1889 - March 15, 1913

There is one other gravestone with a damaged top.

Heinrich & Helena Janzen

Franz & Anna Thiessen

NEUHORST

The village of Neuhorst was established in 1824, one of the smallest villages in the Chortitza Colony. A total of 13 families from the villages of Neuendorf and Schönhorst settled here, hence the name "Neuhorst". It was located along a small stream that ran into the Tomakovka River. The main street ran parallel to the stream on the east side. The farmyards were all located on the west side of the street, backing onto the stream. On the east side of the main street was a tree plantation. To the west of the stream was another street which was connected to the main street by a cross street. Approximately 30 smaller farmyards were located along this street. Their land was rented from a local nobleman.

The original houses were built of wood but through fire and demolition were eventually replaced by new brick houses. Barns and sheds were added to these houses in the traditional manner. In 1874 the village was totally destroyed by fire. It was subsequently rebuilt. Then in 1897, nine buildings were again burnt down and rebuilt.

The village school stood in a wooded area near the centre of the village. It was built of brick. There was no church building since the residents were members of the Neuendorf Mennonite Church. Church services were often held in the school.

During the civil war, the village suffered heavily. In 1919 the Machno bandits continuously plundered it, burning the buildings of the village in the process. By 1920 all the buildings had been destroyed and the original village of Neuhorst ceased to exist. In 1927 a new village of Neuhorst was established, approximately 1 km. south of the original village.

NEUOSTERWICK-KRONSTAL   *Chortitza Colony*

NEUOSTERWICK

The village of Neuosterwick was founded in 1812 by 20 families that came from the already established villages in the Chortitza Colony. Most of them were from Neuendorf but there were also some from Chortitza and Schönhorst. The name of the village was probably based on Osterwick in Prussia, which some of these settlers will have remembered. Neuosterwick was located in a broad valley along which ran a small river by the name of Ritsch, also known as the Middle Chortitza River.

In the early years, a church building of wood construction was built. Eventually it was found to be too small and so in 1872 it was sold and moved away. The same year a new spacious and tastefully appointed church building was opened. It was built of brick and had tall arched windows and a green painted metal roof. The pulpit and platform were located at the east end of the sanctuary. It

served the villages of Neuosterwick, Kronstal, Schöneberg, and Kronsfeld (a village approximately one kilometre south of Schöneberg, founded in 1880). The church was closed in 1935 and the building no longer exists.

It is likely that an elementary school building was also built soon after the village was established. In 1862 a new school building was built. In 1904 it was expanded by constructing another school building on the same yard. The village also had a factory school for about 60 students. In 1912 a third elementary school was built, for Orthodox students. The same year a secondary school was also built. Today only the 1904 elementary school and the former secondary school still exist.

Neuosterwick was one of the more industrially progressive villages in the Chortitza Colony. By 1912 there were two steam-powered flour mills and two factories manufacturing agricultural machinery. There were also several

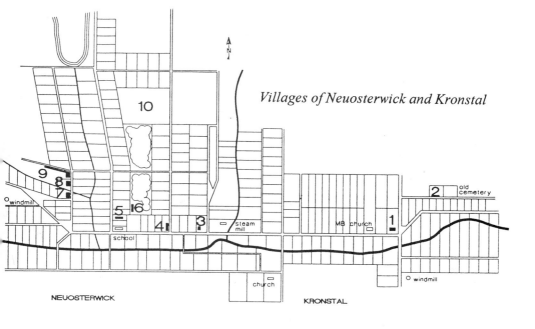

Villages of Neuosterwick and Kronstal

104

NEUOSTERWICK-KRONSTAL *Chortitza Colony*

shops, a pharmacy, and a brick factory.

Over the years there were numerous fires in the village, including a major one in 1863 which destroyed more than 60 buildings (including the roof of the newly constructed village school). Buildings destroyed by fire were replaced by new and more substantial buildings, usually constructed of locally produced brick. As a result, the overall appearance of the village continued to improve.

Over time the name of the village became commonly referred to as Osterwick. In 1910 the name of the village was changed to Pawlowka. After private lands were nationalized, the village became the centre of a collective farm.

Today there are still several significant former Mennonite buildings in the village, including several original houses from around the turn of the century. Also, a number of gravestones can still be found in the cemetery.

KRONSTAL

The village of Kronstal was founded in 1809 by 12 families that came from the existing villages of Kronsweide and Rosental, hence the name "Kronstal". It

was located in a broad valley along which ran a small river known as the Middle Chortitza River.

There was a one room school located near the centre of the village. The village was served by the church in Neuosterwick. Later on a Mennonite Brethren church was built in Kronstal which served its members in both Kronstal and Neuosterwick.

The village had a windmill, built soon after its establishment. By the turn of the century there were also several small factories. Many of the villagers worked in the larger factories in Neuosterwick. Today the village school is still in existence, as are a number of original Mennonite houses, some of which are in reasonably good condition. Several gravestones can also be found in the cemetery.

NEUOSTERWICK-KRONSTAL

After the last Mennonites left in 1943, many of the buildings were demolished and new smaller homes were constructed. The former villages of Neuosterwick and Kronstal are now combined into the village known as Dolinskoye.

House built in 1898, Neuosterwick

House built in 1904, Neuosterwick

NEUOSTERWICK-KRONSTAL *Chortitza Colony*

1. KRONSTAL VILLAGE SCHOOL

The village school was located parallel to the main street. The exterior walls were constructed of brick and are relatively plain. The windows have carved wood decorative frames. Both the frames and the brick have been painted and the roof has been replaced with corrugated cement-asbestos.

Kronstal village school building

NEUOSTERWICK-KRONSTAL *Chortitza Colony*

2. KRONSTAL CEMETERY

The following gravestones have been identified:

- Franz Janzen
  June 26, 1826 - November ..., 1884

  Kath. Janzen geb. Klassen
  ... 23, 1827 - ... 1902

- Gerhard Neufeld
  March 18, 1830 - January 30, 1885

- Abraham Niebuhr
  ... 1807 - ... 1855

  Jakob Niebuhr
  November 20, 18... - ... 1857

- Maria Redekopp
  geb. Funk
  February 13, 1836 - December 24,
  1904

- Gerhard Redekopp
  February 19, 1834 - October 11, 1888

- Jakob Zacharias
  November 17, 1827 - July 7, 1866

Maria Redekopp, 1836-1904

Gerhard Redekopp, 1834-1888

Jakob Zacharias, 1827-1866

NEUOSTERWICK-KRONSTAL *Chortitza Colony*

3. REMPEL FACTORY

The firm of B.W. Rempel, Landwirtschaftliche Maschinenfabrik was founded in 1885. A blacksmith by trade, Bernhard Rempel took over an existing operation from a Franz Peters who moved to Orenburg. Rempel developed and manufactured an improved version of the seeder plow. He also manufactured cultivators, fanning mills, reapers and underground packers that were used to pack newly planted seeds to encourage germination. Apparently these packers were not manufactured by any other factories in the Chortitza Colony.

The factory employed 50 to 75 workers. In 1895 a steam engine was installed to drive all the machines. In 1906 a branch factory was opened in Millerowo. Upon Bernhard's retirement, his son Heinrich Rempel took over the leadership of the business. After the Revolution the factory was nationalized.

Two of the Rempel factory buildings still remain today. The larger building has been painted to emphasize the brick detailing, particularly on the front facade. The building is used today as a community centre. The smaller building, which used to be the factory office, still has its natural brick colour. Today it is used as a library. The roofs on both buildings have been replaced with corrugated cement-asbestos.

Main entrance

Advertisement from 1905

Rempel Factory building

NEUOSTERWICK-KRONSTAL — *Chortitza Colony*

4. KONSUM STORE

A cooperative society was founded in Osterwick in about 1902 for the purpose of establishing a general store. Commonly referred to as the Konsum, this store developed into one of the largest and most stable in the Chortitza Colony. Within a few years of its establishment, this new store facility was constructed.

Its early success is attributed to Wilhelm Klassen, its first manager. The son of a shopkeeper in Kronstal, he was familiar with the retail business, and travelled afar to obtain textiles, leather goods, and other products.

In the 1920's the store was nationalized. The building was constructed of local brick. Although the exterior has been painted, one can still identify the arched parapet on the front wall and the textured brick fascia. The window openings have been enlarged and the front stairs have been replaced. It still operates as a store.

Konsum Store after 1902

Konsum Store today

NEUOSTERWICK-KRONSTAL   *Chortitza Colony*

5. NEUOSTERWICK VILLAGE SCHOOL

The village school consisted of two buildings. One was built in 1862 and was located adjacent and parallel to the main village street. Because of the growth in students more space was required and another school building was constructed in 1904. It was located at the rear of the same schoolyard, parallel to the older school. The new building was officially opened September 19, 1904. In 1912 the two buildings together had 150-160 students. Both buildings also included teachers' quarters. Only the 1904 building exists today. On the west gable are the letters N.O. which stand for Neuosterwick.

Neuosterwick village school building after 1904

NEUOSTERWICK-KRONSTAL   *Chortitza Colony*

6. NEUOSTERWICK ZENTRALSCHULE

This secondary school facility first opened its doors to students on September 3, 1912. The dedication program took place on October 14 of that year, the same day as the 100 year anniversary celebration of the village of Neuosterwick. Almost a dessiatine of land had been assembled for the school site. Funds were raised by the ladies' auxiliary. Local factory owners Dietrich Schulz and Bernhard Rempel each contributed 2,000 Rubles. Construction was supervised by Jakob Dück and David Redekopp along with Board Chairman, Heinrich Rempel. It was completed on time and for less than anticipated - just under 10,000 Rubles.

The building had 4 classrooms plus an assembly room with a stage. A partial basement contained a teacher's residence. To the right of the main entrance hung a Kroeger clock. The exterior walls were constructed of brown bricks produced in Neuosterwick. The brick detailing was fairly restrained. A projected brick course approximately ⅔ of the way up the walls created a horizontal line that tended to reduce the apparent height of the building.

The windows at the entrance were arched. The projected main entrance was emphasized by its peaked parapet wall with intricate brickwork and an unusually steep peaked roof form behind this parapet. This entrance, however, was not normally used by the students. Instead they used two rear entrances that faced the schoolyard.

During the 1930's the stage was removed and the assembly room was converted to a classroom. The assembly room is now used as a gymnasium. The front stairs have been replaced. The steep roof at the entrance is gone and the remainder of the roof has been replaced with corrugated cement-asbestos. Two brick gate posts at the street still identify the entrance to the school yard. A student residence was constructed during the 1930's immediately to the south. Both buildings are used as school facilities today.

Gatepost at the street

NEUOSTERWICK-KRONSTAL   *Chortitza Colony*

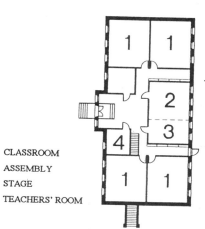

1. CLASSROOM
2. ASSEMBLY
3. STAGE
4. TEACHERS' ROOM

Main entrance today

Neuosterwick Zentralschule in 1912

NEUOSTERWICK-KRONSTAL *Chortitza Colony*

7. PETER D. SCHULZ HOUSE

This residence was built between 1912 and 1914 by Peter D. Schulz, then the head of the Schulz Factory known as "D.B. Schulz & Erben". He was the son of Dietrich B. Schulz, the founder of the factory. The house had hot water heating, running water, water closets and electric lights powered by the factory steam powered generator. The main floor included a kitchen, laundry and servants' quarters. A large veranda faced the yard. The second floor contained a large hall with a balcony facing the front street.

Facade detail

The exterior walls, constructed of locally produced brick, show elaborate detailing, including alternating peaked and flat arched treatments over the windows. The parapet above the second floor has an arched section at the centre, similar to the Volost building in Chortitza. At the rear is a small carriage house, also with fine brick detailing. The original metal roof, however, has been replaced with corrugated cement-asbestos.

During the 1940's this house was used as the village council building. Today it is only partially occupied. It is part of the local collective farm.

Window detail

Peter Schulz House today

NEUOSTERWICK-KRONSTAL *Chortitza Colony*

8. DIETRICH B. SCHULZ HOUSE

This residence, located adjacent to the factory, was built in the late 1800's by Dietrich B. Schulz, the founder of the factory. It had a hip roof with an unusually low slope. An extension at the back of the house featured a parapet with an arched section, similar to the Volost building in Chortitza. This extension is still in place complete with parapet. The original metal roof has been replaced with corrugated cement-asbestos but the original slope has been maintained. The original wood shutters on the windows have been removed and the brick walls have been painted. The building is now part of the collective farm.

Dietrich Schulz House today

Dietrich Schulz House in 1906

NEUOSTERWICK-KRONSTAL   *Chortitza Colony*

9. SCHULZ FACTORY

This factory building was built sometime between 1880 and 1885 by Dietrich B. Schulz to produce various agricultural machinery and in particular to respond to the high demand at the time for fanning mills (Putzmühlen). It grew quickly and soon employed up to 150 workers, and even more during peak periods. In 1893 Dietrich Schulz, a widower, married the widow of Peter Koop, part owner of the Koop factory in Chortitza. She provided capital for the expansion of the factory, and her two sons joined the business. It was then renamed "D.B. Schulz & Erben".

In 1908 an office addition was constructed. It had a parapet with an arched section similar to the Volost building in Chortitza. Then in about 1910 a second storey was added to the south wing of the building. It is likely that the tower over the pass-through was constructed at that time.

The factory included a steel foundry, lathe shop, carpentry shop, paint shop, blacksmith's shop and a steam powered generator that produced electricity for the factory. After the death of the founder in 1908, the leadership of the factory was taken over by his son, Peter D. Schulz. After his death in 1914, his younger brother, Jacob D. Schulz, took over the business. Following the civil war the factory was nationalized.

Today the building is in poor condition, although its aesthetics can still be appreciated. The brown brick walls have an interesting treatment with the large arched windows and the unusual angled arch reliefs above them, whereas the 2 storey wing has curved arch reliefs over the windows. Yet the brick colour and detailing clearly compliment each other. The brick is consistent in colour with that of other buildings in the village and therefore was likely locally produced. The tower over the pass-through was damaged during the civil war. It was rebuilt with the roof ridge running north-south whereas it was originally built with the ridge running east-west. The parapet at the office area is gone and the original metal roofs have been replaced with corrugated cement-asbestos.

LEGEND:

1. ORIGINAL FACTORY BUILDING
2. MACHINE SHOP AND CARPENTRY
3. STABLE
4. OFFICE
5. PAINT AND ASSEMBLY SHOPS
6. WORKERS' RESIDENCE

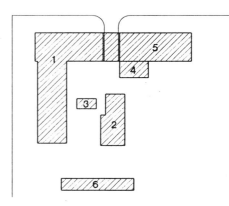

NEUOSTERWICK-KRONSTAL   *Chortitza Colony*

Factory yard in 1910

Entrance to Factory yard   *Addition under construction in 1910*

Window detail   *Schulz Factory building today*

NEUOSTERWICK-KRONSTAL *Chortitza Colony*

10. NEUOSTERWICK CEMETERY

The following gravestones have been identified:

- Margaretha Dyck
  geb. Janzen
  ... 1838 - ... 1901

- Dietrich Dyck
  June 4, 1836 - December 21, 1903

- Anganetha Derksen
  geb. Berg
  November 10, 1858 - October 11, 1905

- Elisabeth Harms
  ... 1823 - November ..., 1905

  Peter Harms
  ... 1813 - January 17, 1897

- ... Klassen
  ... 1783 - ... 1867

- Wilhelm Janzen
  September 27, 1839 - October 12, 1905

- Agatha Letkeman
  July ..., 1892 - May 9, 1900

- Maria Letkeman
  April 20, 1889 - October 20, 1898

- Margaretha Rempel
  geb. Dyck
  November 28, 1840 - June 23, 1906

- Johann Rempel
  July 16, 1841 - June 13, 1905

Helena Rempel
geb. Neudorf
August 11, 1843 - December 5, 1911

- Susana Peters
  August 19, 1842 - March 9, 1893

- Johan Peters
  June 3, 1..9 - June 23, 1918

- Maria Penner
  ... 1807 - ... 1890

- Anna Derksen
  geb. Penner
  August 13, 1835 - September 25, 1897

- Anna Riegert
  geb. Tiessen
  March 29, 1833 - May 27, 1900

- Maria Derksen
  geb. Berg
  July 1, 1843 - May 29, 1887

Klassen, 1783-1867

NEUOSTERWICK-KRONSTAL   *Chortitza Colony*

Margaretha Rempel, 1840-1906

Johann & Helena Rempel

Susana Peters, 1842-1893

Maria Letkeman, 1889-1898

NIEDER-CHORTITZA

Chortitza Colony

The village of Nieder-Chortitza was established in 1803 by 39 families from various existing Chortitza Colony villages. The village was located along the Lower Chortitza River, near where it flows into the Dnieper River, and so was named after this river. The land was made available for settlement by the government which also provided financial support in the amount of 1,000 Rubles.

Nieder-Chortitza had a village school. Church services were held in the school until a small church building was constructed. There were two stores and several other small businesses including a flour mill (C. Wiebe). By 1914 the population of the village was over 800 and there were 175 farms with a total of approximately 2,500 dessiatine of land.

Today the village is known as Nizhnyaya Khortitsa. Several Mennonite buildings still exist in the village. A number of gravestones can also be found in the cemetery.

House in Nieder-Chortitza

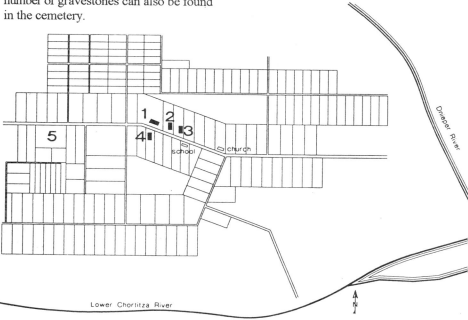

Village of Nieder-Chortitza

NIEDER-CHORTITZA

1. WIEBE MILL

The flour mill owned by the C.P. Wiebe family was the largest business establishment in Nieder-Chortitza. It originally included several buildings constructed of brick.

Today only one building remains. Although it is in poor condition, the decorative brickwork is still evident. The walls have been painted and the original roof has been replaced with corrugated cement-asbestos.

Wiebe Mill

Wall detail

NIEDER-CHORTITZA

2. KRAUSE HOUSE

The former H. Krause house, located next to the flour mill, was constructed of brick with vertical wood siding on the gable ends. The exterior walls have been painted and the original roof has been replaced with corrugated cement-asbestos. The building is still used as a residence.

H. Krause House

NIEDER-CHORTITZA

Chortitza Colony

3. NEUSTATER HOUSE

The former F. Neustater house was constructed of brick. It is similar in its brick detailing to other Mennonite houses of the Chortitza Colony except that the windows in the gable ends are not arched. The building is still used as a residence.

F. Neustater House

NIEDER-CHORTITZA

4. HOUSE

This former Mennonite house, located across from the flour mill, has walls constructed of brick and windows with decorative wood frames. This would suggest that the building is of fairly early vintage. Two small windows in the gable end also have decorative wood frames, a somewhat unusual feature. The building is still used as a residence. The walls have been painted and the roof has been changed to corrugated cement-asbestos.

House in Nieder-Chortitza

NIEDER-CHORTITZA

Chortitza Colony

5. CEMETERY

The following gravestones have been identified:

- Jakob Epp
  April 11, 1847 - November 11, 1889

- Anna Petkau
  ... 1892 - ... 1912

- Katharina Dyck
  June 9, 1886 - March 28, 1918

- H... Dyck
  ... 1888 - ...

- Anna Epp
  geb. Janzen
  August 29, 1850 - ... 18...

- Abraham Winter
  ... 1840 - ... 1903

- Sarah Winter
  geb. Schellenberg
  ... - ...

- ... Klassen
  July 18, 1818 - December 6, 1898

- ... Klassen
  geb. Neufeld
  May 15, 1821 - November 30, 1897

- Gerhard Rempel
  February 10, 1830 - May 25, 1880

- Anna ...
  geb. Neufeld
  ... 1844 - ... 1919

ROSENGART

The village of Rosengart was established in 1824, one of the last villages of the original Chortitza Colony. It was located along the Middle Chortitza River with its main street running generally parallel to the river. The name that was chosen for the village reflected what the settlers expected it to become, a garden of roses. A total of 22 families from various other Chortitza Colony villages settled here. No financial support was provided by the government, since these settlers were already free of previous government debts.

Rosengart had a village school, but no church, since the residents were members of the Chortitza Church. The original houses were quite small, but the residents soon prospered, eventually constructing stately farmyards with large orchards. Local limestone was quarried and sold. When the railroad was constructed, it was located adjacent to the village with a train station close by.

Today very few Mennonite buildings remain in the former village of Rosengart and only a few gravestones can be found in its cemetery. The name of the village is now Novoslobodka.

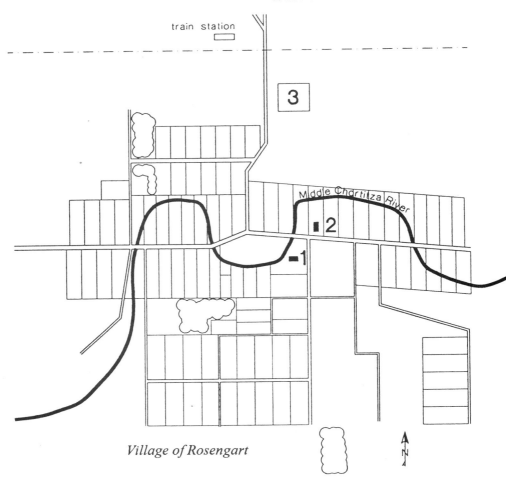

Village of Rosengart

ROSENGART

1. VILLAGE SCHOOL

This village school was constructed in 1909. It was similar in appearance to the houses of the village, with its brick walls and arched gable windows. These gable windows are unusually small and feature brick arches with enlarged keystone designs. The lower windows are framed with fine brick detailing. The building was placed parallel to the street, that is, the side street toward which the entrance faced.

The building is still in use today. The main exterior walls have been painted and the original clay tile roof has been replaced with corrugated cement-asbestos. It is likely that the small entrance was added at a later date.

Wall detail

Rosengart village school building

ROSENGART

2. HOUSE

This former Mennonite house is quite typical of the houses of the Chortitza Colony, with its brick walls and arched gable windows. The lower windows have decorative wood frames. Although in poor condition, the roof appears to have the original clay tiles.

House in Rosengart

ROSENGART

3. CEMETERY

The following gravestones have been identified:

- Margaretha Hamm
  geb. Berg
  ... 1835 - ... 1899

- Isaak Töws
  ... 1825 - ... 1908

- Dietrich Elias
  ... 1842 - ... 1906

SCHÖNEBERG

Chortitza Colony

The village of Schöneberg was founded in 1816 by 14 families from the village of Nieder-Chortitza. The village was located along the Lower Chortitza River with the main street running parallel to the river. The farmyards on the north side of the street backed onto the river. The name of the village was derived from the high hill-like banks of the river valley at this location.

Schöneberg had a village school which no longer exists. There was no church and although the village belonged to the Neuosterwick church district, services were often held in the school. The village also had two windmills and a steam-powered flour mill. There was a blacksmith and several other craftsmen. The Konsum in Neuosterwick had a branch store in Schöneberg.

The name of the village was changed in 1910 to Smolyanoye. Today the village has only a few original Mennonite buildings left, but a number of gravestones can be found in the cemetery.

House in Schöneberg

House and shed in Schöneberg

to Kronsthal

Lower Chortitza River

school

steam | mill

Village of Schöneberg

O windmill

1

N

windm O

SCHÖNEBERG *Chortitza Colony*

1. CEMETERY

The following gravestones have been identified:

●Maria Fröse
  geb. ...
  October 11, 1830 - January 3, 1904

●... Epp
  November 21, 1923 - June 24, 1926

●Heinrich Funk
  February 1, 1850 - August 22, 1914

●Johan Fröse
  March 3, 1827 - February 20, 1889

●...
  geb. Janzen
  ... 1809 - ... 1887

●... Froese
  ... 177. - 1860

●Katharina Klassen
  geb. Bergen
  January ..., 1830 - ... 1896

●Herman Klassen
  February 19, 1840 - ... 12, 1905

●Johann Klassen
  ... 1851 - May 9, 1905

●David Klassen
  July 21, 1882 - March 22, 1905

  Maria
  September 23, 1905 - October 4, 1905

●Katharina Isaak
  geb. Frose
  May 9, 1854 - February 25, 1903

●Peter Peters
  March 23, 1827 - October 15, 1905

SCHÖNHORST
Chortitza Colony

The village of Schönhorst was founded in 1789 by 32 families from West Prussia. The village was located along the Tomakovka River. There were two main streets, Upper Street and Lower Street, both parallel to the river. It was likely named after a village in Prussia.

Schönhorst had a village school. It also had a church building even though it was part of the Neuendorf congregation. The village also had a store, two windmills, and a village granary. Today there are still several Mennonite buildings in the village, which is now known as Vod. Only a few gravestones can be found in the cemetery.

House in Schönhorst

House in Schönhorst

Village of Schönhorst

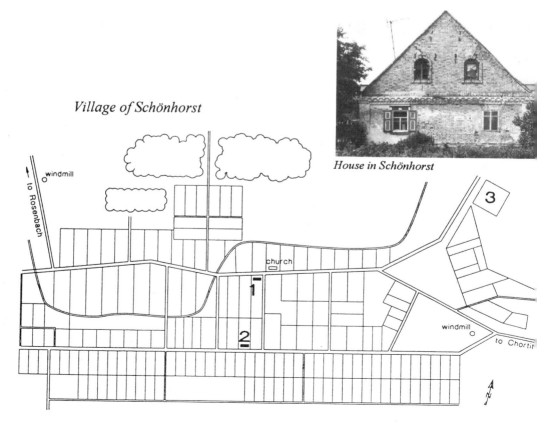

SCHÖNHORST   *Chortitza Colony*

1. VILLAGE SCHOOL

This village school measuring 12 m by 24 m, was built in a style similar to the other schools in the Chortitza Colony. The exterior walls were built of brick and the gable ends had two arched windows. It was located parallel to the street.

The building is still in use today. The wood decorative frames around the lower windows are still in place. The wood carved decoration is particularly evident at the window heads. The original roof has been replaced with corrugated cement-asbestos. A small addition on the south side of the building appears to have been added at a later date.

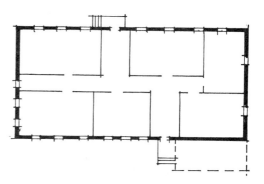

Schönhorst village school building

SCHÖNHORST

2. GRANARY

This village granary was built of brick, in a style similar to other buildings of the Chortitza Colony. This included two small arched windows in the gable end. However, the walls appear more substantial than those of other buildings. The end walls have the structure strongly expressed while the side walls have brick buttresses, required to withstand the weight of the grain.

The building is still in use today and is in good condition. The original roof has been replaced with corrugated cement-asbestos.

Village granary

SCHÖNHORST

Chortitza Colony

3. CEMETERY

The following gravestones have been identified:

- Dietrich Rempel
  May 27, 1808 - July 25, 1900

  Anna Martens
  January ... - June 12, 1892

- Katherine ...
  ... 1837 - November 29, 1882

SCHÖNWIESE

The village of Schönwiese was established in 1797 by 17 families of Frisian Mennonites who had arrived from Prussia between 1793 and 1796. They were skilled farmers and were well supplied with livestock, equipment, and money (an average of 350 Rubles per family).

The village was located in a "beautiful meadow" along the Mokraya Moskovka River, hence its name. The main street, Dachnaya Street, ran parallel to the river with the farmyards located on the north side of the street, backing onto the river. The total area of the village was 1400 dessiatine, one third of which was located north of the river. Since the site was considered to be difficult to settle, four families were soon relocated to the Molotschna Colony, thereby compensating those remaining with more land.

The village school and the church were located on the south side of the main street. The church building was constructed in 1862. Initially it was a branch of the Kronsweide congregation and eventually became the centre of the Kronsweide congregation.

The village eventually developed into a significant industrial centre. Industry soon replaced farming and the village sold most of its land, some of it to the City of Alexandrovsk. Around 1860 there were 12 windmills. After the construction of the railroad through Schönwiese, numerous factories and flour mills were built and expanded. Many of the prominent industrial firms from the other villages established branch factories here, to be nearer to the railroad. Much of the southern part of Schönwiese

became an industrial zone with factories on both sides of Schönwiese Street. This street ran north-south through Schönwiese, intersecting with Dachnaya Street and then crossing the river to the City of Alexandrovsk. The name of the street was later changed to Vokzalnaya Street.

On the west side of Schönwiese St. were located the large Lepp & Wallmann factory and the Koop & Hölker factory. Across the street were the Hildebrand & Priess factory and the largest of the factories, the A.J. Koop factory. Other businesses in Schönwiese included the large H.A. Niebuhr flour mill located adjacent to the railroad, two smaller mills (Niebuhr, H. Janzen), a brewery (H. Janzen), a woodworking shop (H.K. Hübert), a pharmacy, and numerous other stores.

In 1911, the village of Schönwiese was annexed to the City of Alexandrovsk. Because there were so many prosperous businesses, the residents of Schönwiese suffered severely during the civil war. Business eventually came to a halt and after the civil war, most industries were nationalized.

Alexandrovsk, which was named after the former Tsar, was changed to Zaporoshye after the civil war. Today Shenvize is a district of the City of Zaporoshye, a major industrial city. The industrial zone that once covered much of the southern part of Schönwiese is now one large factory, the Kommunar Factory. It is the largest automobile factory in Ukraine, manufacturing the Zaporoshye and Tomnaya cars. Many of the buildings of the original factories (Lepp & Wallmann, Koop & Hölker, A.J. Koop,

SCHÖNWIESE

Chortitza Colony

and Hildebrand & Priess) are still being used today as part of this factory complex.

The Kommunar Factory also has a small museum that depicts the history of the factory including the original factories as well as samples of the products produced there. A large coloured painting created by a factory artist shows the original Mennonite factories. There is also a scale model of the old Koop foundry.

There are still several former Mennonite houses along Dachnaya Street but the cemetery has disappeared, covered by a parking lot within the factory grounds.

Model of foundry, Factory Museum

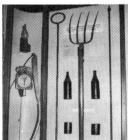

Factory Museum display

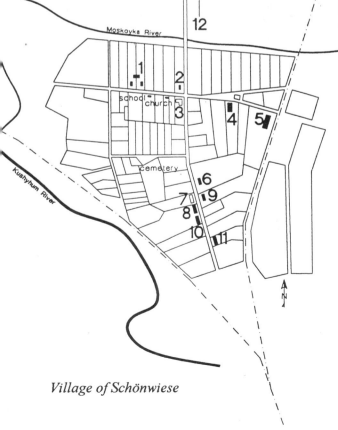

Village of Schönwiese

SCHÖNWIESE

Chortitza Colony

1. JULIUS SIEMENS HOUSE

This complex of buildings at one time was the estate of J.J. Siemens, mayor of the village of Schönwiese. Three separate buildings, two near the street and one set well back, created a fine courtyard with an interesting entrance to it, reminiscent of northern Europe.

The west front building, which measures approximately 21 m by 12 m, was likely the residence, with its front room projecting out toward the street. The fine wooden fretwork and the brick detailing further emphasize this room and present a decorative facade to the street. The rear building measuring 11 m by 22 m was built in 1911.

The decorative fence at the street with its brick posts appears to be as it was originally, except that the brick has been painted. Similarly the brick walls of the buildings have all been painted and the roofs have been replaced with corrugated cement- asbestos. The buildings are still in use today.

Facade detail

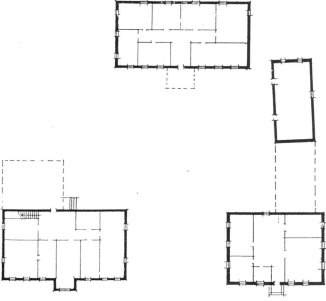

SCHÖNWIESE

Chortitza Colony

Rear building

J. Siemens House

Entrance to yard

SCHÖNWIESE *Chortitza Colony*

2. HEINRICH K. HÜBERT HOUSE

Heinrich K. Hübert owned the property on the west side of Vokzalnaya St., extending from Dachnaya St. all the way to the Mokraya Moskovka River. On this property he had a woodworking enterprise. The family residence was located here as well.

In 1912 this site plan was submitted to the City of Alexandrovsk for approval to construct a small brick office building along Vokzalnaya St. Today only the residence still remains. It is mostly a one-storey building measuring 32 m by 11 m, with a small central section being two storeys. It was constructed of brick. Recently it has undergone major renovations and so the original brick detailing is not obvious. Also the building itself is difficult to find. The property has been fully developed along both street frontages. The only access to the former Hübert residence is, therefore, via a lane off Dachnaya St.

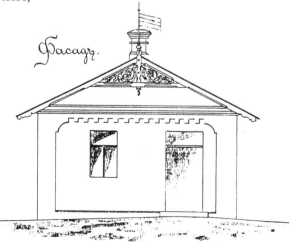

Street facade of proposed office building (No. 1 on site plan)

SCHÖNWIESE

Chortitza Colony

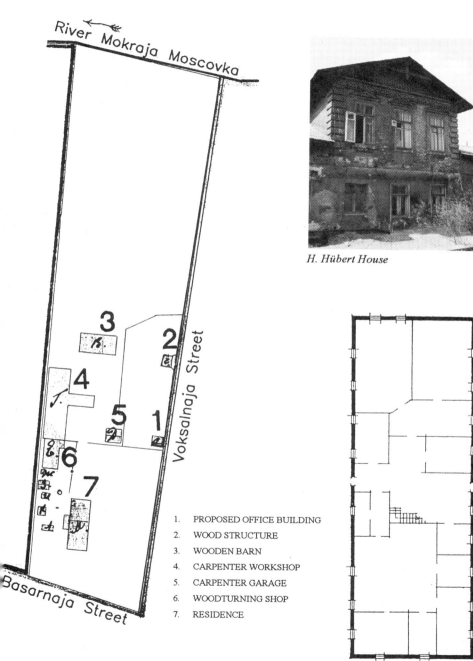

H. Hübert House

1. PROPOSED OFFICE BUILDING
2. WOOD STRUCTURE
3. WOODEN BARN
4. CARPENTER WORKSHOP
5. CARPENTER GARAGE
6. WOODTURNING SHOP
7. RESIDENCE

Plan of H. Hübert House
(No. 7 on site plan)

SCHÖNWIESE

3. TAVONIUS PHARMACY

The building at the southwest corner of Dachnaya St. and Vokzalnaya St. once housed the Tavonius Apotheke on the main floor. Records indicate, however, that the property was owned by Kornelius K. Hübert. It is, therefore, likely that Tavonius was one of several tenants in the building.

The building was constructed of brick and was three storeys in height with a two storey wing along Vokzalnaya St. The street facades were quite impressive with their articulated brickwork and gable-like walls extending above the roof line. Several balconies projected out from the facade.

The building is still in use today. However, it has been modified over time. The gable-like walls and the balconies have been removed, the corner entrance is gone, and the exterior walls have been painted. This has substantially changed the appearance of the building.

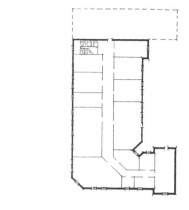

Tavonius Pharmacy building

Tavonius Pharmacy building today

SCHÖNWIESE

Chortitza Colony

4. ABRAHAM A. KOOP HOUSE

This large impressive house located on the south side of Dachnaya Street near the large Niebuhr mill was built for Abraham Koop, one of the owners of the Koop Factory and son of the founder, A.J. Koop. It is of brick construction and is still in fairly good condition. The walls have an interesting mixture of details particularly around the large vertical windows. There is an unusual steep sloped roof over the one angled wall. It is quite similar to western European houses of the time. The intricate metalwork on the upper level balcony and the main interior stair railing show the influence of Jugendstil in their design. The building is now used as a children's TB clinic.

A.A. Koop House

A.A. Koop House today

SCHÖNWIESE

Chortitza Colony

Detail of front wall

Facade detail

Corner detail

Balcony detail

5. H.A. NIEBUHR MILL

Herman Niebuhr started his milling business in Chortitza but in 1880 expanded to Schönwiese where he built his second steam mill adjacent to the railroad. In 1885, together with his brother-in-law Jakob Dueck, he built a third and more modern steam mill. Whereas the steam engine for his previous mill had come from England, the steam engine and boiler for this mill were made by the Lepp & Wallmann factory.

In the fall of 1893 he began construction of his largest mill, after returning from a visit to America, where he toured and was inspired by the Pillsbury Mill in Minneapolis, at that time the largest in the world. Brother-in-law Dueck was in charge of the construction of the mill. The new mill began operation in 1895 but it was too grand for its time and its production capacity too large, so that a large part of it was at first not utilized. In the same year, the business became known as "H.A. Niebuhr & Ko." with Herman Niebuhr and Jakob Dueck as official owners.

After the civil war, this large mill was expropriated. It is still in use today and is still the largest in the area. Built of brick, the main building has shallow arched windows with a horizontal brick pattern at the floor lines. The original two storey administration building which had well articulated brick work with arched windows, vertical column treatment between the windows, and special corner detailing, has recently been demolished to make way for an expansion of the facility.

Advertisement from 1913

Administration building

SCHÖNWIESE

6. A.J. KOOP FACTORY

Founded by Abraham Koop in 1864, when he opened a small blacksmith shop in Chortitza, this firm eventually developed into one of the largest agricultural machinery factories in the region with subsidiaries in Einlage, Schönwiese, and Alexandrovsk. It became known as Gesellschaft A.J. Koop, Fabriken Landwirtschaflicher Maschinen. The Schönwiese subsidiary was built in 1888 near the railroad line so that the agricultural machinery being manufactured could more easily be distributed. Its production soon surpassed that of the main factory in Chortitza. In 1903 it produced 3000 pieces of machinery. In 1911 the A.J. Koop factory employed 800 workers.

The factory buildings ranged from one to three storeys in height. They were constructed of brick and were separated in numerous locations by masonry firewalls. The brick detailing was generally typical for industrial buildings of the time. Large windows provided daylight to the work areas. The foundry building included high level clerestory windows that provided daylight to the centre of this rather wide building. A two storey office building, with its highly decorative brick work, and set back from the street (Vokzalnaya St.), created an impressive entry to the factory complex.

After the civil war, this factory was expropriated and eventually became the main component of the large automobile factory, Kommunar. The main shops of the former Koop factory are still in operation including the boiler house, one of the workshops, and the original steel foundry built around 1900. Also the former technical school that was located on the grounds of the Koop factory is still being used for training the automobile factory workers.

A.J. Koop Factory in Schönwiese

SCHÖNWIESE

Chortitza Colony

Office building

Foundry building today

Molding shop today

SCHÖNWIESE

Chortitza Colony

7. A.J. KOOP & HÖLKER FACTORY

A.J. Koop, who first established his factory in Chortitza in 1864, built another factory in Schönwiese in 1888. The Koop firm then joined with A.J. Hölker, a German, to build a steel tempering factory, to supply tempered steel to the Koop factory. It was soon providing tempered steel to all the other Mennonite factories in the colonies.

This site plan was submitted to the City of Alexandrovsk sometime before 1912, to obtain approval for the reconstruction of one of the buildings. It shows the extent to which this factory had expanded by that time.

The main factory buildings were one-storey brick structures with large arched windows providing daylight to the work areas. The brick detailing was typical for industrial buildings of the time. The factory complex included residences for factory workers which were also constructed of brick. Some had green spaces adjacent to them. The roofs of the buildings were generally of clay tile.

The factory was located adjacent to the Lepp & Wallmann factory. After the civil war it was expropriated and now is incorporated into the large automobile factory known as Kommunar.

1. BUILDING UNDER RECONSTRUCTION
2. PHARMACY
3. SHEDS
4. WORKERS' RESIDENCES
5. STORES
6. STORAGE
7. CANTEEN
8. STABLE
9. SUMMER KITCHEN
10. ICE HOUSE
11. IRON SHOP
12. FOUNDRY
13. STORAGE FOR COKE, CLAY, SAND

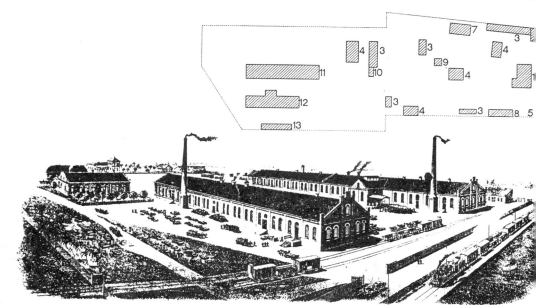

SCHÖNWIESE
Chortitza Colony

8. LEPP & WALLMANN FACTORY

The factory established by Pieter Lepp in Chortitza and known as Gesellschaft Lepp u. Wallmann, expanded to Schönwiese in 1885.

This site plan shows the extent to which the factory had expanded by 1915. This plan was submitted to the City of Alexandrovsk September 30, 1915. The main buildings were constructed of brick and in a style that was typical for industrial buildings of the time. Large windows provided daylight to the work areas. The complex included a number of residences for factory workers.

After the civil war this factory was expropriated. Today parts of it are still in existence, but cannot be recognized, since the factory has been incorporated into the large automobile factory known as Kommunar.

Advertisement from 1915

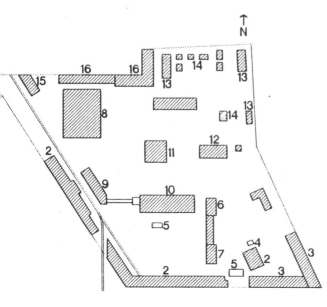

1. OFFICE
2. STORAGE
3. BLACKSMITH SHOP
4. CANTEEN
5. BOILER HOUSE
6. METAL WORK SHOP
7. POWER STATION
8. FOUNDRY
9. TIMBER STORAGE
10. CARPENTER'S SHOP
11. ASSEMBLY SHOP
12. STABLE
13. WORKERS' RESIDENCES
14. SHED
15. COKE STORAGE
16. MATERIAL STORAGE

9. HILDEBRAND & PRIESS FACTORY

Established in Chortitza by Kornelius Hildebrand, the Hildebrand & Priess factory expanded to Schönwiese in 1890 in order to be nearer to the railroad line. By 1911 the firm employed close to 200 people. The factory complex consisted of a series of buildings ranging from one to three storeys in height. They were constructed of brick and had fire separations at various locations. It also included a small hospital where the factory workers were provided treatment free of charge. The factory was known as Handelshaus K. Hildebrand's Söhne & Priess.

After the civil war, it was expropriated and now is incorporated into the large automobile factory, Kommunar.

Advertisement from 1904

SCHÖNWIESE
Chortitza Colony

10. JOHANN G. LEPP HOUSE

This residence was built by Johann G. Lepp, one of the owners of the Lepp & Wallmann factory. It was a long, low one storey brick structure measuring approximately 10 m by 40 m and was located within the grounds of the factory. The brick detailing of the exterior facade was somewhat unique in that there was an arch motif with each of the large arches spanning over two windows.

The building was expropriated after the civil war. It is still in use today, having been incorporated into the large automobile factory, Kommunar.

Johann Lepp House

SCHÖNWIESE
Chortitza Colony

11. ABRAHAM P. LEPP HOUSE

This estate was built by Abraham P. Lepp, one of the owners of the Lepp & Wallmann factory. It was located just down the street from the factory on a separate plot of land. The 17 m by 20 m brick house was one storey in height. A high chateau-like roof at one end emphasized the main entrance to the house. The main roof was metal. The front facade with its articulated brickwork featured fine large windows. Large awnings protected these windows. The wall was partially covered in ivy and the front yard was laid out as a formal garden.

After the civil war, this building was expropriated. It is still used today and is now part of the large automobile factory, Kommunar.

Abraham Lepp House

Abraham Lepp House today

SCHÖNWIESE

Chortitza Colony

12. BÄR HOSPITAL

Located on the corner of Nikolayevskaya Street and Pokrovskaya Street in the City of Alexandrovsk, this two storey hospital was constructed in 1900. It was owned by Doctor Heinrich Bär and his wife who were not Mennonites. This hospital was frequently used by the Mennonites in Schönwiese. It offered services in surgery, gynaecology, and eye surgery. A 1914 list of medical institutions in Alexandrovsk to be used for wounded soldiers, refers to this facility as a Surgical and Gynaecological Hospital, with Dr. Bär as chief doctor, and the Schönwiese Mennonite Society as trustee of the Hospital. It also indicates a capacity of 50 beds for junior officers.

The walls are of brick construction, with very little ornamentation. However, there are brick arches over the different sized lower windows that create an interesting rhythm. The upper windows have a similarly interesting rhythm even though the windows are not arched.

The corner of the building is rounded to respond to the street corner. This is further emphasized by a separate circular steep roof over the corner. Today it is used as a maternity house.

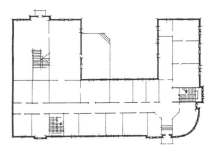

Advertisement from 1912

cade detail

Bär Hospital, Alexandrovsk

4. YAZYKOVO COLONY

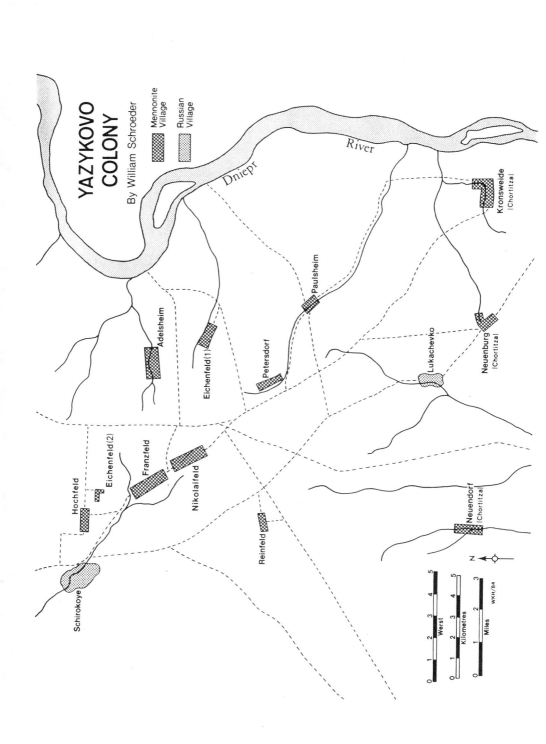

YAZYKOVO
COLONY

By William Schroeder

Mennonite Village

Russian Village

Dniepr *River*

Adelsheim

Eichenfeld (1)

Paulsheim

Petersdorf

Kronsweide
(Chortitza)

Lukachevko

Neuenburg
(Chortitza)

Hochfeld

Eichenfeld (2)

Franzfeld

Nikolaifeld

Reinfeld

Neuendorf
(Chortitza)

Schirokoye

N

Werst

Kilometres

Miles

WKH/84

The former Yazykovo Colony is located immediately north of the former Chortitza Colony. It was established in 1869, the first Mennonite daughter colony to be established after the land reforms of 1866. The Chortitza Colony purchased 7,153 dessiatine on November 8, 1868 from Countess Varvara Koskul for 240,000 Rubles. The name Yazykovo was derived from the name of the nobleman that had previously owned this land. Additional land was purchased from other private sources. Four villages were established: Nikolaifeld, Franzfeld, Adelsheim, and Eichenfeld. A total of 146 families from various villages in the Chortitza Colony settled in these villages. Each family was provided with 50 dessiatine of land, at a cost of 33 Rubles per dessiatine.

In 1872 additional land totalling 1,500 dessiatine was purchased from Countess Eugenia Morozova. The village of Hochfeld was established on this land, with 30 families from the villages of Neuosterwick and Einlage in the Chortitza Colony settling in this village. Again each family received 50 dessiatine of land.

Petersdorf which was established in 1833 as a private estate (chutor), came to be part of the Yazykovo Colony, as did two other estates, Paulsheim and Reinfeld. The Colony was administered from the Volost office in Nikolaifeld.

The villages were generally located and laid out in a manner similar to those in the Chortitza Colony. The single main street with farmyards on either side was usually located parallel to a stream. The lands that belonged to Adelsheim and Eichenfeld extended to the Dnieper River and included an island of 123 dessiatine in the river by the name of Tavolzhansky.

The Colony soon prospered and the early houses were replaced with more substantial brick houses. By the turn of the century there was a population of over 2,000. However, during the civil war, the villages suffered greatly. In the village of Eichenfeld, 82 people were murdered in one night. The remaining people fled and resettled near Hochfeld, creating a new Eichenfeld village. The villages were all eventually collectivized. Following are the present Russian names of the Yazykovo villages:

Adelsheim (No. 3) . . . . Dolinovka
Eichenfeld (No. 4) . . . Novo-Petrovka
Franzfeld (No. 2) . . . . Nikolaipole
Hochfeld (No. 5) . . . . Morozovka
Nikolaifeld (No. 1) . . . . . Nikolaipole

ADELSHEIM

Yazykovo Colony

The village of Adelsheim was established in 1869 by families from various villages in the Chortitza Colony. It was located along a small stream that flows into the Dnieper River. The village street ran parallel to the stream and had farmyards on both sides, with those on the north side backing onto the stream. The stream was dammed off to create a small reservoir.

Adelsheim had a village school. There was no church since the residents were members of the Nikolaifeld Mennonite Church. However, church services were often held in the village school. A small Mennonite Brethren congregation eventually formed in Adelsheim. Over time several small businesses were established. By 1910 there was a brick factory (A. Quiring and A. Siemens), a grocery store (J. Thiessen) and a flour mill (F. Funk). By 1913 there was also a tobacco store (A. Thiessen) and the grocery store had changed hands (P. Willms). By 1918 the village had a total of 64 farms with a population of 334 people and almost 2,000 dessiatine of land.

Today there are only a few Mennonite buildings left in the former village of Adelsheim, now known as Dolinovka. Only a few gravestones remain in the cemetery.

J. Willms House, Adelsheim

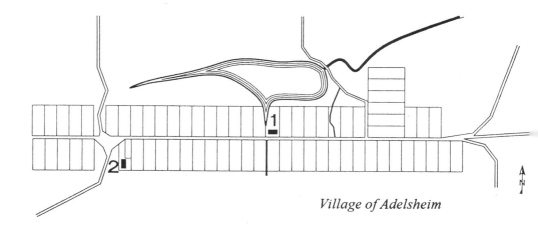

Village of Adelsheim

ADELSHEIM   *Yazykovo Colony*

1. VILLAGE SCHOOL

The village school was located near the centre of the village. It was likely built soon after the village of Adelsheim was established in 1869. The building was placed parallel to the street, as was the tradition. The walls were of brick and the windows had decorative wood frames. However, the hip roof covered with metal gave the building a very different appearance from the village schools in the Chortitza Colony with their gable roofs covered with clay tiles.

The school building was divided into two areas. At one end was the teacher's residence. At the other end were two classrooms. These classrooms were divided by a removable partition. On Sundays this partition would be removed and the double classroom used for church services. The building still exists, although it is not in very good condition. One end of the building is now used as a store. The other end is unoccupied.

Adelsheim village school building

ADELSHEIM

Yazykovo Colony

2. CEMETERY

The following gravestones have been identified:

- Aron Lehn
  May 9, 1838 - May 4, 1906

  Maria Lehn
  geb. Siemens
  September 12, 1845 - June 4, 1898

- Iacob Willms
  September 12, 1820 - June 9, 1903

- Margaretha Peters
  geb. Lepp
  December 23, 1840 - April 30, 1911

The Margaretha Peters gravestone is overgrown with lilac trees.

Aron & Maria Lehn

Iacob Willms, 1820-1903

HOCHFELD

Yazykovo Colony

The village of Hochfeld was established in 1872 by 30 families from the villages of Neuosterwick and Einlage in the Chortitza Colony. It was located approximately one km away from the nearest stream. The village street had farmyards on both sides.

Hochfeld had a village school but no church, since the residents were members of the Nikolaifeld Mennonite Church. By 1910 there was a brick factory (B. Giesbrecht and D. Wiebe), a flour and oil mill (J. Epp) and a grocery and textile store, which was a branch of the Nikolaipole Konsum. By 1918 the village had a total of 92 farms with a population of well over 300 and almost 1,900 dessiatine of land.

Today only a few Mennonite buildings remain in the former village of Hochfeld, now known as Morozovka, and only a few gravestones can be found in the cemetery. Recently the establishment of a new German settlement began in this village.

House built in 1878, Hochfeld

Gable window of house in Hochfeld

Barn in Hochfeld

HOCHFELD *Yazykovo Colony*

1. VILLAGE SCHOOL

This school building was likely built soon after the village of Hochfeld was established in 1872. It was built parallel to the street with the main entrance facing the school yard to the rear. The arched windows in the gable ends were similar to those of the houses in the area and were typical of school buildings in the area and in the Chortitza Colony. The exterior walls were of brick and had fairly modest brick detailing. The decoration over the windows was carved wood rather than brickwork.

The building is still in use today. The original roof has been replaced with corrugated cement-asbestos. The front entrance extension may have been added at a later date.

Gable windows

Hochfeld village school building

HOCHFELD

2. A. REMPEL HOUSE

The Abram Rempel house was not typical of the Mennonite houses of the area. It was placed parallel to the street and had a hip roof rather than a gable roof with arched windows. The exterior brick walls have fine brick detailing around windows and doors, at the corners and along the eaves.

After the owner of the house was exiled in 1931, the building was converted to a community club. It is still in use today.

A. Rempel House

HOCHFELD   *Yazykovo Colony*

3. CEMETERY

The following gravestone has been identified:

- Anna Klassen
  geb. Pauls
  September 17, 1843 - May 6, 1906

  Isaak Klassen
  August 11, 1884

  (und seine Frau)
  Sahra geb. Bergen
  October 11, 1887

There are two more gravestones at the cemetery. One is badly damaged and there is no inscription. The other one is stuck so deep into the ground that the text is not visible.

Anna Klassen, Isaak & Sahra Klassen

NIKOLAIFELD-FRANZFELD *Yazykovo Colony*

NIKOLAIFELD

The village of Nikolaifeld, named after Tsar Nicholas I, was established in 1869 by families from various villages in the Chortitza Colony. It was located less than one km south of the village of Franzfeld, which was established at the same time. Nikolaifeld had one village street with farmyards on both sides. A small stream was located a short distance away from the village.

Nikolaifeld was the administrative centre for the Yazykovo Colony with the Volost (municipal office) located here. A village school was constructed soon after the establishment of the village. By 1910 there was a grocery and textile store which was owned by the Nikolaipole Consumers Society (Konsum). It had branch locations in Hochfeld and Eichenfeld. There was also a book and stationery store (D. Hamm) and a flour mill (P. Schultz). By 1913 there was also a pharmacy (J. Petkau) and two woodworking shops (A. Wieler, J. Dyck). In 1918 the village had a population of well over 200 and approximately 1,600 dessiatine of land.

FRANZFELD

The village of Franzfeld was established in 1869 by 34 families from various Chortitza Colony villages. It was located along the east edge of a fish-filled pond that had been created by the previous land owner. A shepherd by the name of Franz, who had been employed by the previous land owner, still lived in a small house near the village site. Being familiar with bone-setting and the

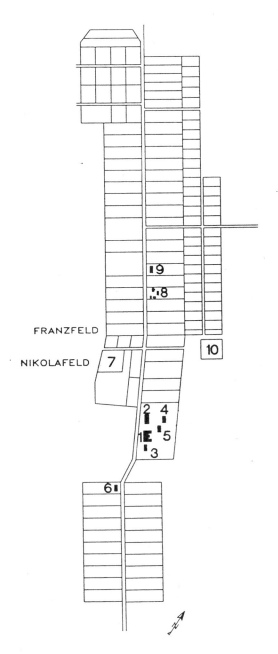

Villages of Nikolaifeld and Franzfeld

NIKOLAIFELD-FRANZFELD   *Yazykovo Colony*

curative characteristics of various wild plants, he assisted the settlers with their health problems. In appreciation the village was named after him.

Franzfeld had a main village street with farmyards on both sides. As the village grew a number of side streets were added. A village school was constructed near the centre of the village soon after it was established. A windmill was located at the north end of the village. Other businesses included a flour mill (D. Letkemann), a large general store (A. Wieler), and a brick factory (G. Wölke). In 1908 a building was constructed to house a doctor's office and a pharmacy as well as separate living quarters for each. By 1918 the village

had 100 farms with a population of approximately 500 and land totalling over 2,000 dessiatine.

NIKOLAIFELD-FRANZFELD

The main streets of Nikolaifeld and Franzfeld were connected by a well-treed road. Approximately halfway between the two villages was the site of the Nikolaifeld church. The Zentralschule along with its teacher's residences were also located here.

When the village names were changed in 1910, Nikolaifeld became Nikolaipole and Franzfeld became Varvarovka. They are now one village, Nikolaipole.

House in Franzfeld

Hübert House built in 1890, Franzfeld

House in Franzfeld

NIKOLAIFELD-FRANZFELD   *Yazykovo Colony*

1. NIKOLAIFELD MENNONITE CHURCH

The Nikolaifeld (Nikolaipole) Church was established in 1869 as a subsidiary of the Chortitza Church. In 1886 the decision was made to construct a new church building in Yazykovo Colony. After some debate, it was decided to locate it in Nikolaifeld which was centrally located. A building committee was established with one representative from each of the five villages and with Peter Töws, Nikolaifeld, as Chairman.

The design was prepared by Dietrich Rempel, a master carpenter at the Lepp & Wallmann factory in Chortitza. He submitted the plans to the authorities and obtained the necessary approval. Construction began in spring 1887. Building materials were brought to the site by the church members. Donations were also received, and so there was very little debt when the building was completed. The dedication service took place October 16, 1888. The key to the new facility was handed to leading minister, Heinrich Epp by the building committee Chairman, Peter Töws. Mr. Epp opened the church door, walked in, and everyone followed. The dedication service then continued with numerous additional speakers.

Built of masonry construction, the exterior walls were plastered and featured subtle decorative details. The Gothic-style windows were located relatively low to the ground creating unusual proportions for the building's exterior. The hip roof was covered with clay tiles.

The building measured 19 m by 28 m. It was located on the east side of the village street and parallel to it. The main

Nikolaifeld Church entrance

NIKOLAIFELD-FRANZFELD

Yazykovo Colony

entrance was at the south end of the building and the pulpit and platform at the north end. There was seating for at least 300. Due to the wide centre aisle, the seating capacity could be increased considerably for special occasions. Men sat on the left and women on the right. The front platform was approximately three feet high. The ministers sat to the left of the pulpit and the song leaders to the right. The pulpit was raised an additional step.

Today the building is used as a gymnasium for the adjacent school. The exterior walls have been painted a dark red/brown and the roof has been changed to corrugated cement-asbestos.

1. SANCTUARY
2. PULPIT
3. MINISTERS' ROOM
4. ENTRANCE/MEN'S COAT ROOM
5. WOMEN'S ROOM

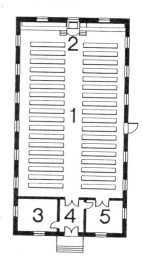

Nikolaifeld Church building

Nikolaifeld Church building today

NIKOLAIFELD-FRANZFELD   *Yazykovo Colony*

2. NIKOLAIFELD ZENTRALSCHULE

Construction of this central secondary school began in 1905 with Architect P. Peters in charge of the construction. It opened in late fall of 1906 with an enrolment of 100 students. The building site was next to the church on land donated by the village of Nikolaifeld.

The main component of the building, 2 storeys high and measuring 15 m by 44 m, was placed parallel to the street. The front facade projected out slightly at the main entrance. In order to emphasize the entrance, the brick treatment of this three storey facade incorporated various Gothic type arches. The main floor contained a dormitory for 50 students while the second floor included four classrooms, a teacher's room, a physics room, and a large hall that was used for music and gymnastics. There was also a library that was well-stocked with both German and Russian books. The central stair also led to a small area on the third floor. Two one storey wings extending out the back of the building. Measuring 12 m by 15 m, each contained a teacher's residence.

The exterior brick detailing is quite elaborate. It varies substantially, for example, between the first and second floors, particularly on the front facade. This seems to express the different functions on the two levels. Similarly, the two rear extensions have a different treatment, again expressing a different function. Yet there is a consistency in the design.

The building is in quite good condition with the exterior brick walls in their original light brown colour. The original tiled floor in a pattern of brown and white squares can still be seen in the front entrance and in the corridors. The original metal roof has been replaced with corrugated cement-asbestos but otherwise the building appears much the way it originally did. Even the brick fence at the street still exists.

After the civil war, this facility became an agricultural school. During the 1930's it was converted to a collective farm school, but eventually became a "Mennonite" school again, functioning with 10 classes and 10 teachers until 1943. It is still used as a school today.

Nikolaifeld Zentralschule entrance

NIKOLAIFELD-FRANZFELD   *Yazykovo Colony*

Nikolaifeld Zentralschule

One storey Teacher's Residence

Two storey facade

NIKOLAIFELD-FRANZFELD *Yazykovo Colony*

3. TEACHERS' RESIDENCE

This building was constructed as part of the school complex and contained two residences for teachers. The brick detailing of the exterior walls complements the design of the school, although it is not as elaborate. The exterior walls have been painted and the original roof has been replaced with corrugated cement-asbestos. The building is still in use today.

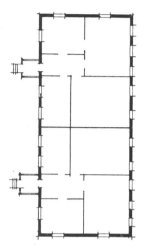

Teachers' Residence from yard

Side view of Teacher's Residence

NIKOLAIFELD-FRANZFELD   *Yazykovo Colony*

4. TEACHERS' RESIDENCE

This building was also constructed as part of the school complex, probably as the principal's residence.   The brick detailing and colour of the exterior walls complement that of the school, although the brickwork is not as elaborate.   The original roof has been replaced with corrugated cement-asbestos but appears very similar to that of the school.   The building is still in use today.

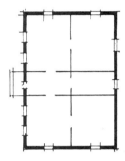

Teacher's Residence at Nikolaifeld Zentralschule

NIKOLAIFELD-FRANZFELD　　　*Yazykovo Colony*

5. BARN

This is the only building remaining of the various barns and sheds that were part of the school complex. The brick detailing and colour complement the other buildings in the complex. However, the roof with its gables of vertical wood siding, contrasts the other buildings and appears more "barn-like". The original roofing material has been replaced with corrugated cement-asbestos.

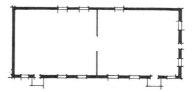

Barn at Nikolaifeld Zentralschule

NIKOLAIFELD-FRANZFELD   *Yazykovo Colony*

6. NIKOLAIFELD VILLAGE SCHOOL

This school building, located on the west side of the village street just south of the Zentralschule, was likely constructed soon after the village was established. It was built parallel to the street with the entrance from the school yard to the rear. It measured 13 m by 36 m. The walls were of brick and the windows had decorative wood frames. The hip roof is not typical for village schools of the area. However, its shape may have been changed when the roofing was replaced with corrugated cement-asbestos. The brick fence posts along the street appear to be original.

After the civil war this facility became a collective farm school. When that function was relocated to the former Zentralschule, this facility became a middle school. Today it houses an outpatient clinic.

Nikolaifeld village school building from street

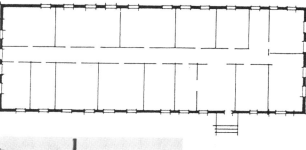

Nikolaifeld village school building

NIKOLAIFELD-FRANZFELD   *Yazykovo Colony*

7. NIKOLAIFELD CEMETERY

The following gravestones have been identified:

- Katharina geb. Penner
  September 13, 1843 - December 2, 1892

- Katharina Friesen
  geb. Peters
  December 4, 1848 - December 10, 1895

- Kornelius Friesen
  October 11, 1845 - March 1, 1916

- Daniel Peters
  August 1, 1814 - September 17, 1905

- Maria Peters
  geb. Janzen
  June 25, 1828 - June 6, 1900

- Sara Ens
  geb. Dyck
  October 21, 1836 - April 6, 1919

- Jakob Ens
  June 30, 1841

  Anganetha Ens
  geb. Janzen
  November 6, 1849 - May 12, 1911
  (in der Ehe gelebt vom 29 Dez 1863 bis zum 12 Mai 1911)

- Johann Dyck
  June 3, 1839 - August 8, 1901

Johann Dyck, 1839-1901

Maria Peters, 1828-1900

NIKOLAIFELD-FRANZFELD   *Yazykovo Colony*

8. STORE COMPLEX

This complex of buildings is located on the east side of the village street near the centre of the former village of Franzfeld. It was established by A. Wieler from Neuenburg soon after the founding of the village. After his death in 1905 it was closed. After three years it was reopened by J. Neufeld. He likely rented it from new owners, a Franz Peters family, who also owned a large estate. When they emigrated to Canada in 1923, they left this complex to Mrs. Peters' brother, Johann Wieler. He then rented out the buildings to various individuals and organizations.

The building closest to the street was the general store. It measured 10 m by 18 m. The exterior walls are of brick but have been covered with plaster. Other changes have been made to the building including the roof. In 1930 the store was relocated to another part of the village. But today it is again used as a store.

The other building close to the street and to the north of the store, was the residence. It measured 12 m by 20 m and had a small extension to the rear. It has some fine brick detailing, although in poor condition. The gable end has vertical wood siding. The roof has been changed to corrugated cement-asbestos. In 1930 it became the administrative office for the local collective farm. Today it is used as a storage shed.

The building farthest from the street was the barn. It was later converted to a granary. The building behind the store was a creamery. Both of these buildings have fine brick detailing although they are in poor condition. Today they are both used as storage sheds.

House

Store

NIKOLAIFELD-FRANZFELD　　　*Yazykovo Colony*

9. FRANZFELD VILLAGE SCHOOL

This school building, located on the east side of the village street, was built in 1872. It was built parallel to the street with entrances from the school yard to the rear. It measured 11 m by 25 m. The walls were of brick and the windows had decorative wood frames. Most windows facing the school yard have no decoration. This may have been removed at a later date. The arched windows in the gable end are typical for village schools of the area.

The building has continued to function as a school. In 1925 there were 63 students and two teachers. The original roof has been replaced with corrugated cement-asbestos and the exterior walls have been painted.

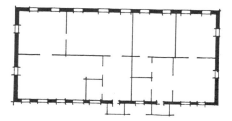

Franzfeld village school building from yard

Franzfeld village school building from street

NIKOLAIFELD-FRANZFELD   *Yazykovo Colony*

10. FRANZFELD CEMETERY

The following gravestones have been identified:

- Johann Dyck
  June 3, 1839 - August 8, 1901

- Sarah Epp
  geb. Redekop
  1865 - 1909

- David Woelk
  July 30, 1842 - July 29, 1902

  Katharina Woelk
  geb. Klassen
  March 15, 1847 - August 1, 1889

- Maria Unger
  geb. Heppner
  February 10, 1839 - December 2, 1903

Sarah Epp, 1865-1909

David & Katharina Woelk

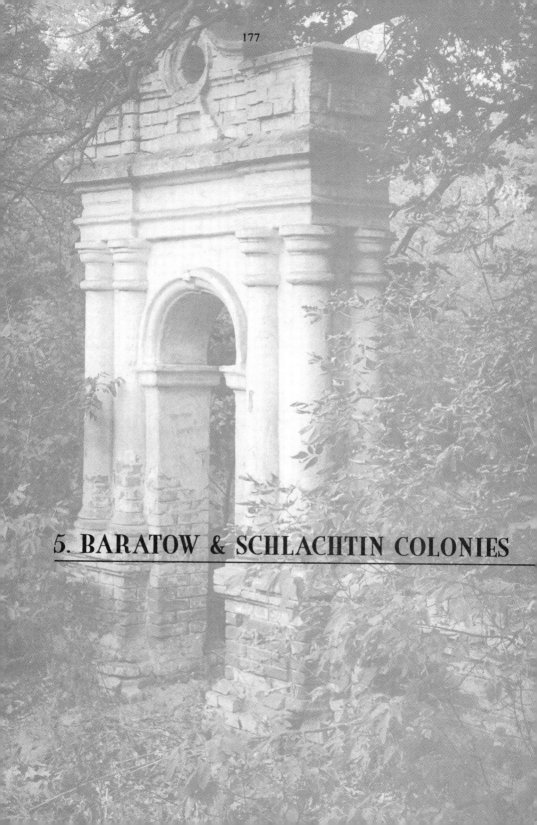

5. BARATOW & SCHLACHTIN COLONIES

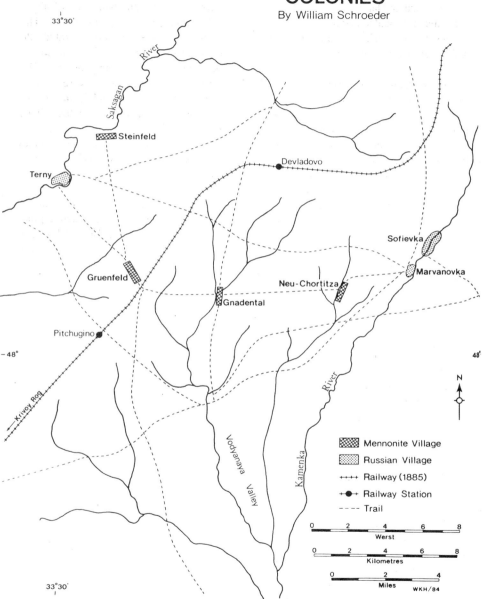

SCHLACHTIN & BARATOV COLONIES

By William Schroeder

33°30'

Saksagan River

Steinfeld

Terny

Devladovo

Sofievka

Marvanovka

Gruenfeld

Neu-Chortitza

Gnadental

Pitchugino

Krivoy Rog

−48°

48°

N

Vodyanaya Valley

Kamenka River

Mennonite Village

Russian Village

Railway (1885)

Railway Station

Trail

0 2 4 6 8
Werst

0 2 4 6 8
Kilometres

0 2 4
Miles

WKH/84

33°30'

The former Baratow and Schlachtin Colonies are located approximately 100 km west of the former Chortitza Colony and 30 km northeast of the City of Krivoy Rog.

The Baratow Colony was established in 1872, when the Chortitza Colony purchased 3,691 dessiatine of land from Prince Repnin. The Prince's daughter, who was married to Count Baratow, helped to expedite the sale, and so the settlement became known as the Baratow Colony. Two villages were established, Neu-Chortitza and Gnadental.

The purchase price was 33 Rubles per dessiatine. A total of 71 families from the Chortitza Colony, most of which were landless, settled in the two villages. Each family received 50 dessiatine of land. Approximately 94 dessiatine were set aside for reserve. Rental income from this land was to be used for future land purchases.

While the representatives of the Chortitza Colony were in the process of negotiating the purchase of the Baratow land, they became aware of additional land that was available immediately to the north of it. So in 1874 they purchased 4,187 dessiatine from Captain Schlachtin for 40 Rubles per dessiatine. A total of 80 families from the Chortitza Colony, most of which were also landless, settled in the two villages which were established, Gruenfeld and Steinfeld. Each family received 50 dessiatine of land.

The locations and layouts of the villages, the allocation of the farmsteads, the planting of trees, and the construction of buildings were all done in accordance with the traditions of the Chortitza Colony. The administration of these settlements, however, differed. The Baratow villages were incorporated into an adjacent Volost which included the Ukrainian village of Maryanovka. The Schlachtin villages were also incorporated into an adjacent Volost which was administered from the village of Terny.

Following are the present Russian names of the Baratow and Schlachtin villages:

Gnadental . . . . Vodyanaya
Gruenfeld . . . . Selenopole
Neu-Chortitza . . . . . . Novo-Khortitsa
Steinfeld . . . . Kamenka

GNADENTAL

The village of Gnadental was founded in 1872 when the Baratow settlement was established by the Chortitza Colony. There were 35 farms of approximately 50 dessiatine each. Almost ⅔ of these were occupied by settlers from the village of Chortitza, while the other settlers came from various daughter colonies.

The village was laid out in the traditional manner with a main street parallel to a stream and farmyards on both sides of the street. The stream was dammed at both ends of the village to increase the water supply. The landless were located along a cross street at the south end of the village referred to as the "Anwohner" street.

A village school was operational by 1873. By 1890 it had expanded into a multi-class school. The village had a treadmill and several windmills. A steam mill was planned for construction in about 1918 but did not proceed.

Between 1907 and 1913, 30 families moved to new daughter settlements in Siberia. In 1918 the population of the village was 300. In 1930 it became a collective farm called "Morganrot". In 1943, Gnadental ceased to exist as a Mennonite village. Today there are three former Mennonite buildings still remaining, the village school and two houses. The village name is now Vodyanaya.

GRUENFELD

The village of Gruenfeld was founded in 1874 when the Schlachtin settlement was established by the Chortitza Colony. The settlers came from the villages of Einlage and Chortitza. There were a total of 40 farms, each with 50 dessiatine.

The village was laid out in the traditional manner, a main street with farmyards on both sides. It was not located adjacent to a stream, but water was available from streams at both ends of the village, which were dammed to create reservoirs. The village had a cross street near its centre, where the church and school were located. There were also several cross streets at both ends of the village for the landless.

The village school building was erected in 1875 and began to be used in the fall of that year. Church services were held in homes and machine sheds until a new church building was built in 1909. A large farm implement factory owned by Johann Froese started operation in 1888. The village also had two large steam mills (Rempel, Schellenberg), a foundry, three blacksmiths, a brick factory, an oil press mill and a cheese factory. Commercial establishments included a drugstore, two general stores, a photo studio, a fire station, a post office and a prison.

The village's importance as an industrial centre increased after 1885 when a railway was built approximately 1 km. south of the village. In 1918 the village had a population of 590. In 1929 it was turned into a collective farm called "May First". Today it is known as Selenopole. There are a number of former Mennonite buildings still remaining and the cemetery still has several gravestones.

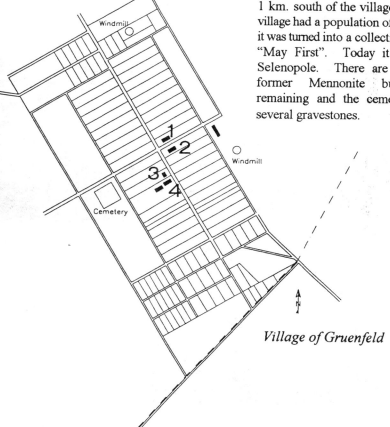

Village of Gruenfeld

GRUENFELD *Baratow & Schlachtin Colonies*

1. GRUENFELD MENNONITE CHURCH

The church in Gruenfeld was constructed in 1909. It was located at the centre of the village where the main village street intersected with the cross street. Placed perpendicular to the main street, the front entrance also faced the main street.

The walls of the church were built of brick, with large Gothic shaped windows. A small circular window in the front gable wall suggested the rose windows of the Gothic cathedrals. A brick fence enclosed the grounds.

The church was closed in 1929. The building was used as a granary for sometime. From 1941 to 1943 it was again used as a church. It was then converted to a clubhouse, and later into a school dormitory. Recently it has been converted back to a church building, utilized by the Selenopole Ukrainian Orthodox Church.

Over time the building has been modified somewhat. The exterior walls have been covered with a light stucco. However, the brick patterning is still evident, including that of the Gothic windows which were filled in after being damaged during World War II. The interior has been substantially modified to meet the liturgical requirements of the new church. The roof structure was replaced, the gable walls have been changed to vertical wood siding and the roofing to corrugated cement-asbestos.

Gruenfeld Church building

Church interior today

Gruenfeld Church building today

GRUENFELD
Baratow & Schlachtin Colonies

2. JAKOB REMPEL HOUSE

This house was constructed by Jakob Rempel, the owner of a steam mill in Gruenfeld. The brick construction featured fine brick detailing, especially around the windows. The house was located parallel to the street and adjacent to the mill.

During the 1920's it was converted to a student dormitory for the secondary school that was established at that time in Gruenfeld. Although the building is still in use today, it is not in good condition. The walls have deteriorated and the roofing has been replaced with corrugated cement-asbestos.

Jakob Rempel House

GRUENFELD *Baratow & Schlachtin Colonies*

3. JOHANN FROESE FACTORY

Johann Froese established this factory in 1888, having moved to Gruenfeld from the Chortitza Colony. The choice of Gruenfeld for the founding of this enterprise was based on its proximity to the newly constructed railroad. The factory produced various farm machinery including plows, drills, binders, and grain cleaning machines.

It developed into a large factory complex and at the height of its operation had some 140 workers. It ceased operation after the civil war. Today several of the factory buildings still exist. Their brick walls have been painted and the roofing has been replaced with corrugated cement-asbestos.

Factory building

GRUENFELD

4. JOHANN FROESE HOUSE

This house was constructed in 1893-1894 by Johann Froese, the factory owner. It was located next door to the factory and was placed parallel to the main street.

The building is still in use today. The roofing has been replaced with corrugated cement-asbestos and the exterior walls have been painted. The fine brick detailing is still evident.

Johann Froese House

NEU-CHORTITZA

Baratow & Schlachtin Colonies

The village of Neu-Chortitza was founded in 1872 when the Baratow settlement was established by the Chortitza Colony. In fact the majority of the settlers were from the village of Chortitza in the Chortitza Colony, hence the name of the new village. It was laid out in the traditional manner with a main street and farmyards on both sides of the street with the farmyards on one side backed on to a stream. The stream was dammed at the south end of the village to increase the water supply. Initially there were 36 farms, each with approximately 50 dessiatine.

The village also had a cross street (Querstrasse) near its centre. At this intersection were located the church, school, and village store. A new area (Neue Ansiedlung) was established for the landless across the stream from the village.

A village school was operational by 1873. By 1890 it had expanded into a multi-class school. Church services were held in homes and machine sheds until 1908 when a new church was built. It was closed in about 1929 and converted to a school.

The village had one windmill. During the 1880's, a large steam mill was built by Heinrich Dyck. Peter Rempel built a second steam mill soon after. Both were built of stone.

In 1918, the village had a population of 300. After 1928 the land was confiscated and turned into a collective farm called "Hope". Today the village is known as Novo-Khortitsa. Only a few former Mennonite homes still exist. The cemetery is gone, the gravestones having been used in the foundations and walls of subsequent buildings.

House in Neu-Chortitza

House in Neu-Chortitza

STEINFELD

The village of Steinfeld was founded in 1874 when the Schlachtin settlement was established by the Chortitza Colony. The settlers came mostly from the villages of Kronsweide and Chortitza. There were 40 farms in total, with 50 dessiatine each.

The village was initially located in the flood plain of the Saksagan River, but after some serious flooding it was relocated in 1877 by approximately one km. It was laid out in the traditional manner of a "Strassendorf", with farmyards on both sides of a main street. There were several cross streets along which the landless lived.

Construction of the village school building was completed in the fall of 1876. Church services were held in homes and machine sheds. In 1898 a Mennonite Brethren church was organized. A large house was purchased and converted to a church building. An Orphans' Administration (Waisanamt) office was established in Steinfeld in 1893 to serve the Mennonite villages of the region. It functioned until 1925.

The village had a flourishing fishing industry form the nearby Saksagan River. Less industrialized than the other Baratow-Schlachtin villages, Steinfeld had several windmills, one steam mill (Willms) which operated until 1930, and an oil press mill which was later converted to dormitories for seasonal workers. A brick factory operated until 1925.

In 1918 the village had a population of 350. Around 1928-29 it was turned into a collective farm called Trud. The A.P. Martens house and the D. Schapansky house, both built in 1910, became the headquarters for the collective farm. Both buildings still exist today, although the village was almost totally levelled as the Russian front moved back and forth through it in 1943. Today the village is known as Kamenka.

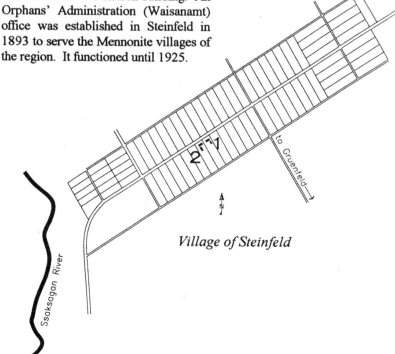

Village of Steinfeld

STEINFELD

1. D. SCHAPANSKY HOUSE/BARN

Built of brick construction in 1910, the D. Schapansky house was placed parallel to the street whereas most Mennonite farm houses were perpendicular to the street. A substantial link connected the house to the barn which in turn was connected to the machine shed. This created an L-shaped layout. The house was somewhat larger than the average house in the village.

After 1929 it became part of the headquarters for the collective farm. The building is still in use today. A small addition has been constructed at the south end. The exterior brick has been covered with stucco. However, the decorative treatment of the exterior walls, especially around the windows, is still visible. The exterior brick of the barn has been whitewashed. The original roofs of both buildings have been replaced with corrugated cement-asbestos.

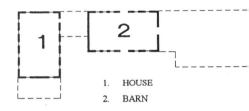

1. HOUSE
2. BARN

D. Schapansky House/Barn

STEINFELD

Baratow & Schlachtin Colonies

2. A.P. MARTENS HOUSE/BARN

The A.P. Martens house was constructed in 1910. It was located parallel to the street and was connected to the barn with a substantial link. The house was built of brick. It was somewhat larger than the average house in the village.

After 1929 it became part of the collective farm headquarters. The building is still in use today. The exterior walls have been painted but the brick detailing is still very evident. Similarly the walls of the barn have been painted and the roofs of both buildings have been replaced with corrugated cement-asbestos. The link between the house and barn is gone.

A.P. Martens House/Barn

1. HOUSE
2. BARN

Facade detail

6. MOLOTSCHNA COLONY

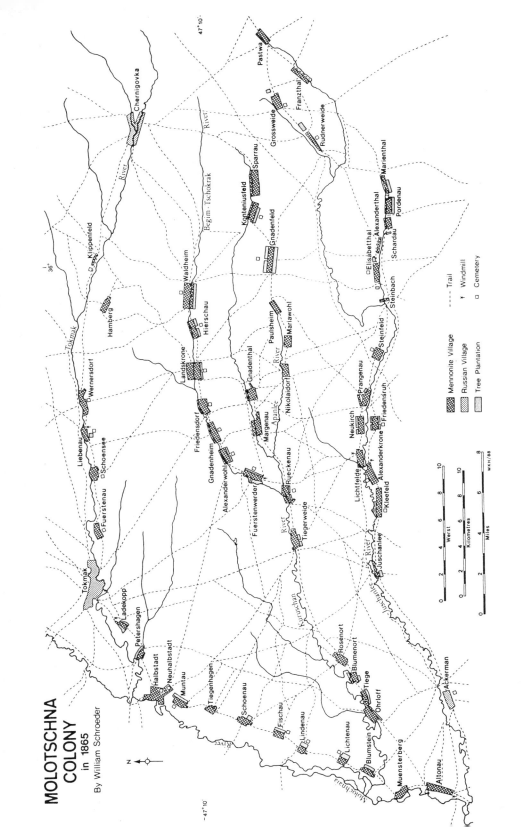

MOLOTSCHNA COLONY
in 1865
By William Schroeder

N

47° 10'

36°

47° 10'

Legend
- Mennonite Village
- Russian Village
- Tree Plantation
- ---- Trail
- ⚑ Windmill
- ▫ Cemetery

Werst: 0 2 4 6 8 10
Kilometres: 0 2 4 6 8 10
Miles: 0 2 4 6 8

wkr/88

Chernigovka
Klippenfeld
Hamberg
Wernersdorf
Liebenau
Schoensee
Fuerstenau
Tokmak
Ladekopp
Petershagen
Halbstadt
Neuhalbstadt
Muntau
Tiegenhagen
Schoenau
Fischau
Lindenau
Lichtenau
Blumstein
Muensterberg
Altonau
Ohrloff
Tiege
Blumenort
Rosenort
Ackerman
Juschanlee
Kleefeld
Alexanderkrone
Lichtfelde
Neukirch
Friedensruh
Prangenau
Steinfeld
Steinbach
Elisabetthal
Alexanderthal
Schardau
Pordenau
Marienthal
Alexanderwohl
Gnadenheim
Friedensdorf
Landskrone
Hierschau
Waldheim
Konteniusfeld
Sparrau
Grossweide
Pastwa
Franzthal
Rudnerweide
Gnadenfeld
Gnadenthal
Paulsheim
Mariawohl
Nikolaidorf
Margenau
Rueckenau
Fuerstenwerder
Alexanderwohl
Tiegerweide

Tokmak River
Begim-Tschokrak River
Apanlee River
Juschanlee River
Kuruschan
Molotschnaia River

The Molotschna Colony, the second major Mennonite settlement in New Russia, was founded in 1804. A tract of land consisting of 120,000 dessiatine east of the Molochnaia River in the Taurida province, had been designated by the government for further Mennonite settlement. This land was located approximately 80 km southeast of the Chortitza Colony.

The first group of settlers consisting of 162 families left West Prussia in the summer of 1803. They spent the winter in the Chortitza Colony. Then, together with another 162 families that arrived that spring, they moved onto the land that had been set aside for them and began to layout the villages. Each family was provided with 65 dessiatine of land.

These first settlers established a line of nine villages along the east bank of the Molochnaia River, starting with Halbstadt in the north and ending with Altonau in the south. The following years more settlers came and additional villages were established along several tributaries of the Molochnaia River.

These settlers were better prepared than those that had settled the Chortitza Colony. Most were experienced farmers who had sold their farms and were able to bring capital with them. They also brought wagons, farm animals and furniture.

The early villages each had 20 farms and were laid out with farmyards on both sides of the street. The street was generally parallel to the river. The farmyards were usually 84 m wide and the houses were set back 29 m from the street to allow for a garden in the front yard. The first houses were made of earth (semlins), or if lumber was available, small wooden huts were built. These were quickly replaced with timber frame houses with walls of clay and straw. Since suitable clay, sand and water were readily available, small brick factories were soon established, after which houses were constructed of burned clay bricks. The houses were based on the model that the settlers brought from Prussia with the barn connected to the house. Usually the house was placed perpendicular to the village street.

There were numerous church congregations in the Molotschna Colony with church buildings usually serving several surrounding villages. Several new church movements began in the Molotschna Colony including the Kleine Gemeinde (small church) and the Mennonite Brethren.

Economically the Colony prospered. Initially sheep raising was the most important economic activity. The silk industry also became significant. Through the influence of Johann Cornies, numerous agricultural reforms were carried out including the four-field system of summer fallowing. Grain growing soon replaced sheep raising. Although farming continued to be the primary economic activity, other businesses also developed including a number of farm machinery factories. In 1910, a railroad was built along the western and northern edges of the Molotschna Colony.

The influence of Cornies was also evident in the appearance of buildings and villages after about 1830. Specifications were established for the layout of villages and the style of farm buildings and school buildings. Farm houses were

194

Molotschna Colony

allowed to be built in two different sizes but with only one standard layout. Barns were to be connected to the houses in the traditional way, separated by a brick fire wall and a metal fireproof door. The machine sheds were attached to the barns either in a straight line or at right angles.

The Molotschna Colony became the most successful Mennonite agricultural settlement in Russia. Up until 1860 the government authorities considered it to be the showpiece of all European settlements. However, with revolution breaking out in 1917 followed by civil war, this prosperity came to an end. The villages of the Molotschna suffered through the terror of Makhno, famine, and the confiscation of property. Many of the residents were exiled during the 1930's and those that remained, left in 1943. Today the Molotschna is still a productive agricultural area, divided into a number of collective farms. The present Russian names of the Molotschna villages are as follows:

Alexanderkrone . . . . Grushevka
Alexandertal . . . . Alexandrovka
Alexanderwohl . . . . Svetloye
Altonau . . . . Travnyeve
Blumenort . . . . Orlovo
Blumstein . . . . Kamenskoye
Elisabethtal . . . . Alexandrovka
Fischau . . . . Rybalovka
Franzthal . . . . no longer exists
Friedensdorf . . . . Khmelnitskoye
Friedensruh . . . . Udarnik
Fürstenau . . . . Lugovka
Fürstenwerder . . . . Balkove
Gnadenfeld . . . . Bogdanovka
Gnadenheim . . . . Balashovka
Gnadenthal . . . . Blagodatnoye

Grossweide . . . . Prostore
Halbstadt . . . . Molochansk
Hamberg . . . . Kamenka
Hierschau . . . . Vladovka
Juschanlee . . . . Kirovo
Kleefeld . . . . no longer exists
Klippenfeld . . . . Stulnevo
Konteniusfeld . . . . Dovge
Ladekopp . . . . part of Tokmak
Landskrone . . . . Lankove
Lichtenau . . . . Svetlodolinskoye
Lichtfelde . . . . Grushevka
Liebenau . . . . Ostrikovka
Lindenau . . . . Lyubimovka
Margenau . . . . no longer exists
Mariawohl . .. . Zelyonyi Yar
Marienthal . . . . Panfilovka
Münsterberg . . . . Prilukovka
Muntau . . . . Molochansk
Neuhalbstadt . . . . Molochansk
Neukirch . . . . Udarnik
Nikolaidorf . . . . no longer exists
Ohrloff . . . . Orlovo
Pastva . . . . Kyitkove
Paulsheim . . . . no longer exists
Petershagen . . . . Kutuzovka
Pordenau . . . . Panfilovka
Prangenau . . . . no longer exists
Rosenort . . . . Orlovo
Rudnerweide . . . . Rozovka
Rückenau . . . . Kozolugovka
Schardau . . . . Panfilovka
Schönau . . . . Dolina
Schönsee . . . . Snegurevka
Sparrau . . . . Dovge
Steinbach . . . . Kalinovka
Steinfeld . . . . no longer exists
Tiege . . . . Orlovo
Tiegenhagen . . . . Levadnoye
Tiegerweide . . . . Mostove
Waldheim . . . . Vladovka
Wernersdorf . . . . Ostrikovka

ALEXANDERKRONE-LICHTFELDE   *Molotschna Colony*

ALEXANDERKRONE

The village of Alexanderkrone was founded in 1857 by 40 families from other villages in the Molotschna Colony. It was located on the south bank of the Juschanlee River, with its main street placed generally parallel to the river. There were 20 farmyards on each side of the street. It was likely named after Tsar Alexander II and the "crown" of land on which it was located.

A village school was constructed soon after the founding of the village. A church building was constructed in 1890 and in 1906 a Zentralschule was built. The village also had a tile factory, a steam mill, two windmills, and a doctor's office and pharmacy.

By 1869 Alexanderkrone had 40 full farms and 25 small farms with a total of 3,000 dessiatine of land. In 1913 the total population of the village was 550. After the civil war, the land was collectivized and many Molotschna farmers were forced out of their homes and onto the open steppe south of Alexanderkrone to survive on their own.

LICHTFELDE

The village of Lichtfelde was founded in 1819 by 18 Flemish Mennonite families. Two more families arrived in 1820. Of the 20 families, 17 were from Prussia, the rest from existing Molotschna villages. Since the settlers were poor, they received an interest free loan of over 2800 Rubles from the government. The total land area provided to the Lichtfelde settlement was 1300 dessiatine. This land was located on the north side of the Juschanlee River and was previously rented from the government by Johann Cornies who in turn had rented it to local Nogai tribes for use as pasture.

The village was laid out with its main street placed generally parallel to the river. It was named after a village by the same name in West Prussia. A village school was not constructed until 1824. In 1834 a 12 dessiatine large tree plantation was started. It was completed in 1847. By 1869 Lichtfelde had 16 full farms, 8 half farms, and 27 small farms with a total land area of over 1,700 dessiatine.

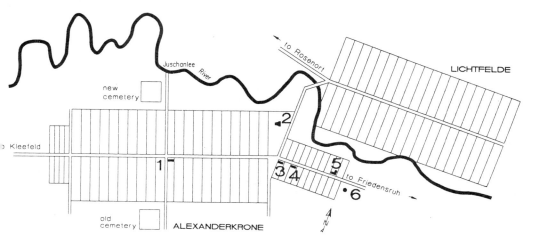

Villages of Alexanderkrone and Lichtfelde

ALEXANDERKRONE-LICHTFELDE   *Molotschna Colony*

The village had a church building which was the home of the Evangelical Mennonite Brotherhood, a new congregation founded in 1905 in Lichtfelde.

ALEXANDERKRONE-LICHTFELDE

The villages of Alexanderkrone and Lichtfelde were located on opposite sides of the Juschanlee River. The main streets of the two villages were connected by a cross street with a bridge over the river. Today the two villages are combined into one, known as Grushevka. There are still several Mennonite buildings in the former village of Alexanderkrone but in the former village of Lichtfelde none are left. The cemeteries of both villages also no longer exist.

House in Alexanderkrone

ALEXANDERKRONE-LICHTFELDE   *Molotschna Colony*

1.   ALEXANDERKRONE VILLAGE SCHOOL

The original village school that was built when the village was founded, was eventually replaced by this ornate brick structure. It was located at the centre of the village and was placed parallel to the street. The brickwork of the exterior walls expressed a series of columns. The window openings were also framed by decorative brickwork and the main entrance, which faced the street, was emphasized by the unique brick detailing above it. It is likely that this brickwork was originally covered with plaster.

Today the building is in poor condition. The window openings have been filled in and brick buttresses have been added to the exterior walls, suggesting that the building is being used for grain storage. The roof has been changed to corrugated cement-asbestos and the gable ends are probably not original. They are now covered with vertical wood siding.

Alexanderkrone village school building

ALEXANDERKRONE-LICHTFELDE   *Molotschna Colony*

2. ALEXANDERKRONE ZENTRALSCHULE

The plans for this secondary school building were prepared by architect Johann Peters from Neuhalbstadt. They called for a substantial building with brick walls covered with decorative plaster and the roof covered with metal sheeting. The entrance had extensive wood fretwork and very thin decorative columns, creating a quite delicate design in contrast to the solid looking exterior walls. The result was a very attractive building with the character of a large residence, rather than the institutional appearance of other schools.

The building was also sited with considerable sensitivity by the architect. Approaching Alexanderkrone from the east (from Lichtfelde), as one crossed the Juschanlee River, the school building suddenly came into view — an impressive sight. The two large gateposts at the entrance to the school grounds further added to the visual impact.

Inside the school there was a central hallway with two classrooms to the left and a classroom and a teachers' room to the right. The hallway led to a larger auditorium with a stage, beyond which was another classroom. Three of the classrooms were large enough to hold up to 50 students each. There was also a basement.

The construction was carried out by a local Russian builder named Matjvai, with most work done by volunteer labour from the surrounding Mennonite villages. The necessary funds needed for construction were raised in a short time with wealthy local estate owners providing substantial funding for it. The ground breaking took place in April 1906 and, although construction was not quite complete, it began to be used by September of the same year. A teacherage was built at the same time. It was quite similar in plan to other Mennonite houses of the time, including a small attached barn.

In 1913 the school was changed to a business school (Handelsschule). After the civil war, the facility continued to function in one way or another as a school until 1941. Today it is used as a dormitory for migrant workers. The teacherage is now a private residence. The buildings are not in good condition. The roofs have been replaced with corrugated cement-asbestos, the walls have been painted and the school's front entrance with its wide stairs is gone. The two gateposts and the fence along the street are also gone.

1.   FOYER
2.   TEACHER'S OFFICE/LIBRARY
3.   CLASSROOM
4.   ASSEMBLY
5.   STAGE

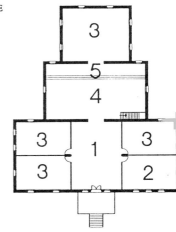

ALEXANDERKRONE-LICHTFELDE *Molotschna Colony*

Alexanderkrone Zentralschule building today

Wall detail

Alexanderkrone Zentralschule after 1906

ALEXANDERKRONE-LICHTFELDE   *Molotschna Colony*

3.   ALEXANDERKRONE MENNONITE CHURCH

The residents of Alexanderkrone originally belonged to the Margenau Mennonite Church but formed their own congregation in 1890. The same year they constructed this church building near the east end of the village. The building was placed parallel to the street with the entrance facing west. It is, therefore, likely that the pulpit and platform were at the east end of the building. The walls were constructed of brick and covered with plaster. The expression of the exterior walls included a series of decorative columns and window frames creating an appearance not unlike the other buildings of the village.

By 1909 the church had close to 600 baptized members and served the villages of Alexanderkrone, Kleefeld, Lichtfelde, Steinfeld, Neukirch, and Prangenau. Today, this building is again being used as a church. It is now a Ukrainian Orthodox Church. It appears to have been modified somewhat particularly at the west end where the original entrance appears to have been expanded. The roof has also been modified and replaced with corrugated cement-asbestos.

Alexanderkrone Church building

ALEXANDERKRONE-LICHTFELDE *Molotschna Colony*

4. DOCTOR'S OFFICE AND PHARMACY

This building housed a doctor's office (Dr. Bittner) and a pharmacy. Its exterior walls were built of brick and covered with plaster. They are similar in their expression to the other buildings in the village, including a series of decorative columns. The gable ends have several arched windows, again similar to other buildings in the village with their decorative brick framing. The brick gateposts and fence at the street, which are still in place, complement the building.

Doctor's office and pharmacy building

Gateposts at street

ALEXANDERKRONE-LICHTFELDE   *Molotschna Colony*

5. HOUSE/BARN

This house and barn located near the east end of the village in the area for the small farmers (Kleinwirte), were built in 1914. The house was placed parallel to the street and the barn perpendicular to it. Both buildings are quite substantial in size and were built of brick. The exterior brickwork of the house was covered with plaster and includes a series of columns and window frames that are very similar in appearance to other buildings in the village.   The gable ends have arched windows with decorative brick framing including small columns at the sides of the windows. The building is still used today as a residence.

House/barn

ALEXANDERKRONE-LICHTFELDE *Molotschna Colony*

6. WINDMILL

This circular brick windmill was an example of the "Dutch" model (Holländer-Mühle) as compared to the earlier wooden model that the Mennonites brought with them from Prussia. These Dutch windmills had four very large blades and a dome-shaped roof with two pairs of small blades that allowed it to automatically set itself against the wind. They were usually 4 storeys high, of wood construction, with exterior brick walls.

These windmills were privately owned and most Mennonite villages had at least one. However, large steam-powered flour mills eventually began to replace them. This windmill was in operation until 1952. It is the last known Mennonite windmill in the former Mennonite Colonies.

Windmill

Interior of windmill

ALEXANDERTAL

Molotschna Colony

The village of Alexandertal was founded in 1820 by 16 families from Prussia. It was located along the north bank of the Tschokrak River, a small stream that flows into the Juschanlee River. The village was laid out parallel to the river, with 10 farmyards on each side of the street. The farmyards on the south side backed onto the river. A short distance down stream, a dam created a small water reservoir. Upon the recommendation of one of the Molotschna church leaders, the village was named Alexandertal to commemorate Tsar Alexander I.

The four farmyards that were not initially settled, were occupied in 1822 by additional settlers from Prussia. In total, the families that settled Alexandertal brought only 6,000 Rubles of their own capital with them. The government, therefore, advanced them somewhat more than 11,000 Rubles as an interest free loan, to assist them with settlement costs. The first houses were earth huts. These were soon replaced by more substantial houses.

The village school was located at the centre of the village. There was also a windmill, a steam mill, and a store. A church building was constructed at the west end of the village. By 1869 there were 15 full farms, 12 half farms, and 26 small farms with a total of about 1,800 dessiatine of land. In 1913 the total population of Alexandertal was 400. Today the village is part of Alexandrovka. There are only a few Mennonite buildings still remaining and the cemetery no longer exists.

G. Spenst House, Alexandertal

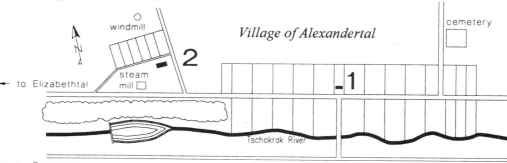

ALEXANDERTAL　　　　　　　　　*Molotschna Colony*

1.　VILLAGE SCHOOL

The village school was located at the village centre and was placed parallel to the street. Being a fairly long building, it probably included both a classroom and a teacher's residence. Its appearance was that of a large residence. The walls were built of brick with very little ornamentation, suggesting that this building was of early vintage. The gable ends are clad in vertical wood siding, the walls have been plastered and the roof has been replaced with corrugated cement-asbestos. The building is used today as a residence.

Alexandertal village school building

ALEXANDERTAL   *Molotschna Colony*

2.   ALEXANDERTAL M. B. CHURCH

The Alexandertal Mennonite Brethren congregation constructed this church building in 1902 to 1903. It was located on a side street and was placed perpendicular to that street. It appears to have had entrance doors at both ends of the south elevation, suggesting that the pulpit/platform would have been located along the north side wall. The exterior walls were built of brick with modest detailing around the windows and the expression of columns at the corners of the building. The original roof has been replaced with corrugated cement-asbestos. The addition on the south side of the building appears to have been added at a later date. Today the west end of the building is used as a private residence and the east end is used as a community club.

Alexandertal M.B. Church building

ALEXANDERWOHL

Molotschna Colony

The village of Alexanderwohl was founded in 1821 by 22 families from Prussia. Seven more families arrived in 1823 and one more arrived in 1824. This group of settlers relocated to Russia as a congregation, an Old Flemish congregation, that had existed as a church in Prussia for over 200 years. On its journey to Russia the group encountered Tsar Alexander I who wished them well (wohl) on the rest of their journey. When the group arrived in the Molotschna, the local government authority named the village Alexanderwohl to commemorate this event. The settlers brought approximately 8,500 Rubles of their own capital and received somewhat over 4,000 Rubles from the government as an interest free loan.

The village was located along the south bank of the Begim-Tschokrak River, with the street running parallel to the river and 15 farmyards on each side of the street. The village school was located at the centre of the village. It was used for church services until a church building was constructed in 1865, across the street from the school. The village also had a windmill. In 1869 the village had 25 full farms, 10 half farms and 26 small farms with a total land area of almost 2,400 dessiatine.

In 1874, the entire village emigrated to America, settling in Kansas. The new occupants of Alexanderwohl came from other Molotschna villages. In 1903 the village had a population of 630. Today there are only a few Mennonite buildings remaining and the cemetery no longer exists. The village is now known as Svetlage.

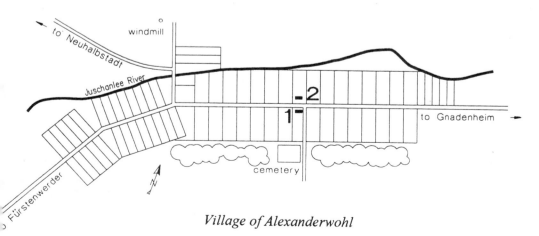

Village of Alexanderwohl

ALEXANDERWOHL   *Molotschna Colony*

1. ALEXANDERWOHL MENNONITE CHURCH

This church building was constructed in 1865. It was a large two storey structure generally based on the traditional Mennonite church design. Located parallel to the street, the building's thick exterior masonry walls had plaster applied to them. The pulpit/platform was located along the long side facing the street. The small shuttered windows were the same size throughout whereas most of the early Mennonite churches had a series of tall windows behind the pulpit/platform. This created the appearance of a large two storey house. The hip gable roof, covered with clay tiles, was similar to that specified by Johann Cornies for village schools during the time of educational reform. It was used in several instances for church buildings.

The main entrance was located at the rear of the building facing the church yard. There were also small side entrances. Two large gateposts at the street emphasized the entrance to the church yard and a masonry fence separated it from the street.

This building still exists today although it is virtually unrecognizable since it has been substantially altered. Only the lower half of the existing walls remain, but the recessed side entrance and the window proportions are still recognizable. A new lower roof structure covered with clay tiles has totally changed the appearance of the building. It is now used as a storage building for the local collective farm.

Alexanderwohl Church building today

ALEXANDERWOHL

Molotschna Colony

Alexanderwohl Church building

Alexanderwohl Church building from street

ALEXANDERWOHL

Molotschna Colony

2. VILLAGE SCHOOL

The village school was located at the centre of the village, parallel to the street and directly across from the church. The exterior walls were built of brick with modest ornamentation. The front entrance faced the street. The building is still in use today. The walls have been plastered and the roof has been replaced with corrugated cement-asbestos.

Alexanderwohl village school building

ALTONAU *Molotschna Colony*

The village of Altonau was founded in 1804 along the east bank of the Molotschnaia River, the last of a string of villages along this river. Initially 13 Flemish Mennonite families from Prussia settled here. Most lived in earth huts during the first winter. The next spring the village was severely flooded after which it was relocated further east to slightly higher ground. It was laid out with the street parallel to the river and farmyards on both sides of the street. There were a total of 22 farmyards. Three settler families received government assistance in the form of an interest free loan of almost 1,200 Rubles from the government. The balance of the families were fairly well off and brought a total of 20,000 Rubles of capital with them.

Initially the village was simply named No. 9 but eventually the authorities required the settlers to give it a name. They chose to name it Altonau, a low German adaptation of Altona, but also meaning "all too close", in reference to the nearby Nogai nomadic tribes which they feared.

The village school which had two classrooms, was located at the centre of the village. There was no church building. The village residents belonged to various congregations in nearby villages. Businesses in the village included a tile and brick factory (B. Enns), a soap factory, a blacksmith shop, a vinegar factory, a fruit tree nursery (B. Friesen) and several mills. In 1869 there were 21 full farms, two half farms and 31 small farms with over 1,900 dessiatine of land. In 1912 its population was 800.

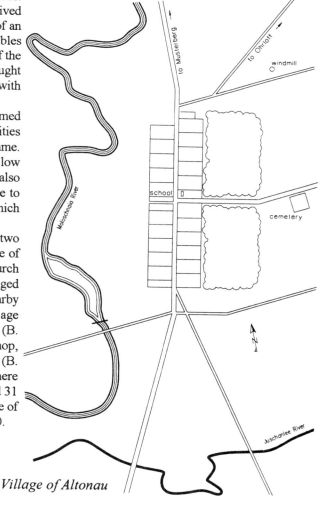

Village of Altonau

ALTONAU

Molotschna Colony

Today the village is called Travnyeve. There are only a few Mennonite buildings left and there are no gravestones in the cemetery. However approximately 10 gravestones have been found in a windbreak along side a road near the village. They are badly damaged and only the following three have been identified:

● Abr. Matthies
September 29, 1824 - April 10, 1898

Anna Matthies
April 15, 1833 - June 23, 1899
On the opposite side of this stone there is an inscription: "Die dankbaren Kinder und Grosskinder, 1903." (presumably the date when the monument was erected).

● Wilhelm Bar(ch)
... 1841 - ... 1903

● Katharina Neufeld
geb. Töws
December 19, 1819 - July 1, 1896

House in Altonau

Building in Altonau

House in Altonau

BLUMSTEIN

The village of Blumstein was founded in 1804 by 21 Flemish Mennonite families from Prussia. It was located east of the Molotschnaia River and just north of the Kuruschan River. It was laid out with the village street parallel to the Molotschnaia River and farmyards on both sides of the street. A small dam on the Kuruschan River created a reservoir for watering the cattle.

The village was originally referred to as No. 4, but was later named after a village in Prussia. In 1817, two thirds of the village was destroyed by fire but was soon rebuilt. By 1869 there were 20 full farms, two half farms and 51 small farms with a total land area of almost 2,200 dessiatine. In 1911 the population was over 600. There was a village school with two classrooms, but there was no church building as most residents belonged to the Lichtenau Mennonite Church. There were several small industries in the village.

Today the village is known as Kamenskoye. There are no Mennonite buildings left in the village but a number of gravestones have been found in the cemetery, located to the east of the village. A number of them are in the shape of frames with inscriptions on them. The following have been identified:

- Jakob Joh. Riediger
  ... 8, 1895 - December 13, 1895

- Jakob ... Riediger
  ... 1899 - January 18, ...

- Jakob Jak. Riediger
  ... - ...

- Katarina ... Riediger
  February 17, 1880 - June 1, 1886

- Abraham Jak. Riediger
  June 9, 1886 - June 6, 1887

- Johann Joh. Riediger
  January 23, 1904 - October 20, 1909

- ...ob Riediger
  ... - ...

- Kornelia Riediger
  January 28, 1929 - February 1, 1929

Jakob Riediger, 1895-1895

Riediger

ELISABETHTAL
Molotschna Colony

The village of Elisabethtal was founded in 1823 along the north bank of the Tschokrak River. Initially 22 Flemish Mennonite families settled here. Another three families joined them in subsequent years. Most had arrived from Prussia before 1823. An interest free loan of almost 11,000 Rubles was provided by the government to 14 of the families. The other families brought their own financial resources amounting to over 14,000 Rubles. They named the village in honour of Empress Elisabeth, wife of Tsar Alexander I.

The village was laid out with the village street placed parallel to the river. Farmyards were located on both sides of the street. A cross street at the centre of the village led to the cemetery. The land on which Elisabethtal was established had previously been rented to Klaas Wiens, owner of the nearby Steinbach estate, who in turn had rented it to local Nogai tribes.

The first houses were earth huts and small wooden huts. These were soon replaced with more substantial houses and barns. A village school was located at the centre of the village. There were also two windmills. The village had no church building since most inhabitants were members of the Pordenau Mennonite Church. In 1869 Elisabethtal had 22 full farms, six half farms and 29 small farms, with a land area totalling just over 2,000 dessiatine. In 1913 it had a population of 436.

Today Elisabethtal together with the former village of Alexandertal are known as Alexandrovka. Only a few Mennonite buildings still remain. A number of Mennonite gravestones can be found in the cemetery.

House in Elisabethtal

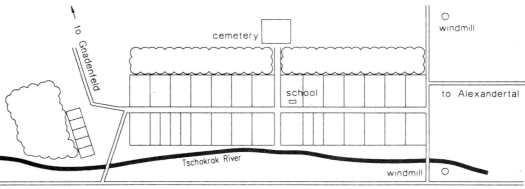

Village of Elisabethtal

FISCHAU

The village of Fischau was founded in 1804 along the east bank of the Molochnaia River by 22 Flemish Mennonite families from Prussia. Initially the village was known as "No. 4", but later was named after a village in Prussia. In 1832 the village was relocated to a better site, as directed by Johann Cornies and the Agricultural Society. It was laid out with farmyards on both sides of the village street. There was a village school but no church building.

In 1869 there were 16 full farms, 12 half farms and 23 small farms with a total land area of approximately 1,800 dessiatine. Today the village is known as Rybalovka. The school building is the only remaining Mennonite building. Two gravestones have been identified in the cemetery, which is located southeast of the village:

●Katharina Enns
   geb. Friesen
   September 11, 1839 - January 24, 1906

●... Wiebe
   ... - ...

Katharina Enns, 1839-1906

FISCHAU   *Molotschna Colony*

1. VILLAGE SCHOOL

This school building was constructed in 1896. It was placed parallel to the street. The exterior walls have fine brick detailing above and below the windows. The brickwork at the corners of the building suggests structural columns. These columns also occur at the centre of the long facade facing the street. This may have originally emphasized an entrance.

The entrance extension on the opposite facade appears to have been added at a later date. The building is not in good condition and is no longer in use. The walls have been painted and the original roof has been replaced with corrugated cement-asbestos.

Fischau village school building

FRIEDENSDORF

The village of Friedensdorf was founded in 1824 along the south bank of the Begim Tschokrak River by 30 families. Of these, 14 arrived in 1825. The majority of these were Flemish Mennonites from Prussia but three families were from the Chortitza Colony and two were from other villages in the Molotschna Colony. An interest free loan of almost 4,000 Rubles was provided by the government to 17 of the families. They also had about 1,000 Rubles of their own. The other 13 families brought 3,000 Rubles of their own capital. Several settlers wanted to name the village Friedberg, to remind them of a village in Prussia. But the local authority, noting that the new village was not located on a large hill (Berg), decided that Friedensdorf was more appropriate.

The village was laid out with the street parallel to the river and farmyards on both sides of the street and the farmyards on the north side backing onto the river. The land had been previously rented by Johann Cornies who in turn had rented it to neighbouring Russians and Nogai tribes for pasture.

In 1830 the village school was built. In 1869 there were 27 full farms, 6 half farms and 26 small farms with a total land area of almost 2,400 dessiatine. There are no Mennonite buildings remaining today. The remains of several gravestones can be found in the cemetery, but none of the inscriptions are legible. The village is now called Khmelnitskoye.

Gravestone in Friedensdorf Cemetery

FRIEDENSRUH

The village of Friedensruh was founded in 1857 along the south bank of the Juschanlee River. It was one of the last villages to be established in the Molotschna Colony. The village was laid out in accordance with regulations established by Johann Cornies and the Agricultural Society. There was a single village street with farmyards on both sides. The street was placed parallel to the river. The buildings were constructed in accordance with the Agricultural Society's regulations which included the use of brick walls and clay tile roofs.

The land on which Friedensruh was established had been part of the Molotschna Colony's lands that were reserved for expansion. The families that settled Friedensruh were primarily from the villages along the west edge of the Molotschna. In 1869 the village had 28 full farms, four half farms, and 24 small farms with a total land area of over 2,300 dessiatine. Today the village together with the former village of Neukirch across the river are known as Udarnik. Little is left of the former Mennonite buildings. One gravestone has been identified in the cemetery, which is located to the south of the village:

• Bernhard Harms
  January 21, 1881 - ... 1896

FÜRSTENAU

The village of Fürstenau was founded in 1806 by 12 Flemish Mennonite families from Prussia. By 1810 another nine families had joined them. The settlers received an interest free loan from the government of over 10,000 Rubles. They brought no more than 2,000 Rubles of their own capital. The village was located on the south bank of the Tokmak River about three km. east of the town of Tokmak. The village street was placed parallel to the river, and had farmyards on both sides. The total land area of the village was 1,365 dessiatine. It was named after a village in Prussia by the same name.

In 1869 Fürstenau had 20 full farms, two half farms and 37 small farms with a total land area of almost 2,000 dessiatine. In 1915 the village was renamed Dolinka and since 1945 it is known as Lugovka. During the years 1919 to 1922 the villagers suffered more than most people in the Molotschna, first from a serious typhoid epidemic and then from severe hunger. Today only a few Mennonite buildings remain. The cemetery no longer exists.

FÜRSTENAU

Molotschna Colony

1. VILLAGE SCHOOL

The village school in Fürstenau had a classroom at one end and a teachers' residence at the other end. The older students were separated from the younger students by a folding wall. Enrolment was usually 30 to 40 students.

The school was located near the centre of the village. It was built with brick exterior walls and a hip gable roof covered with clay tiles. This roof shape was referred to as the "Johann Cornies" style since it was prescribed by the Agricultural Society. This and the minimal brick detailing suggest that the building was built around the mid-1800's.

In 1921 the school was taken over by the authorities and converted to a Russian school, with the Mennonite students being sent elsewhere. The building is still in use today. A row of clay roof tiles is still in place at the gable ends but the main roof has been replaced with corrugated cement-asbestos.

Fürstenau village school building

FÜRSTENAU

2. WILHELM NEUFELD HOUSE

This large residence was part of the Wilhelm and Maria Neufeld estate located across from the village school in Fürstenau. The building was expanded and remodelled over time resulting in a rather grand home. It featured a Grand Salon decorated in a Victorian style and filled with classical works of art, a large family room with a gramophone and record library and a dining room with a table for over 50 guests and a large electric chandelier powered by the estate's own generator. Other features included a full glazed veranda, a second floor glass skylight covered "arboretum" filled with large flowers and plants, several guest bedrooms, bathrooms, and extensive servants' quarters. The exterior masonry walls of the house were up to two feet thick. The front facade was uniquely decorative with a large second floor gable wall. The grounds surrounding the house included a flower garden, a large orchard with numerous types of fruit trees, landscaped areas, a gazebo, and a bowling lane. The estate also included a variety of large barns, sheds, and storage buildings. A brick fence with decorative posts surrounded the estate.

As a result of the post civil war situation, the Neufeld family was forced to abandon the estate in about 1921. It was subsequently incorporated into a collective farm. Today only the house remains and it has changed substantially in appearance. The second floor has been removed and the gable wall over the front entrance has been rebuilt. The end balconies are gone and the original clay tile roof has been replaced with corrugated cement-asbestos. The exterior walls have recently been plastered, covering much of the ornate brick detailing. The building is now used as a community centre.

Wilhelm Neufeld House

FÜRSTENAU

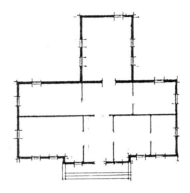

Entrance to garden

Wilhelm Neufeld House before 1920

Wilhelm Neufeld House in 1994

FÜRSTENWERDER   *Molotschna Colony*

The village of Fürstenwerder was founded in 1821 by 30 Flemish Mennonite families, four of which were from within the Molotschna Colony. The others were from Prussia, having arrived between 1816 and 1819. Since these settlers were quite poor, they received an interest free loan from the government of almost 20,000 Rubles.

The village was located along the east bank of the Begim Tschokrak River with its street parallel to the river and farmyards on both sides of the street. It was named after a village of the same name in Prussia.

By 1848, eight of the farmyards had houses built of burned clay bricks while the other 22 had houses built of air-dried bricks. They all had connected barns. A village school and a windmill had been built. There were close to 10,000 fruit trees and a tree plantation with over 11,000 mulberry trees and over 20,000 other trees. In 1869 the village had 18 full farms, four half farms and 33 small farms with a total land area of almost 2,500 dessiatine.

In 1915 the village name was changed to Poworotnoje. Then in 1917 it was changed back to Fürstenwerder and since 1945 it is known as Balkove. The former village school still exists but the cemetery is gone.

1. VILLAGE SCHOOL

The village school was located near the centre of the village. It was placed parallel to the village street. Since it is quite a long building it probably had a classroom at one end and a teacher's residence at the other end. The building looked like a large residence. The walls were built of brick with very little ornamentation and the gable ends were clad with vertical wood siding, suggesting that this is probably the original school building built prior to 1848. The exterior walls have been painted and the roof has been replaced with corrugated cement-asbestos. The building is used today as a residence.

Fürstenwerder village school building

GNADENFELD

Molotschna Colony

The village of Gnadenfeld was founded in 1835 by a congregation of Old Flemish Mennonites from the villages of Brenkenhofswalde and Franztal in the Brandenburg province in Prussia. Under the dynamic leadership of their elder, Wilhelm Lange, the spiritual life of the congregation had recently been revitalized. He worked to obtain permission from Tsar Nicholas I for his congregation to immigrate to southern Russia, even though by that time the Tsar had forbidden any further immigration. Forty families eventually moved to the Molotschna Colony where they established a new village which they called Gnadenfeld. Its name was derived from the fact that the Tsar had shown mercy (Gnade) bending the rules to allow this group into Russia, and field (feld) because of the location of the new village in the middle of the bald treeless steppes. Whereas most new Mennonite villages were located in valleys, near streams, Gnadenfeld was located on a slight hill.

The village was laid out with two main streets parallel to each other, each with 20 full farms (with farmyards of approximately 107 m wide by 214 m deep, equalling 2 dessiatine) on one side and 40 smaller farmyards on the other side. Between the two main streets, separating the full farms was an 8.5 m wide walkway referred to as the church path (Kirchensteg). Water was obtained from several wells.

The members of this congregation were spiritually very active and were highly cultural, more so than the people in the other villages. A village school was established when the village was founded. A fine church building was constructed in 1854. A Zentralschule was established in 1857.

The congregation was somewhat pietistic and had practices unknown in other Mennonite churches, such as having small children blessed in its services, Bible study groups, mission festivals, footwashing, and emphasis on

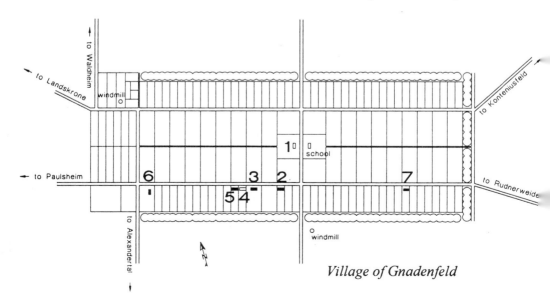

Village of Gnadenfeld

GNADENFELD

Molotschna Colony

temperance. Gnadenfeld became the centre of a new type of spiritual life, but soon theological disagreements developed, and in 1860, a group broke away and formed the Mennonite Brethren Church. This created a profound change in Mennonite church life in Russia.

In the 1860's the population of Gnadenfeld was more than 580. There were 34 full farms, 12 half farms and 38 small farms with a total of 3,200 dessiatine of land. In 1870 the municipalities in Russia were reorganized including the Molotschna Colony which was separated into two districts or Volosts. Gnadenfeld at that time became the administrative centre for the Gnadenfeld Volost, the eastern part of the Molotschna, consisting of 27 villages.

Eventually the village also had an inn (Gasthaus), a doctor's clinic, a private girls' school, a post office and several stores. Over time forests of trees and shelter belts were planted around the village. Around 1900 it was considered to be one of the most attractive among the many beautiful Mennonite villages in the Molotschna.

In 1918 the population of Gnadenfeld was approximately 800. During World War I the village name was changed to Bogdanovka. It suffered through the Revolution of 1917 and the postwar famine. A significant number of the

villagers emigrated in the 1920's. In the 1930's it underwent collectivization like the rest of Russia. It became the headquarters for the Karl Marx Collective Farm. Most of the remaining Mennonite population left in 1943.

The village still exists today and is still known as Bogdanovka. Many of the buildings are still there, such as the Zentralschule, the post office, and the doctor's clinic. The church was demolished some time ago. The girls school and the Volost building have recently been demolished.

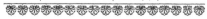

GNADENFELD

Molotschna Colony

1. GNADENFELD MENNONITE CHURCH

Although this building no longer exists, its prominent location within the village and its somewhat unique design make it of interest. Gnadenfeld is the only village in the Molotschna Colony to have had two parallel streets with a walkway in between referred to as the Kirchensteg (church path). Several other villages had two parallel streets but they did not have a walkway. The walkway led directly to the main church entrance which was opposite the cross-street. A brick fence complete with turnstile gates separated the church grounds from the street.

The church building was built in 1854 and appears to have been modelled after the Mennonite Church in Danzig which was built in 1819. The long vertical arched windows, the building proportions, and the roof shape were very similar. The interior was also similar with the pulpit/ platform located along the long side opposite the main entrance, and balconies along both short sides. There were also separate side entrances for men and women. The main entrance was only used on special occasions such as funerals and weddings. On these occasions the benches were laid out so as to create a centre aisle from the main entrance to the front platform. Normally the benches were laid out so as to create two side aisles since only the side entrances were used.

The church was designed to have a capacity of 500 people. In 1895 a pipe organ was installed on one of the balconies, the only Mennonite church in the Molotschna to have one. It is said that the organ music could be heard throughout the surrounding countryside. It is also said that the church had excellent acoustics and that on special occasions, two choirs, one in each balcony, would sing to each other, effectively demonstrating the acoustics.

In 1909, the Gnadenfeld Church had 620 baptized members and 13 ministers. The church was closed in 1933, reopened for a short time in 1941 and then converted to a movie theatre. It has since been demolished but its site is still recognizable. A memorial garden is now located there.

Gnadenfeld Church building from Kirchensteg

GNADENFELD

Molotschna Colony

5

1

2

4

3

1. SANCTUARY
2. PULPIT
3. STUDY
4. WOMENS' ROOM
5. MENS' ROOM

denfeld Church building from yard

Gnadenfeld Church building from cross street

GNADENFELD *Molotschna Colony*

2. GNADENFELD ZENTRALSCHULE

The origins of this facility go back to the 1850's at which time it was decided to establish a new secondary school in Gnadenfeld. A society was established at that time for this purpose. The school program was to be based on religious principles that would combine education with religious and philanthropic ideals. Funding was provided through substantial individual contributions from as far away as Charkov, Moscow and the Baltics. Also a brick factory and a lumber yard were established by the school society, the profits from which were to support the school including the construction of a new building. In 1857 government approval was received to establish this school, and in 1859 a fine new school building was opened. The Brotherhood School operated until 1863 when it was closed due to a division within the Church. The Gnadenfeld Volost purchased the building in 1870, renovated and used it as an administrative office. After the Volost constructed a new administrative building, this building was made into a Zentralschule. It opened in 1873. It had a 6 year course like other Mennonite secondary schools in Russia.

In 1914, in order to avoid the controls of the Russian Ministry of Education which was determined to end the autonomy of local school boards, the school was changed to a business school (Handelsschule). This way it fell under the control of the Ministry of Trade and Industry, which was more lenient in terms of controlling curriculum. In 1914 there were 150 students in 4 classes, plus 5 teachers.

The building located parallel to the street, had 4 classrooms, a large assembly area, a teachers' room and a teachers' residence on the main floor. At one time there was a veranda on the street side where stuffed animals and other items were displayed. In the basement was the cloak room with a direct entrance stair from the school yard. The toilets and barn were located elsewhere on the school yard. The exterior walls were constructed of brick and the roof covered with clay tile. Large ornamental brick gateposts at the street identified the entrance to the school yard.

After the civil war it was combined with other village schools and turned into a 7 class trade school (Arbeitsschule). In subsequent years the building was substantially enlarged. The construction of this addition was the responsibility of Peter Voth, a resident of Gnadenfeld. Today it is used by the local collective farm. The roof has been substantially changed and the building is generally not in good condition.

Basement entrance

GNADENFELD

Molotschna Colony

Gnadenfeld Zentralschule from street

1. TEACHERS' RESIDENCE
2. TEACHERS' ROOM
3. ASSEMBLY
4. CLASSROOM

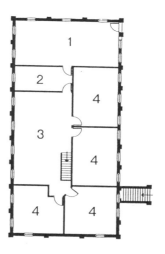

Gnadenfeld Zentralschule from yard, after 1917

Gnadenfeld Zentralschule today

GNADENFELD *Molotschna Colony*

3. JOHANN REMPEL HOUSE

This large brick house, constructed by the Johann Rempel family, was placed parallel to the street. The exterior walls are covered with plaster and are particularly ornate. The detailing of the walls suggests a structural column between every window which extends up into the eave. The gable end wall is particularly ornate with its two arched windows, each flanked by half-round columns. The original roof has been replaced with corrugated cement-asbestos. After the civil war, this building was used as a bookstore for a period of time. It is now used to house migrant workers.

Window detail

West facade

Johann Rempel House from yard

GNADENFELD

4. VOLOST

When the Molotschna Colony was separated into two districts in 1870, Gnadenfeld became the administrative centre for the eastern district which included 27 villages. The office was initially located in the former school building that the Volost purchased.

In 1872 this new Volost building was constructed of masonry and was used to carry out the administration's various responsibilities. For a short time in 1923 it was used as an agricultural school. This building has recently been demolished.

Volost building

Volost building in 1978

GNADENFELD   *Molotschna Colony*

5. POST OFFICE

This large brick building was placed parallel to the street. Its appearance is that of a large house and its ornamentation is similar to other houses in the village. The exterior brick walls are covered with plaster. The detailing of the end walls suggests structural columns between the windows. The two gable windows have detailing around them similar to the lower windows. The original roof has been replaced with corrugated cement-asbestos but the brick gateposts and fenceposts appear to be original.

Post Office building

GNADENFELD

6. DOCTOR'S CLINIC

This long rectangular building was located perpendicular to the street and appeared somewhat similar to the village houses, although larger. The exterior walls were built of brick and had fine detailing around the windows.

It was originally a doctor's clinic and day hospital. During the 1930's it functioned as a maternity hospital and during World War II it served as the regional headquarters for the German Army. Today it is used as a granary. The windows have been bricked in, the roof structure has been altered and the roofing changed to corrugated cement-asbestos.

Doctor's Clinic today

Doctor's Clinic in the 1940's

GNADENFELD   *Molotschna Colony*

7. KLAAS HEIDE HOUSE

This brick house, built by the Klaas Heide family, was placed parallel to the street. The exterior brick walls are quite ornate, particularly the detailing around the windows. The brick detailing also suggests a series of structural columns. The east portion of the rear wall is devoid of ornamentation. This is where the barn originally adjoined the house. The original gable roof has been replaced with a hip roof covered with corrugated cement-asbestos. The original gable walls had the initials K.H. and the date of construction (18...) indicated on it. Subsequent owners of the house were the H. Becker family and the H. Unruh family. Today it is used as a veterinary pharmacy.

Klaas Heide House from yard

HALBSTADT-MUNTAU
Molotschna Colony

HALBSTADT

The village of Halbstadt was founded in 1804, the first to be established in the Molotschna Colony. It was located on the east bank of the Molochnaia River near the northern border of the Colony. A total of 21 Flemish Mennonite families from Prussia settled here. The village was named after a village in Prussia by the same name, from which some of the settlers came.

The village was laid out with farmyards on both sides of the village street. The street was parallel to the river and the farmyards on the west side of the street backed on to the river. Many of the settlers built their houses the first summer. The wood for these timber frame houses with walls of clay and

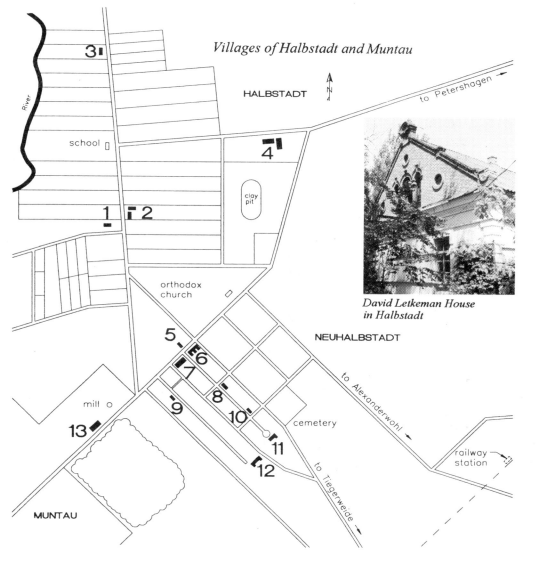

Villages of Halbstadt and Muntau

David Letkeman House in Halbstadt

straw, was provided by the government. It also provided each family with an interest free loan of 125 Rubles to buy livestock and equipment.

After many difficult years, the village began to prosper. In 1825 a 10½ dessiatine tree plantation was established north of the village. Gradually small businesses were established to meet local needs. These included a brewery, a distillery, three vinegar breweries, a watermill, two dye works and a cloth factory which by 1843 employed 48 workers.

In 1842 an industrial suburb was established by Johann Cornies, chairman of the Agricultural Society. Located southeast of Halbstadt, it became known as Neuhalbstadt and provided 200 craftsmen each with 3 dessiatine of land. As a result more industries developed including two large steam-powered mills,

a starch factory, a barley mill, a motor factory, two tile factories, two oil presses, and a print shop (Raduga). A number of retail shops and a credit union were also established. Thus, Halbstadt became the largest industrial and commercial centre in the Molotschna Colony.

In 1816 Halbstadt became the administrative centre for the Molotschna Colony and in 1870, when the Molotschna Colony was separated into two districts or Volosts, it became the administrative centre for the Halbstadt Volost, the western part of the Colony, consisting of 30 villages. In 1869, Halbstadt still had 21 full farms. Another 28 small farms had been added by that time, increasing its total land area to over 1,900 dessiatine.

In addition to a village school, Halbstadt also had a Zentralschule which included a teachers' college, as well as a

Heinrich Dyck House in Halbstadt

HALBSTADT-MUNTAU

school of commerce, and a girls' school. Whereas the residents of Halbstadt originally belonged to the Ohrloff-Petershagen congregation, in 1858 a new church building was constructed in Neuhalbstadt. Eventually a Mennonite Brethren Church building was also built. When a railroad was built through the Molotschna Colony in 1910 one of the three railroad stations was located in Neuhalbstadt.

Whereas Halbstadt was originally made up of only Mennonite families, its development as an industrial and commercial centre resulted in the population gradually changing. By 1917 the Mennonites were no longer the majority and by 1925 only about ⅓ were Mennonite.

MUNTAU

The village of Muntau was also established in 1804. It was located immediately south of Halbstadt and was settled by 21 Flemish Mennonite families from Prussia. An interest free loan of 12,600 Rubles was provided to them by the government. Initially the village was referred to as No. 2. But soon it was given the name Muntau, after a village of the same name in Prussia. The village was laid out in the traditional manner, with farmyards on both sides of the village street and the street placed parallel to the Molochnaia River.

The early years were difficult and for various reasons the construction of the first houses was not completed until 1805 and 1806. During that time some lived in earth huts and others utilized the barns that they had built. Eventually the village

prospered and the first houses were replaced with large houses built of burned clay brick. In 1869 the village had 17 full farms, eight half farms and 38 small farms with a total land area of almost 2,000 dessiatine. In 1913 the population was about 400.

The village school was built in 1852 and in 1889 a hospital was established. Industries included a mill and a starch factory.

HALBSTADT-MUNTAU

The former village of Muntau and Halbstadt, including its suburb of Neuhalbstadt, are now one village called Molochansk. It is the second largest centre in the Tokmak district, after the City of Tokmak. There are still a large number of Mennonite buildings but the cemeteries no longer exist.

HALBSTADT-MUNTAU
Molotschna Colony

1. H.H. WILLMS MILL

At seven storeys in height, this flour mill was reputed to be the tallest mill constructed by Mennonites in Russia. It was owned by the firm of H.H. Willms & Ko. and was run by a large steam-operated engine located in a separate power house. Large steel rollers were used to crush the wheat. Each floor contained a separate operation. A balcony was located on the 6th floor from which an excellent view of the surrounding countryside could be enjoyed.

The brick walls of the mill were quite decorative with a circular motif expressing an industrial theme, as well as brick pilasters expressing the structure of the building and an interesting brick cornice above the 5th floor reducing the apparent height of the building. This building is still being used, producing condensed milk.

H.H. Willms Mill

H.H. Willms Mill today

HALBSTADT-MUNTAU *Molotschna Colony*

2. HERMANN NEUFELD BREWERY

The Hermann Neufeld Bier-und Essigbrauerei und Limonadenfabrik was established in 1832. The brewery primarily produced beer and vinegar. The firm also sold and repaired products from England, Germany, and USA, including stationary engines, sewing machines, cream separators, and various other household products.

Most of the brewery buildings were destroyed in 1918 by retreating German troops. Only the former beer hall remains. Located adjacent to the street, its brick walls are in fairly poor condition and its roof has been changed to corrugated cement-asbestos.

Advertisement from 1904

st remaining building

rman Neufeld Brewery

HALBSTADT-MUNTAU   *Molotschna Colony*

3. DAVID WILLMS HOUSE

This large private residence belonged to David Willms, one of the owners of the large flour mill in Halbstadt. The brick walls of the house are articulated to express large strong vertical columns between the windows. Most have been painted and are not their original colour. The roof still has some of the original clay tiles.

The ancillary buildings, also have brick walls, but have much simpler decoration. They too have been painted and the roofs have been replaced with corrugated cement-asbestos.

Near the house there is a gazebo. It appears to be an original structure, with its wood posts and wrought iron fence. The roof has been changed to metal sheeting. Today the former house is a part of a silkworm factory.

Gazebo

David Willms House

Gatepost

HALBSTADT-MUNTAU   *Molotschna Colony*

4. HEINRICH SCHROEDER ENTERPRISE

This business was primarily involved in the sales and services of various agricultural products including threshing machines, binders, plows, pumps and watering systems. The business was housed in two long brick buildings located at right angles to each other. These buildings are still in use today. They have large arched windows and hip roofs covered with clay tiles.

Advertisement from 1905

Advertisement from 1905

Heinrich Schroeder building

5. KREDITANSTALT

This banking facility was established as a mutual credit organization, to provide farmers with loans at reasonable interest rates. It probably also provided services to the local business owners.

This fine building had a large central element that appears to have been the banking hall, and smaller elements at either end that included the entrances. It was built of brick and had unusually tall narrow windows. The decorative treatment of the brick pilasters between the windows and the ornamental treatment of the parapet with the name of the building incorporated into it, show the influence of the Jugendstil movement.

The parapet is no longer there and the roof has been changed. But the decorative brick treatment is still clearly visible. The building is still in fairly good condition and is now used as a gymnasium for the nearby school.

Window detail

Kreditanstalt building

Kreditanstalt building today

Wall detail

HALBSTADT-MUNTAU   *Molotschna Colony*

6. HALBSTADT ZENTRALSCHULE

Erected in 1895, this was the third building to be constructed for the Halbstadt secondary school for boys which was founded in 1835. It had a three year educational program and in 1878 a two year co-educational pedagogical program was introduced for the training of future teachers.

The most unique feature of the building is its main entrance which is emphasized by a "Greek temple" design. Although it was not unusual at the time for various types of institutional buildings in Europe and elsewhere to be built in this style, it appears that the Zentralschule in Halbstadt was the only Mennonite building in Russia to utilize this style. Four large (almost Doric) columns with a pediment above create a canopy over the wide steps that lead to the entrance doors.

The exterior walls were built of brick with a design that suggested the use of columns between windows. At both ends of the front facade there are projected sections complete with gables that complement the front entrance.

Inside, the school building had eight classrooms, a laboratory, a library, and offices. There was a large wing

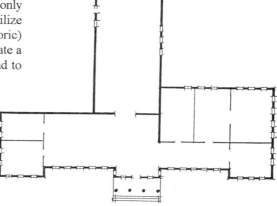

Halbstadt Zentralschule

HALBSTADT-MUNTAU

extending out the back which was the auditorium. The north wing consisted of classrooms for the secondary school and the south wing was used for the teachers training institute.

There was a fence along the street with brick pillars and wrought iron pickets. Large decorative gateposts with an ornate wrought iron gate marked the entrance to the grounds. The grounds were landscaped and bordered with trees including large chestnut trees.

Until recently the building was used as a local party headquarters, but now the Lenin bust and the large party signs are gone. The fence and gate are no longer there and the outer walls have been painted. The roof, which until recently had the original clay roof tiles, is now covered with corrugated cement-asbestos. A large addition has recently been constructed at the rear of the building.

Entrance

Southwest wall

Wall detail

HALBSTADT-MUNTAU

Molotschna Colony

7. VOLOST

This building was the administrative centre for the western portion of the Molotschna Colony, which included 30 villages. It may have been built in 1870 when the Molotschna administration was divided into two districts. However, it could have been built earlier, since prior to this, Halbstadt was the administrative centre for the entire Molotschna Colony. This building is actually located in the former Neuhalbstadt, a suburb of Halbstadt, which was developed in 1843. It measures 13 m by 30 m.

The building is still in use and is now a shop. The brick walls have been painted and the original metal roof has been replaced with corrugated cement-asbestos. The building has an official brass plaque on the roadside wall referring to the events of 1917-1918 and the fact that the Volost was a significant site of Soviet activity during the Revolution and civil war. It shows the head of a soldier striving to achieve Bolshevik power.

Volost building

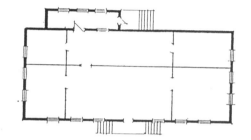

Volost building today

HALBSTADT-MUNTAU *Molotschna Colony*

8. DIAKONISSENHEIM "MORIJA"

The "Morija" Deaconess Home was a private charitable institution established in 1909 for training nurses. It was closely associated with the Muntau and Ohrloff hospitals where the student nurses were able to receive practical training as part of the three year course. The various courses were taught by teachers from the other schools in Halbstadt, as well as by Dr. E. Tavonius from the Muntau hospital.

Construction of this first "Morija" building started in late spring of 1909 and opened on December of that year. The cost of construction was covered by donations. The dedication took place on May 23, 1910. The building's amenities included central heating, bathing rooms and running water. It had brick exterior walls that were plastered and painted several colours. Soon this building became too small for the program and so it was decided to build a new facility. This facility was sold in 1912 to Johann Schröder who used it as a residence until 1922.

This building still exists today. Its walls are now painted white. The roof has been substantially changed with a partial second floor having been removed and corrugated cement-asbestos replacing the clay tiles. But the interesting details of the walls are still distinguishable.

Diakonissenheim "Morija" in 1910

Wall detail

First Diakonissenheim "Morija" building today

HALBSTADT-MUNTAU

9. DIAKONISSENHEIM "MORIJA"

Construction of the new 2 storey "Morija" Deaconess Home was completed in December 1912. In 1913 a new nursing program was introduced. Total enrolment was around 35. Nurses that graduated from this course found employment at the various Mennonite hospitals, as well as at the Bethania Mental Institute and the Grossweide Orphanage. Some also were employed in private service.

The facades of the new building showed an interesting use of ornamentation. The decorative brick-work around the windows was subtly different between the first and second floors. The brickwork between the windows was used to express columns. The ornamentation on these columns included the use of three vertical lines and a circle, similar in design to the Kreditanstalt in Halbstadt. The arched parapets repeated this theme. This decorative treatment shows the influence of the Jugendstil movement.

The building still exists today. The roof has been altered and a dormer window eliminated. A small canopy has also been added over the front entrance.

Diakonissenheim "Morija" in 1913

Second Diakonissenheim "Morija" today

HALBSTADT-MUNTAU   *Molotschna Colony*

10. HALBSTADT MÄDCHENSCHULE

The Mädchenschule in Halbstadt was established in 1882, the first girls' school in the Molotschna Colony. In 1910 it was upgraded to a full secondary school for girls with five grades.

The walls were built with brick and portions of the exterior walls were then plastered to create decorative facades. The front of the building has two facades that are particularly ornate. The gables of these facades have exposed brick and short clay tile roofs at their base. The roof itself was also originally clay tile but is now covered with corrugated cement-asbestos.

The building is still in fairly good condition. The area between the two extended facades has been enclosed to create a larger entrance area. It is now used as an elementary school.

Mädchenschule   *Facade detail*

Mädchenschule today

HALBSTADT-MUNTAU

11. HEINRICH WILLMS HOUSE

This large private residence belonged to Heinrich Willms, one of the owners of the large flour mill in Halbstadt. It was built of masonry with an exterior plaster finish in a neo-Renaissance style not unlike what was common in western Europe at the time. The ground floor alone contained over 7,000 square feet of area.

The building is still in good condition today, retaining much of its grandeur although the original roof has been replaced with corrugated cement-asbestos. Today it is being used as a recreational facility for the workers of a nearby furniture factory. Also, a portion of the house has recently been converted to a commercial bank (Bank of Ukraine).

Main entrance

Heinrich Willms House

HALBSTADT-MUNTAU

Molotschna Colony

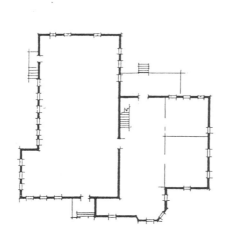

Heinrich Willms House today

Wall details

HALBSTADT-MUNTAU

Molotschna Colony

12. FRANZ & SCHRÖDER FACTORY

This building was constructed in Neuhalbstadt, probably in 1860. Built by non-Mennonites, it was initially used for a large-scale silk industry that soon failed. In 1874 the Franz & Schröder Fabrik Landwirtschaftlicher Maschinen was established in this building. It became one of the largest industries in the Halbstadt area, producing large quantities of farm machinery. It specialized in the production of threshing machines and binders and also manufactured numerous items such as plows, cultivators, seeders, feed mills, hydraulic presses, roof tile presses and wood working machinery. The firm also sold and repaired equipment manufactured by others. Near the factory were large barracks for the factory workers. The building is still in use today and is now a furniture factory.

Advertisement from 1903

Franz & Schröder Factory building

HALBSTADT-MUNTAU *Molotschna Colony*

13. MUNTAU HOSPITAL

Sometimes referred to as "Wall's House for the Ill", this hospital was established in 1889 as a private initiative by Franz Wall. After obtaining the site in Muntau, he built a small hospital with three 2 bed wards, an operating room and other support areas, using his own funds. In 1892 an 8 bed wing was added and in 1899 an addition and renovations were carried out to meet the requirements of the authorities. In 1907 a department for infectious diseases was added at a cost of 2,500 Rubles.

As the need for medical services increased significantly the decision was made to construct a new facility. Substantial financial support was provided by both churches and individuals. Construction was carried out in 1911 and, after receiving approval from the authorities, the new facility was occupied in spring of 1912. The new facility incorporated much of the original building and included two new 2 storey wings, one parallel to the street and the other extending into the yard. The main floor of the front wing included the main entrance, an office and waiting area, a large hall for sick children, and a nurses' residence. The main floor of the other wing included a doctor's waiting and reception room, a laboratory and a pharmacy. The second floor of the front wing contained the wards and the second floor of the other wing included an operating room with its support facilities. There was also an X-ray room and patient bathing facilities. The new facility could accommodate 40 patients.

The building was of brick construction and had hot water heating, warm and cold running water and electric lights. The total cost was 45,000 Rubles. The construction created some inconvenience to the ongoing operation of the facility, but it was not significant. Temporary barracks were constructed in the yard during the period of warm weather. Dr. Erich Tavonius was the head doctor for many years and provided leadership in carrying out the expansion plans. In 1911 the hospital staff included three doctors, one head nurse, 11 nurses, and one seamstress. In 1913, over 9,500 days of patient care were provided with an average stay of 12 days.

After the civil war the hospital was nationalized. Today it is used as a children's sanitorium. The institutional expression of the building is still apparent, although the roof structure has been substantially altered. The exterior brick walls covered with plaster still appear the same, although they are now one colour and the fence and gateposts at the street are still in place, although somewhat deteriorated.

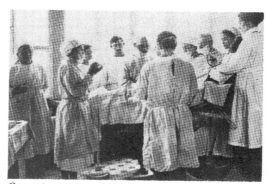

Operating room in 1912

HALBSTADT-MUNTAU
Molotschna Colony

Muntau Hospital after 1912

Muntau Hospital today

HAMBERG

The village of Hamberg was founded in 1863 by families from existing villages along the west edge of the Molotschna Colony. It was one of the last two villages to be established in the Molotschna and was located some distance away from the Tokmak River, on land reserved for expansion.

The village was laid out in accordance with the regulations established by the Agricultural Society. There were 26 full farms and three small farms, with 1,735 dessiatine of land in total. By 1869 there were 25 full farms, two half farms and five small farms with 1,770 dessiatine of land.

There was a village school, but there was no church building as most villagers were members of the Schönsee Mennonite Church. It became a prosperous village but suffered unusual hardships during and after the civil war. Today few Mennonite buildings remain. The village is now known as Kamenka and the land is part of the Gorki Collective Farm which is centered in Vladovka, formerly Waldheim.

1. VILLAGE SCHOOL

The village school was located near the centre of the village. It was set back somewhat from the street and was placed parallel to it. The building that still exists today appears to be the original school since there is very little ornamentation on the exterior brick walls. They have been covered with plaster and the roof has been replaced with corrugated cement-asbestos. It appears that more significant changes have also been made to the building, including a front entrance addition and the roof shape.

Hamberg village school building

HIERSCHAU

The village of Hierschau was established in 1848 by 30 families from other Molotschna villages. It had been planned by Johann Cornies and the Agricultural Society as a model village and was laid out in accordance with the Society's requirements. The village may have been named by Cornies since the name suggests "here (hier), look (schau) at this model village".

The village was located on the south bank of the Begim Tschokrak River, with the village street placed parallel to the river. There were 15 farmyards on each side of the street with those on the north side backing onto the river. There were cross streets at each end, both crossing over the river. Another cross street at the centre of the village extended south to the cemetery. The farmyards measured 64 m wide by 256 m long. The houses and barns were built of burned clay bricks. In 1852 a village school was built at the centre of the village. Since the village was served by the Margenau-Schönsee Church, there was no church building in Hierschau. A windmill was constructed at the west end of the village, on the north side of the river. In 1869 there were still 30 full farms and 30 small farms had been added. The total land area was over 2,400 dessiatine.

Today little is left of the former village of Hierschau. One gate post still exists and the remains of several gravestones can be found in the cemetery, although there are no inscriptions on them. It is now part of the village of Vladovka and the land is part of the Gorki Collective Farm.

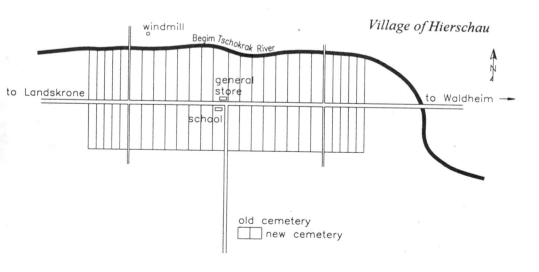

Village of Hierschau

JUSCHANLEE

Juschanlee was established by Johann Cornies in 1830 as an experimental farm. It was located along the Juschanlee River south of the village of Ohrloff and initially consisted of 500 dessiatine of land that he had rented from the government. At this location Cornies built a model farm including a large residence, numerous barns and various outbuildings. A large kiln provided the bricks and roof tiles. The breeding of high quality farm animals was developed and large orchards and gardens were established. Silk, tobacco and honey were also produced.

In 1836, as a reward for his contributions to the state, the Juschanlee land was presented by Tsar Nicholas I to Cornies and his descendants as a private estate. After Cornies' death in 1848, the Juschanlee Estate was inherited by his son-in-law, Philip Wiebe. He founded a school on the estate in 1850.

In 1879 ownership of the estate changed. A Reimer family took possession, demolished many of the buildings and constructed a large castle-like residence. After the civil war the estate was nationalized. Today it is a regional psychiatric hospital. Numerous buildings, including the large Reimer residence, still exist, as do the ornate gateposts at the street. The statues of the owner, his wife, and other family members, which once dotted the property, however, are gone.

Wall detail

House on Juschanlee Estate

JUSCHANLEE

Molotschna Colony

REIMER HOUSE

Built sometime after 1879, this very large house was built of red brick, with gables and other details in a style common to northern Europe. The building was heavily damaged during World War II. A new roof, substantially different from the original, has been added. A balcony on the rear facade of the house is gone. The building is now part of the psychiatric hospital.

Wall detail

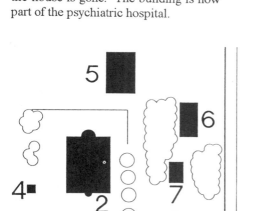

Wall detail

1. GATEPOSTS
2. REIMER HOUSE
3. BARN
4. SMALL SHED
5. LARGE BARN
6. BARN
7. HOUSE
8. HOUSE

Reimer House and gatepost from street

KURUSCHAN

Molotschna Colony

Kuruschan was not a village, but rather a large community sheep pasture owned by the Halbstadt Volost and located along the Kuruschan River northeast of the village of Rosenort. A number of small estates were established on the north side of the river and several homes and small farmyards were established on the south side. There was also a brick factory (Wiebe) on the south side.

A home for the elderly was built to the west of this settled area on land that was previously part of the community sheep pasture. A heavily wooded area separated it from the farms and houses. The home for the elderly no longer exists today and very few of the other Mennonite buildings still exist.

1. ALTENHEIM KURUSCHAN

In 1903 the villages in the Halbstadt Volost decided to establish a facility for those elderly people that could no longer be cared for by family. This was done as a centennial project to commemorate the establishment of the Molotschna Colony.

A fairly central site was selected along the Kuruschan River, northeast of the village of Rosenort where the Halbstadt Volost designated 35 dessiatine of its large community sheep pasture for this purpose. To the east of the site was a forest which was to protect the facility from the east winds.

In 1904 a building committee was appointed. Members were Gerhard Neufeld, Johannes Wiebe, and Peter

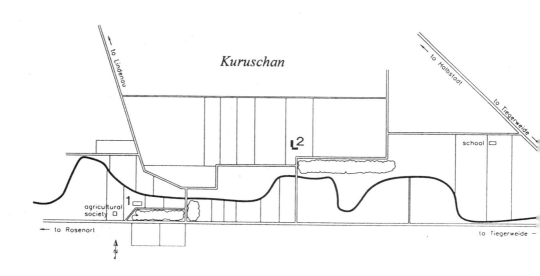

KURUSCHAN

Loewen. Plans were then prepared by the regional architect, Johann Braeul, and construction was begun. During construction a shortage of bricks caused some delays. The official opening was finally held December 6, 1906. The total cost was 40,000 Rubles, which was raised partly through an assessment of land owners and partly through church collections.

The facility had accommodation for approximately 60 residents. There were 18 living rooms. The dining room had 5 large tables that could accommodate all the residents and staff. It was also used for church services. There were 2 bathing rooms and 2 toilets. There were also 2 empty rooms in the attic at the gable ends.

The construction included wood framing and burned clay brick walls. The floors were wood, except for the kitchen floor which was concrete. The roof was covered with cement tiles. Lighting was provided by petroleum-fuelled hanging lamps. In the attic there were two steel water tanks that were filled by pumping water from a well. These tanks provided water to the kitchen, bathing rooms, and toilets.

A barn on the property had space for 12 cows and 8 horses, as well as a room for several servants and a room for the laundry mangl. The property also included a 2 dessiatine orchard and a 1½ dessiatine vegetable garden. These facilities contributed to the home's food supply.

In 1913 there were 64 residents. Consideration was given to expansion. However, this did not occur and today this facility no longer exists.

Altenheim from street

Altenheim from front drive

KURUSCHAN   *Molotschna Colony*

2. WILHELM NEUFELD HOUSE/BARN

The Wilhelm Neufeld estate was located on the north side of the Kuruschan River. The house and barn were connected. The house was located parallel to the street and the barn at right angles to it. Both buildings were built of brick, with vertical wood siding on the gables and clay tile roofs.

The house and barn still exist today although the connection between them no longer exists. They are in poor condition but the brick detailing is still evident.

Wilhelm Neufeld House and Barn

LADEKOPP

The village of Ladekopp was founded in 1805 by 16 Flemish Mennonite families from Prussia. Four more families arrived later. They named Ladekopp after a village in Prussia by the same name. The village was located approximately two km south of the Tokmak River. The village street had farmyards on both sides. Six of the families had adequate financial means to build small wooden huts, the lumber for which they obtained in the City of Alexandrovsk. Their total capital amounted to approximately 11,000 Rubles. The other families did not have adequate resources of their own and so they received an interest free loan of almost 5,000 Rubles from the government. They ended up living in earth huts for the first winter.

The conditions gradually improved. In addition to farming, the village also engaged in the silk industry. A spacious village school was built, but there was no church building since most of the villagers belonged to the Petershagen Mennonite Church. In 1869 Ladekopp had 20 full farms and 29 small farms with a total of almost 1,800 dessiatine of land. In 1914 the population was 460. Today the village has become integrated into the City of Tokmak and is no longer recognizable. Very few Mennonite buildings still remain.

1. VILLAGE SCHOOL

Beginning in the 1890's, the Russian government placed great emphasis on improving the educational system throughout Russia. As part of this program, regulations were developed for the construction of new school buildings in the Russian villages, with emphasis on providing adequate light, warmth and space. Many new schools were built during this time, spearheaded by the zemstvos, i.e. the local self-government agencies. Standard plans for school buildings were developed and made available to the zemstvos. In some cases the Mennonite villages also took advantage of the availability of standard plans.

When the village leaders in Ladekopp decided to replace their existing school with a new village school, they wrote to the government officials in the City of Charkov, requesting modern school plans. The price that the architects responsible for these plans quoted them was at first considered too high. But after much discussion and deliberation, they decided to proceed with the project and order the plans. The village school building was constructed in approximately 1910.

At the time of construction, this

LADEKOPP   *Molotschna Colony*

school had one large classroom and one small classroom. The large classroom was like a small auditorium and was used for community activities and church services. The school also had two teachers' residences, one larger and one smaller. The building plan was in the shape of an "H" with a central section and short wings at each end with gables both to the front and rear. There was also a gable roof over the front entrance but it has been removed.

The brick-pillared fence along the street has been replaced with an ordinary metal fence. The brick walls have been painted. The roof clay tiles are still in place. The building is in quite good condition and is still in use.

Ladekopp village school building

LANDSKRONE

Molotschna Colony

The village of Landskrone was founded in 1839 along the Begim Tschokrak River on land that had been rented by Johann Cornies who in turn had rented it to Heinrich Janzen of Schönsee. Because the river valley was so small, the village was laid out with two streets, both parallel to the river, and 470 m apart. The southerly street was considered to be the main street of the village. It was planned for 40 families from other Molotschna villages and in accordance with the requirements of Johann Cornies and the Agricultural Society. The first year 26 families arrived. Another 11 families came the following year and in 1842 the last three families arrived. The village was named by Cornies but he never explained to the village leaders why he named it Landskrone.

During the first few years, the river flooded in the spring causing considerable damage. So in 1844 a 21 m wide canal was constructed through the centre of the village. The river was rerouted through this canal and the original river bed partially filled in. The settlers built their houses mostly out of red clay bricks in accordance with specifications of the Agricultural Society. The village's Russian neighbours, therefore, referred to Landskrone as the red village.

The village had a few small businesses and a village school. By 1848 it had 5,500 fruit trees. In 1869 there were 36 full farms, eight half farms and 34 small farms. In 1910 a new church building was constructed. Today the village is called Lankove. There is very little left of the former Landskrone other than a few sections of wall from the church.

Gatepost in Landskrone

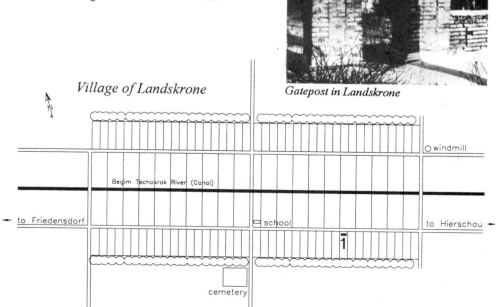

Village of Landskrone

LANDSKRONE   *Molotschna Colony*

1. LANDSKRONE MENNONITE CHURCH

On October 21, 1909, a petition was submitted to the Taurida Provincial Government Building Department requesting permission to construct a new prayer house in Landskrone. It was submitted on behalf of the Margenau and Schönsee parish by representatives Johann G. Derksen and Peter A. Martens. Drawings for the new building were submitted at the same time. Approval was given on October 31, 1909, signed by the Berdjansk Regional Department.

Construction was carried out in 1910. Designed in a neo-gothic style complete with gothic-shaped windows and buttresses between the windows, the building measured 14 m by 28 m. The pulpit/platform was at one end of the rectangular shaped sanctuary and the centre aisle was parallel to the long walls. This interior layout and the exterior brick ornamentation presented a major contrast to the early Mennonite prayer houses built in Russia. Today only portions of the walls of this church building remain standing.

Wall detail

Front elevation

Remains of Landskrone Church building

LANDSKRONE

Molotschna Colony

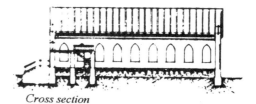

Cross section

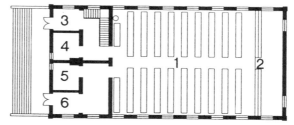

1. SANCTUARY
2. PULPIT
3. MEN'S ENTRANCE
4. MINISTERS' ROOM
5. WOMEN'S ROOM
6. WOMEN'S ENTRANCE

LICHTENAU

The village of Lichtenau was founded in 1804 by 21 Flemish Mennonite families from Prussia. They received an interest free loan of over 10,000 Rubles from the government to assist them with settlement costs. Initially referred to as No. 6, the village was soon named after a village in Prussia.

The village was laid out with farmyards on both sides of the village street. The street was placed parallel to the Molochnaia River. Lichtenau belonged to the large Lichtenau-Petershagen congregation and so in 1826 a church building was constructed in Lichtenau. In 1860 a larger church building was constructed. Built of brick, it was constructed under the direction of Johann Wall, a carpenter and cabinetmaker by trade. There was also a village school and several businesses including a farm machinery dealership (Hamm & Hübert). In 1869 Lichtenau had 18 full farms, six half farms and 26 small farms with a total land area of almost 1,800 dessiatine.

When a railroad was built through the Molotschna Colony in 1910, Lichtenau became one of the three train stations within the colony. Today the village is known as Svetlodolinskoye. There are almost no Mennonite buildings left in the village. In the cemetery which is located at the northeast end of the village, approximately a dozen gravestones have been found and brought together in one location. Most are in the shape of rectangular frames but there are no inscriptions on any of them.

LICHTENAU   *Molotschna Colony*

1. LICHTENAU TRAIN STATION

The Lichtenau train station was built soon after the railroad was constructed in 1910. It was located northeast of the village. The exterior walls were built of brick with fine detailing around the large windows. The building is still used as a railroad station. The walls have been painted and the roof has been replaced with corrugated cement-asbestos.

Lichtenau Train Station

LIEBENAU

Molotschna Colony

The village of Liebenau was established in 1823. From a group of Frisian Mennonites that immigrated to the Molotschna Colony, nine families, including the group leader, Peter Franz, joined together with another 11 families who had previously arrived in the Molotschna. Together they settled in the village of Liebenau. Thirteen of the families did not have adequate capital and received an interest free loan of over 10,000 Rubles from the government. The others had a total of between 18,000 and 24,000 Rubles of their own capital. The name was arrived at when the local authority showed the settlers the site of their new village, which looked like a lovely (lieblich) meadow (Aue), hence Liebenau.

The village was located along the south bank of the Tokmak River, with the village street parallel to the river. Farmyards were located on both sides of the street, with those on the north side backing onto the river. Liebenau had a village school and a factory that manufactured feed mills (Jakob Franz). In 1869 the village still had 20 full farms. Twenty-two small farms had been added. The land area was a total of over 1,600 dessiatine.

Today the village is known as Ostrikovka. A few Mennonite buildings still exist, as do a number of gateposts and fences.

Fence in Liebenau

Gatepost and fence in Liebenau

LIEBENAU

Molotschna Colony

Gateposts in Liebenau

Gateposts in Liebenau

Neufeld House in Liebenau

LIEBENAU
Molotschna Colony

1. JAKOB FRANZ FACTORY

The factory owned by Jakob Franz manufactured feed mills which were sold to farmers and estate owners. The factory building was constructed of brick and the roof was covered with clay roof tiles. Large arched windows provided adequate daylight into the factory. The building is in very poor condition but the brick detailing at the eaves and around the windows is still evident.

Advertisement from 1915

Jakob Franz Factory building today

MÜNSTERBERG

The village of Münsterberg was founded in 1804 by 21 Flemish Mennonite families from Prussia. It was located on the east bank of the Molochnaia River. The village street with farmyards on both sides, generally followed the curvature of the river. Initially the village was referred to as No. 8, but then was named Münsterberg, after a village by the same name in Prussia. The settlers received assistance from the government including provisions, lumber and an interest free loan. The value of this assistance was over 12,000 Rubles.

In 1869 Münsterberg had 22 full farms and 24 small farms with a land area of approximately 1,800 dessiatine. In 1913 its population was 400. In addition to the village school, the village had two motor-driven mills, a tile factory and four large shops.

Today the name of the village is Prilukovka. There are virtually no Mennonite buildings left but a number of gravestones have been found in the cemetery. On several of them, the inscriptions have been deliberately damaged. But the following have been identified:

- Herman Neufeld
  January 2, 1806 - September 8, 1882

- Peter Neuman
  January 20, 1784 - November 13, 1860
  (This gravestone was erected in 1867)

- Katarina Neuman
  geb. Neufeld
  ... 1779 - December 20, 1845

- Maria Neuman
  geb. ...
  ... 1822 - June 19, 1851

- ... Barch
  ... 1807 - ... 1823

- Franz Janzen
  February 25, 1865 - October 15, 1905

Peter Neuman, 1784-1860

Franz Janzen, 1865-1905

NEUKIRCH

The village of Neukirch was founded in 1820 by 20 Flemish Mennonite families from Prussia, many of which had immigrated in previous years, some as early as 1804. It was located on the north bank of the Juschanlee River. The village street was placed parallel to the river with farmyards on either side of the street. The settlers initially wanted to name the village Schöneberg, but since there already was a village by that name in the Chortitza Colony, this was not accepted. They then chose to name it Neukirch after a well-known village in Prussia. The settlers that had no capital of their own, received an interest free loan from the government of over 7,500 Rubles. The others had their own capital of about 4,000 Rubles.

The first winter was spent in earth huts and wooden huts, but the following year 22 houses were built, 20 for the farm families and two for the families of craftsmen. The total land area of Neukirch was 1,300 dessiatine based on 65 dessiatine per family. In 1848 there were 540 dessiatine of cultivated land, 60 dessiatine of hayland and 700 dessiatine of pasture land. Since the pasture land was not adequate to feed their 500 head of cattle, additional land was rented each year. By 1848 the village had 48 houses, four of which were built of burned clay bricks. There was also a spacious village school, a dye works and a brick factory. In 1865 a new church building was erected. By 1869 there were 17 full farms, 6 half farms and 26 small farms with a land area of just over 1,700 dessiatine. By 1910 the population of the village was 526.

Today the village, together with the former village of Friedensruh across the river, is known as Udarnik. Little is left of the former Mennonite buildings. However, a number of gravestones have been found in the cemetery. They have been brought together near the entrance to the cemetery. Two of them have been identified as follows:

- Agatha Hildebrand
  geb. Wiebe
  August 15, 1855 - May 13, 1909

- Bernhard Toews
  November 21, 1821 - M... 4, 1896

OHRLOFF-TIEGE   *Molotschna Colony*

OHRLOFF

The village of Ohrloff was founded in 1805 along the south bank of the Kuruschan River. The village was laid out with 12 farmyards on the north side of the village street and 9 farmyards on the south side. Initially 12 families settled in the village. Another 8 families arrived the following year. They were Flemish Mennonites from Prussia. At the request of several of the settlers the village was named Ohrloff, after their home village in Prussia. Due to a shortage of workers, the first settlers were only able to complete a few houses the first summer. So during the following winter, these houses were shared by two to three families each. These first settlers brought close to 30,000 Rubles of capital with them. In addition they received an interest free loan of almost 3,800 Rubles from the government.

In 1869 Ohrloff still had 21 full farms. In addition, there were 26 small farms. The total land area was almost 1,800 dessiatine. By 1910 the population was 548. Ohrloff became one of the most important Mennonite communities in the Molotschna Colony, particularly in terms of educational and cultural development. In addition to the traditional village school, Ohrloff had a Zentralschule, the first secondary school among the Mennonites in Russia, as well as a girls' school (which was actually located in Tiege). There was also a church building, home of the Ohrloff congregation, and a hospital.

TIEGE

The village of Tiege was also founded in 1805, along the south bank of the Kuruschan River, and was located immediately east of Ohrloff. It was settled by 20 Flemish Mennonite families from Prussia. The village street was located parallel to the river. There were 10 farmyards on each side of the street.

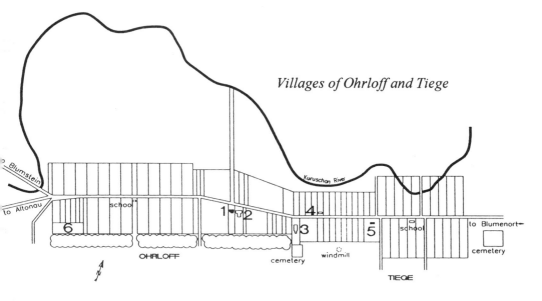

Villages of Ohrloff and Tiege

OHRLOFF-TIEGE

The settlers brought a total of 8,500 Rubles of capital with them. In addition, they received an interest free loan from the government. One of the settlers found that the Kuruschan River reminded him of the Tiege River that ran through his home village in Prussia. At his request the village was, therefore, named Tiege.

The village soon prospered and its residents participated actively in the life of the Molotschna Colony. In 1869 there were still 20 full farms but an additional 23 small farms had been established. The total land area was almost 1,700 dessiatine. In addition to the traditional village school, Tiege had a special school for the deaf. It was also the location of the Ohrloff girls' school. There was a small Mennonite Brethren congregation which had its own church building. A doctor's office and a drugstore provided medical services to the area. There were also several commercial enterprises including a windmill, a general store, a bookstore, and a small factory (K. Funk) that manufactured various types of wagons.

OHRLOFF-TIEGE

As the villages of Ohrloff and Tiege developed, they expanded towards each other, since their village streets were connected. The space between them became occupied, mostly with small farms, but many of the public buildings were also located in this area.

During the 1930's the villages were collectivized. They were subsequently incorporated into one village known as Orlovo. Very few of the Mennonite buildings still remain. The Tiege cemetery no longer exists but a few gravestones have been found in the Ohrloff cemetery. However, the memorial to Johann Cornies, which was a broken marble column expressing his incomplete work, no longer exists.

OHRLOFF-TIEGE

Molotschna Colony

1. OHRLOFF MENNONITE CHURCH

In 1809 the first church building in the Molotschna Colony was constructed in Ohrloff. It was built by a man from the Chortitza Colony by the name of Siemens with funds largely provided by Tsar Alexander I. Later on the church building was considerably enlarged. In 1905 the congregation, which included neighbouring villages of Tiege, Rosenort and Blumenort, had 475 baptized members.

The former Ohrloff Church building still stands today. Its design was in the tradition of the early Mennonite churches. The exterior masonry walls were covered with plaster featuring subtle decorative details particularly around the windows. The windows suggested a 2 storey building with the lower level windows being slightly taller than the upper ones.

The building is located parallel to the street. A large 2 storey extension, which once included the main entrance, extends into the former church yard at the rear. The pulpit and platform were located opposite the main entrance, along the long side of the building. Two tall vertical windows facing the street were located behind the platform. There was a decorative fence along the street made of bricks and clay roof tiles. Two large gateposts of similar construction marked the entrance to the church yard.

The roof, originally metal sheeting, is now covered with corrugated cement-asbestos. The building is not in good condition and is difficult to recognize as the former church building. The fence and gateposts are gone. It seized to function as a church in 1932. It is now a facility for the severally mentally handicapped.

Ohrloff Church building

Ohrloff Church building today

OHRLOFF-TIEGE   *Molotschna Colony*

2. OHRLOFF ZENTRALSCHULE

The first Mennonite central secondary school in Russia was established in Ohrloff in 1822 under the leadership of Johann Cornies. In 1847 the school building burned down and a new one was built in 1860. It was demolished in 1913 to make way for a new school building.

It was a rather unique building, designed by Johann Braeul, an architect and bridge engineer, whose father was the principal of the school at the time. The massing of the building was similar to the Chortitza Mädchenschule, i.e. a two storey central element with one storey wings on either side. The hip roofs were partially hidden by the high decorative parapets. The ground floor had a very large entrance foyer, off which were located the classrooms. At the end of the foyer was a grand stair leading to the second floor where a large auditorium was located, with very high windows overlooking the street.

The exterior design was very different from any of the other Mennonite buildings. The decoration on the facade seems to indicate a certain Jugendstil influence, but the facade also suggests a structural system, with its slightly angled and arched element. The windows were made to fit the opening created by this structural element, rather than being the traditional "holes in the wall". This created large areas of glass similar to modern day glass curtainwalls. The design was quite advanced for its time.

On July 18, 1913 a petition was submitted to the Taurida Provincial Government Building Department requesting permission to construct a new Zentralschule in Ohrloff. It was submitted along with the drawings, by Kornelius K. Toews, on behalf of the school. The Building Department which was located in Simpferopol, capital of Taurida, approved the project on August 2, finding it technically satisfactory. It then instructed the Berdjansk Regional Police Department to pass on this technical approval to Mr. Toews, provided that it would be "safe for the attending students". This may have referred to its involvement in the overseeing of education during a time of distrust and government restrictions on higher education. The approval to build was passed on and construction began. The official opening took place May 20, 1914.

The school yard was separated from the street by a rather simple picket fence with masonry posts. Adjacent to the school was a teachers' residence behind which was a large shed. The yard also included a vegetable garden and an area for drying laundry. Unfortunately this building no longer exists today.

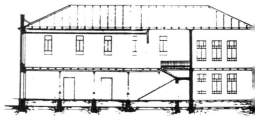

Cross section

OHRLOFF-TIEGE

Molotschna Colony

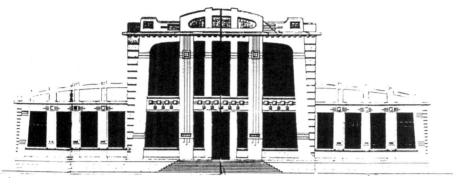

Front elevation

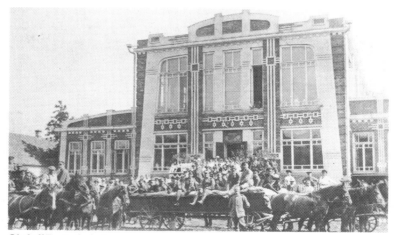

Ohrloff Zentralschule

OHRLOFF-TIEGE

3. OHRLOFF HOSPITAL

Construction of the Ohrloff hospital began in 1908 and was completed in 1909. The official opening was held on January 7, 1910. It was considered to be a stately structure, large and practically appointed. The funding for its construction was provided by the heirs of the estate of H.H. Reimer from Ohrloff. After its completion, it was taken over and sustained by the surrounding community.

By 1911 the facility was becoming overcrowded due to the demand for surgery. The wing for infectious diseases was, therefore, converted to surgery. But because of a subsequent outbreak of various infectious diseases, an infectious disease department was again established. Several donors funded the construction of barracks on the hospital grounds for this purpose.

The same year the hospital acquired an X-ray cabinet. One of the hospital doctors, Dr. G. Dürksen, while in Germany, had purchased the equipment from Sanitas, an electrical company in Berlin. Several estate owners donated the necessary funds for this purchase.

In 1912 the hospital had three doctors and provided over 6,000 days of patient care with an average stay of 13 days. The same year a total of 325 operations were performed including stomach, chest, head and throat operations. Substantial donations were made to the hospital including support for four hospital beds that were made available free of charge to those who could not afford to pay. During World War I, 15 beds were allocated to the care of wounded soldiers.

The building was quite inviting and non-institutional in appearance, with its delicately detailed entrance porch and its large windows, particularly the arched windows at the ends of the wings. A second floor sunroom overlooked the beautifully landscaped yard. Unfortunately this facility no longer exists today.

Ohrloff Hospital

OHRLOFF-TIEGE *Molotschna Colony*

4. TIEGE M.B. CHURCH

This small church building was constructed by the Mennonite Brethren congregation in Tiege after submitting a petition and the necessary drawings to the Taurida Provincial Government Building Department.   The petition requested approval of the plans for the proposed prayer house.   Once approval was received the construction proceeded.

The building was fairly modest in appearance although it featured gothic-shaped windows, a style that was common at the time.   It was placed parallel to the street. The pulpit/platform was located at one end of the rectangular shaped sanctuary and separate men's and women's entrances were located at the other end.   A modest picket fence separated the church yard from the street. This building no longer exists.

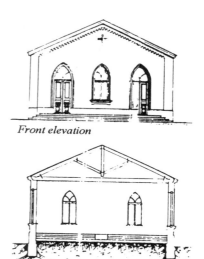

Front elevation

Cross section

1. SANCTUARY
2. PULPIT
3. MEN'S ENTRANCE
4. STUDY
5. WOMEN'S ENTRANCE

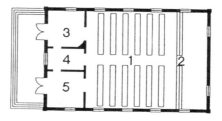

Tiege M.B. Church building

OHRLOFF-TIEGE

Molotschna Colony

5. MARIENTAUBSTUMMENSCHULE

The Maria School for the Deaf was founded in 1881 by the Halbstadt Volost to commemorate 25 years of Tsar Alexander II's government. It was named after his wife. In 1890 this large and impressive building was constructed. It cost 40,000 Rubles. The windows and other items were paid for by individual benefactors. It contained classrooms, bedrooms, and a dining room for 40 students, and in addition some teacher residences. There were several other buildings including a workshop. A water system supplied by an artesian well served the kitchen, bathroom, laundry and barn. A 9 year course equivalent to the elementary education in the village schools was provided. Also handicrafts training in such things as woodworking, basket weaving and sewing was provided with excellent results. Once a year a sale of crafts produced by the students was held to raise money for the school. The building was designed to recreate a family setting in order to be able to deal with each child's individuality. Originally there were two sick rooms but one was converted to a maids' bedroom and the other to teachers' quarters.

This facility was considered to be one of the best schools for the deaf in Russia because of its family character, low student/teacher ratio, and well-trained teachers who were decently paid. The teachers received their training in places such as St. Petersburg and Frankfurt (Vatterschen Anstalt). They also attended conferences regularly in Russia and Germany.

The building is still in use today. It is now an administration centre. The exterior walls have been painted, the metal roof has been replaced with corrugated cement-asbestos, and a non-descript canopy has been added at the front entrance.

School for the Deaf

Front entrance today

OHRLOFF-TIEGE
Molotschna Colony

School for the Deaf from street

School for the Deaf from yard

School for the Deaf building today

OHRLOFF-TIEGE

Molotschna Colony

6. OHRLOFF CEMETERY

The following gravestones have been identified:

●Agnes Reimer
geb. Schröder
February 4, 1839 - October 15, 1883
(This beautiful gravestone is in fairly good condition. The inscription on it is in Russian and German.)

●Heinrich Heinrich Reimer
... - ...
(This gravestone is badly damaged and is located deep in the ground.)

●David Cornies
June 1, 1797 - October 7, 1873

There are also three gravestones that look like rectangular frames without any inscriptions on them, plus the remains of four other gravestones.

David Cornies, 1797-1873

Agnes Reimer, 1839-1883

PETERSHAGEN

Molotschna Colony

The village of Petershagen was founded in 1805 by 20 Flemish Mennonite families from Prussia. It was located on the south side of the Tokmak River. A small stream ran through the village and into the Tokmak. The village was named at the request of one of the settlers after a village in Prussia where many of the settlers came from. Eight of the families had no capital of their own and, therefore, received an interest free loan from the government of over 4,500 Rubles. The other 12 families brought 15,500 Rubles of their own capital.

A village school was built soon after the village was established. A church building was constructed in 1810 with financial assistance from the government. In 1852 the congregation decided to demolish this church building and construct a new one in Neuhalbstadt. The material from the demolition was hauled to Neuhalbstadt and used for the foundation of the new church building. In 1892 a new church building was again constructed in Petershagen.

In 1869, there were 17 full farms, six half farms and 19 small farms with a total land area of 1,600 dessiatine. Today the village is known as Kutuzovka. Little is left of the former village of Petershagen, other than the church building.

PETERSHAGEN

Molotschna Colony

1. PETERSHAGEN MENNONITE CHURCH

This church building was constructed in 1892 replacing the first church building built in Petershagen in 1831. It was built in a neo-Gothic style, including Gothic-shaped windows and brick buttresses between the windows. The walls were all brick and the roof was covered with clay tiles. The main body of the church building measured 12 m by 26 m.

The church was located at the east end of the village and was placed parallel to the street. The pulpit and platform were at one end of the long rectangular sanctuary rather than the traditional layout with the pulpit and platform along the long side of the sanctuary. At the end of the rectangle, opposite the pulpit/platform, there was a 6 m extension which was the main entrance. The actual entrance door faced the yard which was away from the street. There was another extension along the main wall facing the yard, which was a side entrance.

In 1909 the church had 350 baptized members and four ministers. Today this building is in poor condition. The walls have been painted and the roof replaced with metal sheeting. The main entrance extension is still in place but the side extension has been removed. It is now used as a storage building.

Petershagen Church building

Wall detail

Petershagen Church building today

RÜCKENAU

The village of Rückenau was founded in 1811 along the south side of the Kuruschan River at the point where the Begim Tschokrak River runs into it. The village street was laid out with a gentle curve and was generally parallel to the river. Twenty farmyards were established, all located on the north side of the street, with the river running through them. The river was eventually dammed just east of the village to control the water flow and to create a reservoir. The south side of the street was reserved for community facilities. Rückenau was named after a village of the same name in Prussia.

Initially 11 families settled in Rückenau, eight of which were Flemish Mennonite families from Prussia and two from the Palatinate area. Since they were very poor, they received an interest free loan from the government of almost 4,600 Rubles. The first winter was spent in earth huts. Over time another nine families from Prussia settled in the village.

The early years of the settlement were difficult since occupants of the land to the north of the village seriously interfered with their farming activities and with the construction of their houses. This problem was eventually resolved and the village began to prosper. In 1844 a new village school was constructed and a tree plantation was established along the south side of the village. In 1869 there were 14 full farms, 12 half farms and 34 small farms with a total land area of over 1,800 dessiatine. The village also had a tavern which was later converted into a Mennonite Brethren church. In 1883 this congregation built a new church building and in 1895 it built a home for the elderly on land donated to it for this purpose. The village also had a store and a windmill.

Today the village is known as Kozolugovka. The church and a few Mennonite houses still remain, but the cemetery no longer exists.

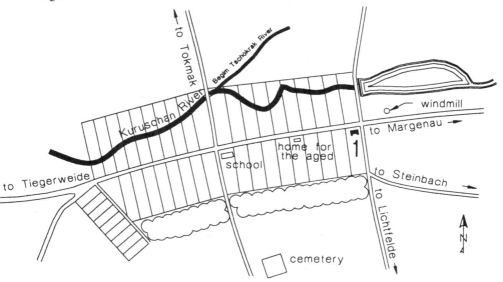

Village of Rückenau

RÜCKENAU

1. RÜCKENAU M.B. CHURCH

The Rückenau Mennonite Brethren Church was founded in 1860. Its first facility was a converted tavern in Rückenau. In 1883 a new church building was constructed. Johann Koop from Fürstenau was responsible for the planning of it and for overseeing its construction. The cost of construction was 8,500 Rubles. Large amounts of material and labour were contributed by members. The dedication service took place on October 2, 1883.

The building was located parallel to the street with the church yard behind it. There was an extension toward the yard near one end of the building which included the main entrance. The building measured approximately 26 m by 13 m and had an inside ceiling height of 4.4 m. The exterior walls were of brick, covered with plaster and painted dark red. The hip roof was covered with metal sheeting. A decorative masonry fence was located along the street and an "L" shaped horse barn built of wood was located in the church yard.

In 1909, the church had 485 baptized members and 22 ministers. For a period of time during the 1930's it was used as a school. It was then converted to a feed mill. The roof structure was substantially altered and the roofing changed to corrugated cement-asbestos. The windows have been filled in and the walls painted. The fine detailing, especially at the window heads, is still evident, however.

Rückenau M.B. Church building

Window detail

Rückenau M.B. Church building today

RUDNERWEIDE

Molotschna Colony

The village of Rudnerweide was founded in 1820, one of eight villages established at the east end of the Molotschna Colony. The majority of the settlers were members of a Frisian congregation from the village of Rudnerweide in Prussia. The new village of Rudnerweide, therefore, became the church centre for the villages of Pastwa, Franztal, and Grossweide.

Rudnerweide was located along the southeast bank of the Sassikulak River, a small stream that runs into the Juschanlee River. It was laid out with farmyards on both sides of the village street. The farmyards on the northeast side of the street backed onto the river. Initially 24 families settled in the village. Then in 1826 another nine families arrived.

During the first summer, the settlers built their barns which they used for their own accommodation until they were able to built their houses the following summer. Most of these first settlers were poor and so were provided with an interest free loan of over 12,500 Rubles by the government. Some of the first settlers and a number of the later settlers had sufficient capital of their own, totalling some 30,000 Rubles.

In 1822 a church building was constructed with financial assistance from Tsar Alexander I. There was also a village school as well as a two storey vinegar distillery and a large one storey beer brewery. These buildings were built of stone with clay tile roofs.

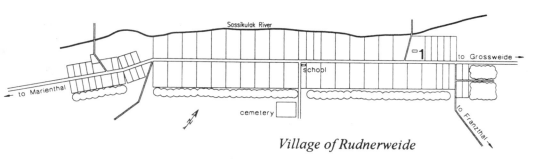

Village of Rudnerweide

House in Rudnerweide

House built in 1901, Rudnerweide

RUDNERWEIDE

Molotschna Colony

A village report from 1848 provides an interesting description of Rudnerweide.

"As one gradually climbs up the hill that is separated from the village by the small stream, one can easily see the two rows of houses of Rudnerweide. All the houses are similar in style, practically planned, and pleasing to look at. What makes these houses even more beautiful are the orchards planted around them, with wild pear trees along the street, mulberry hedges between neighbours, and olive trees along the rear.

To the northeast there is the village plantation, a third of which is mulberry trees which provide the opportunity to make silk. This plantation covers 16½ dessiatine of land. Every farm owner possesses therein an area of ½ dessiatine. Each such area is surrounded by a mulberry hedge and the entire plantation is surrounded by a wild olive hedge.

Along the southeast side of the village one finds the newly established shelter-belt that is to protect the orchards from storms and snow storms. At the southwest end of the village is where the landless people live, in houses that are also built in similar fashion and surrounded with orchards."

By 1855 there were 28 full farms, 10 half farms and 46 small farms with almost 2,900 dessiatine of land in total.

During World War I the name of the village was changed to Rozovka. The village is still identifiable today, although only a few houses are left at the south end of the village. It is incorporated into the collective farm that is headquartered in the neighbouring village of Prostore, formerly Grossweide.

House in Rudnerweide

RUDNERWEIDE   *Molotschna Colony*

1. RUDNERWEIDE MENNONITE CHURCH

The church building in Rudnerweide was built in 1822. It served the Molotschna villages of Grossweide, Franztal, Pastwa and Rudnerweide. A grant of 10,000 Rubles was provided by Tsar Alexander I in accordance with the original agreement that funding would be provided for the construction of Mennonite Church buildings. This was the last Mennonite church to receive this assistance. Additional funds required for the construction were donated by the villagers.

It was a large plain building in the tradition of earlier Mennonite churches in Prussia and Holland. The exterior brick walls were up to 2 feet thick, plastered and painted. The interior construction was mostly wood including large posts and beams supporting the roof and balcony.

The pulpit and platform were located along the long side of the building. The ministers and deacons sat to one side of the pulpit and the song leaders (Vorsänger) to the other side. Behind the pulpit was a sofa for the speakers. There were two entrances, one for the women and the other for the men, both located in the end wall. The women and girls sat on the main floor. The men and boys sat in the balcony, in order of age with the younger to the front and the older to the rear.

The balcony extended along the wall opposite the pulpit and across both ends. The speaker at the pulpit could be seen from the last rows of benches on both the main floor and the balcony. The speaker could also be easily heard since the acoustics were very good.

The choir used one of the end balconies, except in winter when they sat on the main floor opposite the song leaders. There was no piano or organ. In winter both end balconies were closed off to conserve heat and because attendance was lower. Heating was provided by two wood stoves. In the ceiling there was a hatch which could be opened up to provide extra seating on special occasions. Usually the young boys would sit up there.

The windows all had shutters and were generally small except for four large windows behind the pulpit which provided considerable daylight to the interior. For the occasional evening services such as Christmas Eve, petroleum lamps were used to provide lighting.

The church building was located parallel to the street with the large windows behind the pulpit facing the street. Behind the church was the caretaker's house and barn as well as the toilets and a horse barn for those attending in winter.

In the 1840's the original straw roof was replaced with clay roof tiles and in the 1890's the building was extended by 8.5 m in length. Then in 1900 major repairs were undertaken, although some church members were in favour of constructing a new church building. At that time it was repainted in brighter colours giving it a more friendly appearance.

Around 1909, the Rudnerweide church had over 1,300 baptized

RUDNERWEIDE

members, one leading minister, and two deacons.

The church was closed in 1933 and converted to a club house. Later it was used for storing grain and in 1940 it was demolished, its bricks reused for the construction of other buildings.

1. SANCTUARY
2. PULPIT
3. MINISTERS' ROOM
4. COATS
5. MEN'S ENTRANCE
6. WOMEN'S ENTRANCE
7. WOMEN'S ROOM
8. BALCONY

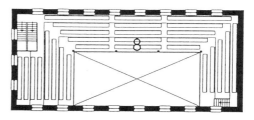
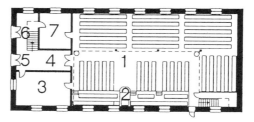

Rudnerweide Church building from street

SCHÖNSEE
Molotschna Colony

The village of Schönsee was founded in 1805 on the south bank of the Tokmak River between the villages of Ladekopp and Petershagen. The first settlers were 19 Flemish Mennonite families from Prussia. They brought approximately 5,000 Rubles of capital with them, but also received an interest free loan from the government of over 8,500 Rubles, including funds for provisions and lumber. Schönsee was named after a village of the same name in Prussia. The site was not surveyed properly and it was soon determined that the three villages were too close together. Schönsee was, therefore, relocated to a site approximately 10 km. east of Tokmak, again along the south bank of the Tokmak River. The village was laid out with farmyards on both sides of the village street. There were a total of 20 farmyards. However, only 10 of the original families relocated. They were joined by 10 other families that had recently immigrated.

After some difficult years, the village began to prosper. In 1869 there were 19 full farms, two half farms and 26 small farms with a total land area of over 1,700 dessiatine. There was a general store, a small factory manufacturing agricultural machinery, a large flour mill, a blacksmith shop, and a large Dutch-style windmill used for milling feed grain. There were also a number of craftsmen living in the village.

The village school had two classrooms. In 1831 a church building was constructed behind the village orchards. Built out of wood, it was a small, plain building in the tradition of the early Mennonite churches. It was replaced in 1909 by a large ornate church building that was constructed at the east end of the village.

Today the village is known as Snegurevka. Very little is left of the Mennonite buildings other than the remains of the Schönsee church building.

Building in Schönsee

SCHÖNSEE

Molotschna Colony

1. SCHÖNSEE MENNONITE CHURCH

On April 15, 1909, the Schönsee community submitted a petition along with two sets of drawings to the Taurida Provincial Government Building Department, requesting approval to construct a new prayer house. The application was made on behalf of the villages of Klippenfeld, Hamberg, Wernersdorf, Liebenau, and Schönsee-Fabrikerwiese. The petition was signed by N.F. Von-Garnie, a Baltic German from Revel, but living in the City of Orekkov, who used his social-political connections to support the application. Approval was received and construction began the same year.

The Schönsee church building was one of the most ornate Mennonite churches in Russia. It was built in a neo-Gothic style complete with Gothic shaped windows and buttresses between the windows. The style was further emphasized by the use of light coloured plaster around windows and other details.

This church was located at the east end of the village. It was placed parallel to the street with the pulpit/platform at one end of the long rectangular sanctuary. At the other end of the building, opposite the pulpit/platform, was an extension which was the main entrance. The actual entrance door faced the yard which was away from the street. There was another extension along the main wall facing the yard, which was a side entrance. Large ornate gateposts at the street complemented the design of the church building.

In 1909 the church had 745 baptized members and 6 ministers. The seating capacity of the building was 700. The interior had a fresco ceiling painted by an Italian artist. After the civil war the building was turned into a granary and then into a club.

Main entrance extension

Interior

SCHÖNSEE

Molotschna Colony

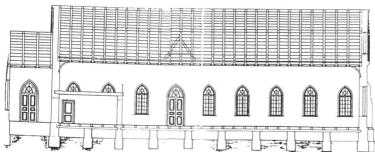

Cross section

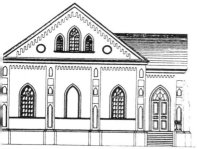

West elevation

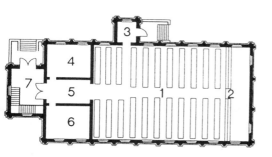

Side entrance extension

1. SANCTUARY
2. PULPIT
3. SIDE ENTRANCE
4. MINISTERS' ROOM
5. COATS
6. WOMEN'S ROOM
7. ENTRANCE FOYER

Schönsee Church building

STEINBACH   *Molotschna Colony*

Steinbach was a large private estate located along the Juschanlee River, at the southern edge of the Molotschna Colony, between the villages of Steinfeld and Elisabethtal. It was established in 1812 by Klaas Wiens, the first Oberschultz of the Molotschna Colony, who had originally settled in the village of Altonau. In 1825 Tsar Alexander I visited the estate and was so impressed by the successful tree planting that had been carried out on the bare steppes, that he granted Wiens large land holdings. This also led to the establishment of the Agricultural Society.

Through marriage, ownership transferred to Pieter Schmidt, and stayed in the Schmidt family until the civil war.

The estate's land holdings eventually grew to 11,000 dessiatine, probably one of the largest Mennonite land holdings in southern Russia.

After the civil war the owners of the estate were forced to occupy the former tavern. The estate was then converted into an orphanage. Today many of the buildings still remain and are still used as an orphanage. Several gravestones can also be found in the cemetery. The following have been identified:

●Heinrich Schmidt
February 2, 1821 - July 29, 1881

●Maria Schmidt
..., ... - June 5, 1860

Steinbach Estate today

Steinbach Estate, Jakob Dick House (left) and Barn (right)

STEINBACH
Molotschna Colony

1. JAKOB DICK HOUSE
2. JAKOB DICK BARN
3. KLAAS WIENS HOUSE/BARN
4. NIKOLAI SCHMIDT HOUSE
5. PIETER SCHMIDT HOUSE
6. PRIVATE SCHOOL
7. BARNS
8. GARAGE
9. GENERATOR
10. KITCHEN
11. CEMETERY
12. TAVERN
13. BLACKSMITH SHOP
14. BLACKSMITH'S HOUSE
15. WORKER'S KITCHENS
16. PRIVATE RESIDENCES
17. GARDENER'S HOUSE

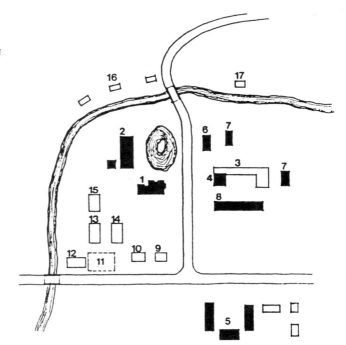

JAKOB DICK HOUSE

Jakob Dick, who married into the Schmidt family, had this house built in 1880. The exterior walls of brick have very ornate detailing, similar in style to what the Russian nobility built at the time. At the main entrance there were steps on either side leading to an entrance platform. What is now the entrance door was originally a window. The wall facing the road had a large bay window and a large domed roof over it. However the ceiling inside, under the dome, was flat. This and several other ceilings had artwork painted by a Belgian artist.

For many years this house stood in a state of serious disrepair, with its original roof completely gone. Recently a new roof was constructed and the building was upgraded for use by the orphanage.

Jakob Dick House

STEINBACH *Molotschna Colony*

Jakob Dick House today

JAKOB DICK BARN

This barn was also built of brick and had very fine detailing around doors and windows, at corners and along the eaves. The original one and two storey building has been altered so that now the entire building is two storeys. The roof has been changed from its original metal sheeting to corrugated cement-asbestos and the fine arched parapets have been removed. It is now being used as a residence for the orphanage.

Jakob Dick Barn today

STEINBACH

Jakob Dick Barn

Jakob Dick Barn today

NIKOLAI SCHMIDT HOUSE

This house was constructed by Nikolai Schmidt and was added to the original house-barn built by Klaas Wiens, the founder of the estate. Today only the house itself still remains. The brick walls still show the fine detailing although they have been painted. The gable end still shows the original brick colour but has been altered substantially. The upper arched windows have been bricked in and the decorative parapet has been mostly removed. It still functions as a private residence.

Nikolai Schmidt House (left)

Nikolai Schmidt House today

STEINBACH

PRIVATE SCHOOL

The school was founded by Pieter Schmidt in 1838. It was considered to be a secondary school, providing higher education for the children of wealthy and progressive Mennonites as well as children of Russian nobility and other non-Mennonites. It became a centre for reform-minded teachers. The building still exists today.

GARAGE

There were originally two separate garage buildings. One was only large enough for one large vehicle. The other had two large garage doors as well as several large windows. All wall openings were slightly arched and again the brick walls had fine detailing. The larger building also had a small tower projecting above the roof. Both buildings had chimneys, suggesting that they were heated.

Today the two buildings have been connected and made into one long building. The roof structure has been completely altered and the tower is gone. The walls have been painted and are not in good condition.

Garage buildings

Garage building today

STEINFELD

The village of Steinfeld was established in 1857, along the north bank of the Juschanlee River at the south edge of the Molotschna Colony. It was one of the last villages to be established in the Molotschna. Its name was likely derived from the local conditions, i.e. Stein (stone), feld (field).

The land on which Steinfeld was located had been part of the Molotschna Colony's lands reserved for expansion. Since the farms in the previously established villages could not be subdivided, there were large numbers of landless in these villages that were anxious to establish farms. Steinfeld was one of several new villages settled primarily by people from the villages along the west edge of the Molotschna. Thirty families settled in Steinfeld.

The village was laid out parallel to the river and in accordance with regulations established by the Agricultural Society under the leadership of Johann Cornies. Similarly the farm buildings were constructed in accordance with these regulations. This included the use of brick walls and clay tile roofs. In 1869, Steinfeld had 29 full farms, 2 half farms, and 6 small farms, with a total land area of just over 2,000 dessiatine.

During the civil war, the village suffered the same fate as the other Molotschna villages. It survived until 1943, when all the remaining Mennonites left. The village no longer exists today.

WALDHEIM

The village of Waldheim was founded in 1836, along the Begim Tschokrak River by a group of Groningen Old Flemish Mennonites from Volhynia, and originally from Prussia. Eight families arrived the first year, 12 more in 1838, and another 20 in 1840. The village was laid out with two streets that were parallel to the river. The street on the north side of the river was for the 40 landowners and the street on the south side of the river was for factory workers and small farm owners. They were connected by three cross streets.

Although the settlers had very little of their own capital, they received no financial assistance from the government. They were, however, given some support by their neighbours. Since the settlers had lived in a forested area in Volhynia, Johann Cornies named the village Waldheim (forest home).

Waldheim eventually became the largest village in the Molotschna Colony, in terms of land area and number of farms. In 1869 there were 34 full farms, 12 half farms, and 56 small farms, with a total land area of 3,500 dessiatine. There was also a considerable amount of industry in Waldheim, with a large number of factory workers. Two factories (J.J. Neufeld, Koehn) produced a variety of agricultural equipment. There were large steam mills and several windmills. The village also had three stores, a post office, a doctor's office, and after 1912, a hospital. There were two church buildings, the original Mennonite Church and a Mennonite Brethren Church. There was also a village school and a high school was added later.

Because of the many factory workers,

the village of Waldheim was more directly involved in the political upheavals of the Revolution and civil war. Many of the village leaders were executed during the 1920's. After the collectivization of the 1930's, the population of the village was just over 1,000, half of which were Mennonite. The last Mennonites left the village in 1943.

Today the village is known as Vladovka. It is the administrative centre of the Gorki Collective Farm. Little is left of the Mennonite buildings other than the hospital which still operates as a 50 bed facility. Also one gravestone, resembling a tree, has been identified in the cemetery:

- David Goerzen
  January 27, 1846 - August 1, 1917

David Goerzen, 1846-1917

WALDHEIM

Molotschna Colony

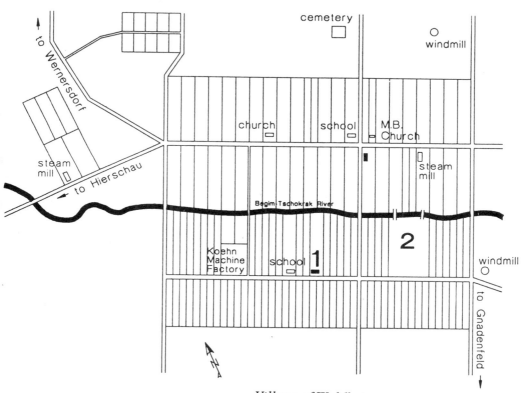

Village of Waldheim

WALDHEIM

1. WALDHEIM HOSPITAL

Since the village of Waldheim had several factories and since there were many Mennonite and Russian villages nearby, Waldheim was considered a good location for a hospital. The Kornelius Warkentin family, therefore, established this private hospital in Waldheim. It was the second hospital to be established in the Molotschna Colony. The building was officially opened January 13, 1908 with many guests in attendance.

The facility consisted of several buildings and was considered quite modern at the time. It could comfortably accommodate 50 patients and included a pharmacy. In its first year of operation it had one doctor and three nurses and provided 1,617 patient days of care with an average stay of 13 days. During World War I, 30 beds were allocated to care for wounded soldiers. It eventually experienced financial difficulties and did not operate for very many years.

However, the buildings still exist and still function as a 50 bed hospital. The brick walls are painted red with white trim and the main entrance to the hospital building is emphasized by a white painted gable projection. The lab and pharmacy are in an adjacent building. The original roof has been replaced with corrugated cement-asbestos. The grounds are landscaped and well kept.

Waldheim Hospital

WALDHEIM

2. J.J. NEUFELD FACTORY

In 1890, Isaak J. Neufeld established a factory in Waldheim that specialized in producing threshing machines and a variety of agricultural machinery. In 1900 it was reorganized as a joint-stock company and became known as J.J. Neufeld & Ko. The factory was located approximately 7 km. from the Stulnevo train station allowing its products to be shipped by rail after 1913.

After the civil war the factory was nationalized. It eventually ceased to operate and today none of the buildings exist anymore.

Advertisement from 1915

WALDHEIM

Molotschna Colony

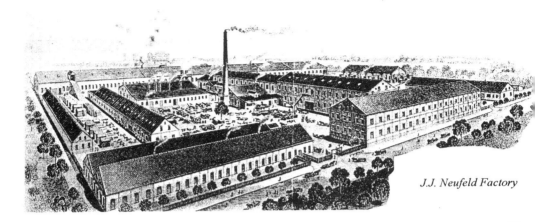

J.J. Neufeld Factory

1. JOINER'S SHOP
2. MECHANIC'S SHOP
3. CAST IRON CLEANING
4. PAINTING HOUSE
5. LUMBER STORAGE
6. WEIGH BOOTH
7. SPARE PARTS STOREHOUSE
8. STOREHOUSE
9. MACHINE ASSEMBLY
10. OFFICE
11. ENGINE DEPARTMENT
12. SMITHY
13. FOUNDRY
14. DRIVE ASSEMBLY
15. COVERED STORAGE
16. DRYING ROOM
17. ENGINE DEPARTMENT
18. INDOOR LUMBER STORAGE
19. SHOP FOR THRESHING MACHINES
20. SHED FOR TESTING THRESHING MACHINES
21. WATCHMAN'S SHED
22. LUMBER STORAGE
23. OIL TANK

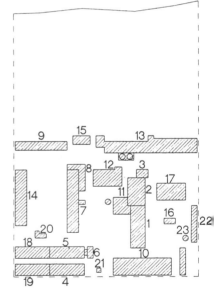

7. ZAGRADOVKA COLONY

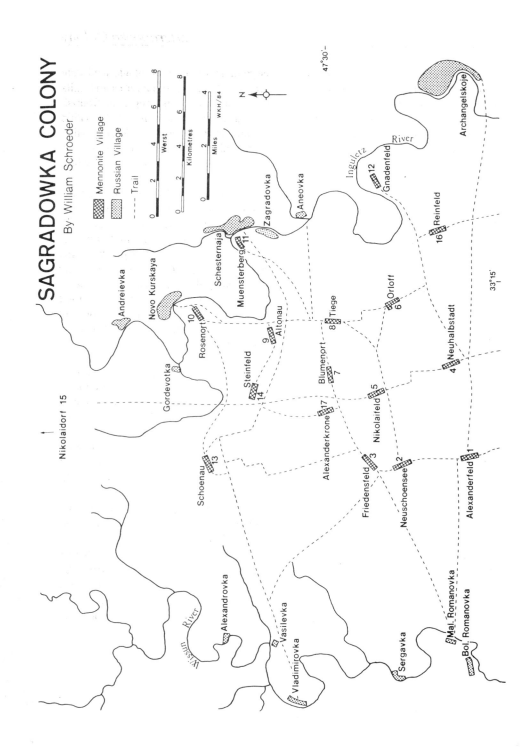

SAGRADOWKA COLONY

By: William Schroeder

Mennonite Village

Russian Village

- - - - - Trail

Werst
0 2 4 6 8

Kilometres
0 2 4 6 8

Miles
0 2 4
WKH/84

N

Nikolaidorf 15

Andreievka

Novo Kurskaya

Gordevotka

Rosenort 10

Steinfeld

Altonau 9

Schoenau 13

Schesternaja

Muensterberg 11

Zagradovka

Aneovka

Alexanderkrone 17

Blumenort 7

Tiege 8

Orloff 6

Gnadenfeld 12

Reinfeld 16

Inguletz River

Steinfeld 14

Friedensfeld 3

Nikolaifeld 5

Neuschoensee 2

Neuhalbstadt 4

Alexanderfeld 1

Archangelskoje

Wisun River

Alexandrovka

Vasilevka

Vladimirovka

Sergavka

Mal. Romanovka

Bol. Romanovka

47°30'

33°15'

The former Zagradovka Colony is located approximately 100 km. northeast of the City of Kherson and 50 km. south of the City of Krivoy Rog. It was established by the Molotschna Colony when 21,276 dessiatine were purchased from Count Leo Kochubey for 500,000 Rubles. The land purchase was concluded on June 15, 1871.

It was named after the large Russian village of Zagradovka located nearby. The Inguletz River, a tributary of the Dnieper, ran along the east edge of the Colony.

A total of 484 families settled in the 16 villages that were established between 1872 and 1879. Each family was provided with 32.5 dessiatine of land which they purchased for 25 Rubles per dessiatine. The exception was the village of Orloff which had farms of 65 dessiatine.

A 17th village, Nikolaidorf, was established in 1879 on land that was purchased privately. It was located north of the Colony, but considered itself to be part of the Zagradovka Colony. However, it was not administered by the Zagradovka Volost office which was located in the village of Tiege.

Generally the villages were named after those in the Molotschna from where most of the settlers came. They were also designated by numbers for the benefit of the neighbouring people. They were laid out in accordance with the traditions of the Molotschna Colony, including single main streets with farmyards on either side and large areas of planted trees.

In the early years the settlement was quite poor but by the turn of the Century most inhabitants were fairly well off with large houses built of brick and well-kept gardens. A number of factories and mills were established and began to flourish after a railroad was built in 1916 within 10 km. of the Colony. The population increased and soon this daughter colony began to establish its own daughter colonies.

However, during the civil war the Colony suffered tremendously. In a number of the villages serious atrocities were carried out including murder, confiscation of property and the destruction of buildings. Of the inhabitants that survived, many were exiled during the 1930's and the rest left in 1943. Following are the present Russian names of the Zagradovka Colony villages:

Alexanderfeld (No.1) . Novo-Alexandrovka
Alexanderkrone (No.17) .... Lugovka
Altonau (No.9) .... Prigorye
Blumenort (No.7) .... Svetlovka
Friedensfeld (No.3) .... Ozerovka
Gnadenfeld (No.12) ...... Gnadovka
Münsterberg (No.11) .... Dolinovka
Neuhalbstadt (No.4) .... Rovnopolye
Neuschönsee (No.2) ...... Ozerovka
Nikolaidorf (No.15) ..... Nikolaevka
Nikolaifeld (No.5) ...... Nikolskoye
Orloff (No.6) .... Orlovo
Reinfeld (No.16) .... Sofievka
Rosenort (No.10) .... Rozovka
Schönau (No.13) .... Krasnovka
Steinfeld (No.14) .... Kamenka
Tiege (No.8) .... Kochubeyevka

NIKOLAIFELD

The village of Nikolaifeld was established in 1872 and settled by 40 landless families from the Molotschna Colony. The village was laid out with farmyards on both sides of the village street. Each family received 32.5 dessiatine of land at a cost of 25 Rubles per dessiatine. The village was named after Tsar Nicholas I but was also known as village No. 5.

Although the settlers were quite poor, the village soon prospered and the original houses were replaced with large brick houses. A village school was constructed soon after the village was established. A church building was constructed at the south end of the village for the Nikolaifeld Mennonite Church.

The village of Nikolaifeld is now known as Nikolskoye. The church building still exists but few other Mennonite buildings remain.

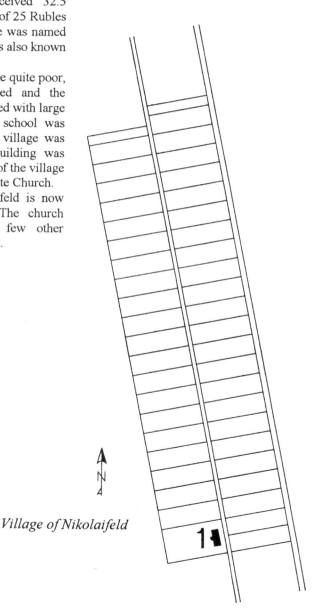

Village of Nikolaifeld

NIKOLAIFELD

Zagradovka Colony

Gerhard Dyck House, Nikolaifeld

Isbrand Friesen House, Nikolaifeld

NIKOLAIFELD

1. NIKOLAIFELD MENNONITE CHURCH

Construction of the church building in Nikolaifeld began in 1888 and was completed in 1891, with the first service held on May 5 of that year. In 1922 it had 1,241 members.

The design of the church building was in the tradition of the earlier plain Mennonite churches but some decorative features were added. The windows had wood shutters and wood trim around them while the brick walls were covered with decorative plaster.

The building was located parallel to the street with the church yard behind it. There was a two storey extension toward the yard, which included not only the main entrance but also a large kitchen. Meals were prepared for occasions such as Thanksgiving and were eaten outdoors.

The pulpit and platform were located along the long side of the building, parallel to the street. Four tall vertical windows were located behind the platform, facing the street. There were narrow balconies along the short sides. In winter the building was heated by a large stove that burned sunflower husks.

The hip roof which was originally covered with metal sheeting, now has corrugated cement-asbestos. The building is generally in poor condition, although traces of the exterior decorative details are still visible. In 1931 the building was converted to a granary and is still used for that purpose today.

Window detail

NIKOLAIFELD

Zagradovka Colony

Nikolaifeld Church building today

Nikolaifeld Church building from yard

ORLOFF

Zagradovka Colony

The village of Orloff was established in 1872 and settled by families from the Molotschna Colony who had some available capital. The village was laid out with farmyards on both sides of the village street. Each family received 65 dessiatine of land at a cost of 25 Rubles per dessiatine. The village was named after Ohrloff in the Molotschna Colony which was also sometimes spelled "Orloff", as the original village in Prussia was. Orloff was also known as village No. 6.

The village soon prospered and became one of the most important in the Zagradovka Colony. Although the Volost office was located in Tiege, it was named Volost Orloff. In addition to the village school, there was a private three classroom Zentralschule for a period of time. A church building was constructed at the north end of the village for the Allianz Church. The village also had a small factory (Wiebe) that manufactured farm machinery.

The village suffered tremendously during the civil war. In 1919, Machno terrorists murdered 45 villagers in one night. The victims are buried in a mass grave near the cemetery.

The village is now known as Orlovo. Several Mennonite buildings still exist including the church building. There are also a number of traditional masonry Mennonite fences remaining. A number of gravestones have also been identified in the cemetery.

Village of Orloff

Fence in Orloff

House in Orloff

ORLOFF

1. ALLIANZ CHURCH

This church was organized in 1907 when a group led by Franz Martens broke away from the mainstream Mennonite Church to form the Altonau, later Orloff, Evangelical Mennonite Church. It attempted to serve as a bridge between the Mennonite Church and the Mennonite Brethren Church and had its roots in the Blankenburg Allianz, an evangelical movement in Germany. In 1922 the Orloff Church had 214 members.

This building was constructed in 1914 on land donated by Heinrich Wiebe. It was placed parallel to the street and featured Gothic-style windows. The pulpit and platform were located at one end of the rectangular shaped building. The brick walls were covered with plaster which featured fairly subtle decorative details. A decorative fence along the street utilizing curved clay roof tiles was consistent in appearance with the fences throughout village. Two large decorative gateposts with a wrought iron gate emphasized the entrance to the church yard.

The cottage-style roof was covered with metal sheeting. It is said that in 1943 the villagers removed the roof structure and used the material for building wagons for the Great Trek to the west. It has since been replaced with a substantially different roof. The building is now used as a granary.

Wall detail

Allianz Church building today

Allianz Church building

ORLOFF

2. CEMETERY

The following gravestones have been identified. They are rectangular concrete frames with the names and dates imprinted on the top. On the sides of the frames are the names (shown below in brackets) of the firms that made them.

●Maria Friesen geb. Löwen
June 2, 1848 - June 24, 1902
(Braun Volk 10.5.1913)

●Isbrand Friesen
August 17, 1839 - October 4, 1908
(Braun Volk 10.5.1913)

●Jakob Köhn
September 10, 1840 - March 13, 1901
(Braun & Woelk 1.6.1913)

●Helena Isaak
September 5, 1908 (?) - April 19, 1910
(Auf Wiedersehen)
(Braun & Co. 10.6.1910)

●Maria Martens
July 3, 1898 (?) - April 18, 1910
(Braun & Co. 23.4.1911)

●Johann Bargen
June (?) ..., 1871 - December 26, 1913

●Names and dates not legible
(Braun & Co. 20.8.1911)

●Names and dates not legible
(Braun & Woelk 8.6.1913)

●Katherina Isaak geb. Bärg
August 8, 1887 - July 17, 1904

●Helena Martens geb. Regehr
December 20, 1882 - April 30, 1914
(Braun & Woelk 19.8.1914)

●Maria Wall geb. Dückmann
December 14, 1844 - March 15 (?), 1914
(8.5.1914)

TIEGE

The village of Tiege was established in 1873 and settled by landless families from the Molotschna Colony. Each family received 32.5 dessiatine of land at a cost of 25 Rubles per dessiatine. The village was laid out with farmyards on both sides of the village street. The village was named after the village of Tiege in the Molotschna Colony but was also known as village No. 8.

Tiege was one of the most significant villages in the Zagradovka Colony. It was the location of the Volost, the administrative centre for the Colony, which was responsible for constructing a pharmacy and a small hospital in 1877. A village school was constructed soon after the village was established, and a church building was built in 1888 for the Tiege Mennonite Brethren Church. The village also had a large flour mill, a post office, a bank, and a store.

The village is now known as Kochubyeyevka. A number of Mennonite buildings still remain, although some are no longer recognizable. For example, the church building has been substantially altered and is now used as a mill.

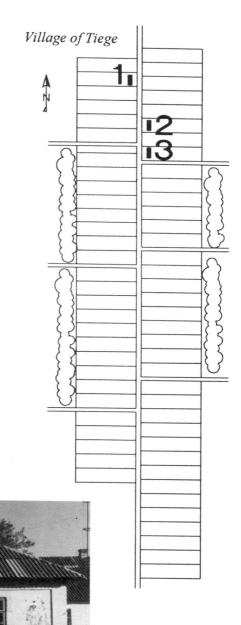

Village of Tiege

Post Office building in Tiege

TIEGE

Zagradovka Colony

1. VILLAGE SCHOOL

The village school was constructed soon after the village of Tiege was established in 1873. It was located at the north end of the village and was placed parallel to the village street. The exterior brick walls were covered with plaster and had a modest amount of ornamentation over the windows and along the eaves. A series of columns were also expressed on the exterior walls.

Because of the length of the building and because of the change in roofing material, it appears that the building may have been expanded at one time. The building is now part of a larger school complex.

Window detail

Tiege village school building

TIEGE

Zagradovka Colony

2. STORE

This store building was placed parallel to the village street. Its exterior brick walls included ornamentation along the eaves and around the windows. The gable windows had similar detailing around them.

The building is still in use today. The walls have been painted and the original roofing has been replaced with corrugated cement-asbestos. Curved metal canopies have been installed over the entrance doors.

Window detail

Store

TIEGE

3. TIEGE HOSPITAL

This small hospital was constructed by the Volost in 1877 along with an adjacent pharmacy, to serve the entire Colony. It was placed parallel to the village street. The exterior brick walls were covered with plaster and have minimal detailing. The original roofing has been replaced with corrugated cement-asbestos.

The building is still used as a hospital. The facility has been expanded with an additional building that is placed perpendicular to the street.

Tiege Hospital

8. CRIMEA

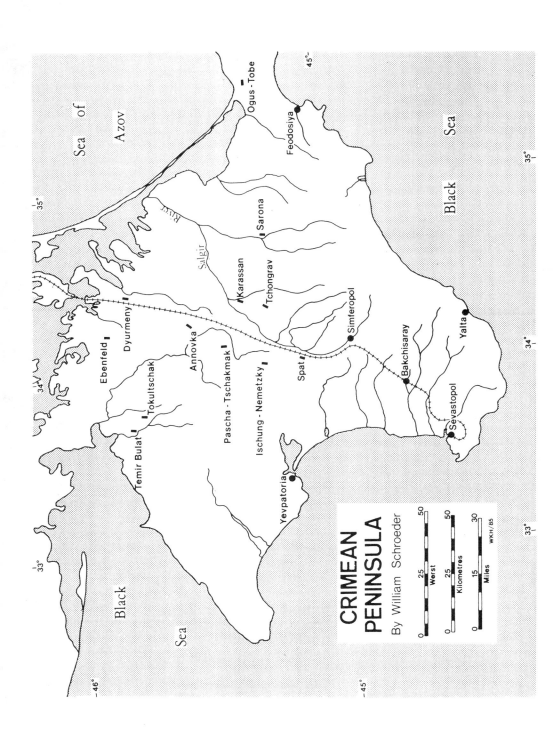

CRIMEAN
PENINSULA

By William Schroeder

Werst
0   25   50

Kilometres
0   25   50

Miles
0   15   30

WKH/85

Sea   of   Azov

Black   Sea

Black   Sea

Ogus - Tobe

Feodosiya

Sarona

Karassan

Tchongrav

Simferopol

Salgir   River

Bakchisaray

Yalta

Ebenfeld

Dyurmeny

Tokultschak

Annovka

Pascha - Tschakmak

Ischung - Nemetzky

Spat

Sevastopol

Temir Bulat

Yevpatoria

45°

35°

35°

45°

34°

34°

33°

46°

45°

33°

Mennonite contact with Crimea began during the early years of the Molotschna Colony. The occasional entrepreneur such as Johann Cornies would haul agricultural products to the cities of Crimea where they would be sold for a good profit. However, it was during the Crimean War of 1853 to 1856 that the Mennonites became well acquainted with the area, providing transportation services for the Russian war effort. While hauling food to the front and bringing wounded soldiers back to the Molotschna Colony, they became familiar with the fertile and inexpensive land there.

Soon after the war, Mennonite land scouts began to search for appropriate places for settlements in Crimea. By the mid-1860's several Mennonite villages had been established. Most settlers came from the Molotschna Colony. Some also came from the other Mennonite colonies and others came directly from Germany.

The Mennonite settlements in Crimea were different from those in other parts of Russia in that the land purchases were made privately, not by the mother colony, as was the case elsewhere. Settlements were established on both rented and purchased land. Several large villages were established such as Karassan and Spat, but most were small, some as small as four to five farmyards. There were also numerous private estates, some of which had their own tenant (Anwohner) villages. By 1926 there were some 70 Mennonite settlements, spread throughout Crimea, with a total population of close to 5,000 and 55,000 dessiatine of land.

Since these settlements were not concentrated in one area, there were no Mennonite districts or Volosts. Instead they were incorporated into regional administrative districts which often included Russian, Tatar and other German settlements. The Mennonite villages were administered by a mayor (Schulze) and a village assembly (Schulzenbott).

Since most settlers came from the Molotschna Colony, the style of buildings tended to be very similar to that of Molotschna. The houses were usually located perpendicular to the street with the barn and machine shed at right angles to the house (Querscheune). Most buildings were constructed of a locally quarried limestone, although, after brick factories were established, brick was often used. Clay roof tiles were commonly used, initially imported from France and later manufactured locally. In some cases the roofs of public buildings were covered with painted metal.

The Mennonite settlements in Crimea did not experience murder, rape and plundering that most other Mennonite villages in southern Russia experienced during the Revolution and civil war. However, eventually the Communist regime took control here as well, expropriating all land. Most of the Mennonite population was evacuated from Crimea prior to the German invasion in 1941.

KARASSAN   *Crimea*

Karassan was established in 1865, one of the first Mennonite villages in Crimea and the second largest. Sixty-five dessiatine of land were allocated to each farm, the same as in the Molotschna Colony. This, however, changed as individual farmers purchased additional land nearby, some owning as much as 800 dessiatine. Initially the village was laid out with farmyards along one side of the street only, but eventually farmyards were built on the opposite side as well. At the centre of the village was a large open area where the church building was located.

The village obtained its water from two large wells. Large pumps imported from England were used to provide running water to the individual houses and farm buildings. The houses were similar to those in the Molotschna Colony, but were generally larger. They were constructed of local limestone with clay tile roofs. The fences along the street were also made of limestone.

In addition to the church building, Karassan also had a two-room elementary school, a secondary school (Zentralschule), a girls' school and a small hospital. There was also a large general store, a bookstore, and a lumber and iron business, all owned by J. Janzen, and a large steam mill (Tjart and Fast). A brick factory (G. Wall) produced brick and clay roof tiles for the region.

In the early 1930's the land was confiscated and became part of a collectivized farm. At the beginning of the Second World War, all remaining Mennonites were exiled, bringing to an end this Mennonite settlement. Today the village is known as Rownoje. A number of former Mennonite buildings are still in existence and several gravestones can still be found in the cemetery.

Village of Karassan

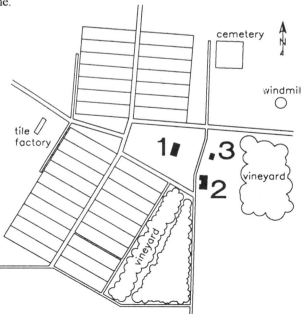

Cemetery in Karassan

KARASSAN   *Crimea*

1. KARASSAN MENNONITE CHURCH

The Karassan Mennonite Church was organized soon after the village of Karassan was established. Until 1884 it was the main Mennonite congregation in Crimea, with affiliates in several other settlements. In 1905 it had 846 members.

The church building in Karassan was probably the largest in Crimea. It was built of local limestone and was placed parallel to the main street. However, it was set well back from the street, creating a rather large town square.

In 1930 the church was closed and the building converted to a clubhouse. A rather non-descript addition was constructed at one end of the building. The walls were covered with stucco and the roofing replaced with corrugated cement-asbestos. The building is still in use today.

Karassan Church building

KARASSAN
Crimea

2. KARASSAN ZENTRALSCHULE

The Karassan secondary school was established in 1905 and this school building constructed the same year. The school was administered by a society and, similar to the secondary schools in the Molotschna Colony, had three classes. It also had a small meteorological station where students were able to study and practise weather observation.

The walls of the building were constructed of local limestone, and covered with stucco. The parapets, and the entrance gate and fence at the street were made of brick, and the roof was covered with metal. While most buildings had two large gateposts to define the entrance to the yard, the Karassan school had only one large entrance gate located symmetrically with the school building. The main entrance to the building was not, however, on axis with this gatepost. Instead, the front steps and landing extended the full width of the area between the projecting wings, from which there were entrance doors into these wings.

The school building was set well back from the church building. Teacherages were constructed on either side. In the mid-1920's the school was taken over by the Communist government. Today the building is still used as a school. One can still identify much of the original detailing including the parapets, the treatment around the windows and the metal roofing. Remains of the brick fence along the street are also evident.

Typical classroom

Karassan Zentralschule

KARASSAN

Karassan Zentralschule today

KARASSAN

3. KARASSAN HOSPITAL

A small hospital was established in Karassan to provide medical services to the surrounding Mennonite community. These services were provided by Mennonite doctors. The hospital building was similar in size and appearance to a large house. It was located behind the church building and down the street from the secondary school.

The building generally still resembles its original appearance except that an extension has been added to one end and the roofing has been changed to corrugated cement-asbestos. It is still used as a hospital today.

Karassan Hospital

SPAT *Crimea*

The village of Spat was established in 1881 when a group of Mennonites from various villages in the Molotschna Colony purchased 5,000 dessiatine of land from an estate owner's wife at a cost of 40 Rubles per dessiatine. The land was located near the Sarabus station of the recently constructed railroad and was utilized to establish two villages, Spat, which became the largest Mennonite village in Crimea, and the much smaller village of Menlerchik.

Spat was laid out in the traditional manner, with a main street running parallel to the Salgir River, and farmyards on both sides of the street. There were three side streets, one leading to the train station, one to the cemetery, and one to the village of Menlerchik. The houses were built of local limestone, and later of brick. As in the Molotschna Colony, most were placed perpendicular to the street, although some were built parallel to the street.

There were two elementary schools in Spat. The main village school was a large two-classroom building with two teacherages. A second school was provided for the children of the factory workers. Spat also had a Zentralschule that also accepted girls, and a Mennonite Brethren church building. There was also a large general store, a bookstore, a lumber and iron business, a binder twine factory and a windmill. A large factory owned by J. Langemann produced agricultural machinery and employed up to 450 workers. There were also two large steam mills, one owned by Langemann and Janzen, the other by F. Toews.

In the early 1930's the land became part of a collective farm. All the Mennonites that were still in Spat at the beginning of the Second World War, were exiled, thereby ending this Mennonite settlement. Today the village is known as Gwardejskoje. Several original Mennonite buildings can still be identified.

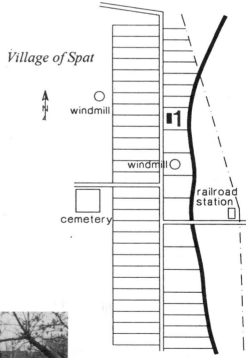

Village of Spat

House in Spat

SPAT   *Crimea*

1. SPAT ZENTRALSCHULE

The secondary school in Spat was established in 1906 and its construction completed the same year. Significant amounts of voluntary labour and materials were provided. Three teacherages were also constructed, all in a style that complemented the design of the school. Local limestone was used for the buildings as well as for the fence and gateposts. Large windows provided substantial daylight to the classrooms. As with secondary schools in the Molotschna Colony, the school had three classes and was administered by a society.

The building is still in use today, although it has been substantially altered. The fence-like parapet has been changed, the roofing has been replaced with corrugated cement-asbestos, and the walls have been covered with stucco. Windows have been added to the front wings, but the proportions of the windows can still be identified as being the same as the original windows. The fence and gateposts are gone, as are the teacherages.

Spat Zentralschule today

Spat Zentralschule

TCHONGRAW   *Crimea*

The village of Tchongraw was established in the 1890's by Mennonites from Blumenfeld. It was located 10 km south of Karassan. It was a fairly small village but was noted for having the only Mennonite Bible School in Russia. The Tchongraw Bible School was founded in 1918 to provide biblical training for congregational workers and preliminary training for prospective missionaries. It was closed by the authorities in 1924. The building has since been demolitioned. However, several other Mennonite buildings still remain.

House in Tchongraw

TCHONGRAW *Crimea*

1. GERHARDT WIENS HOUSE

The Gerhardt Wiens house was set well back from the street. The walls were built of masonry covered with plaster. The house featured a recessed entrance area with two decorative columns. The gable windows featured a unique decorative design, which was the same as that used on the Tchongraw Bible School building. The building is still in good condition and is now used as a municipal administration facility (Volost).

Gable detail

Gerhardt Wiens House

APPENDICES

INFORMATION SOURCES

PREFACE
- *Mennonite Historian*, published by the Mennonite Heritage Centre and the Centre for MB Studies in Canada, Winnipeg, Canada
- *Der Bote*, a German language Mennonite weekly, published by the Conference of Mennonites in Canada, Winnipeg, Canada

EXPLANATORY NOTES
- *Mennonite Encyclopedia*
- *None But Saints*, J. Urry
- *Die Gemeinde Berichte von 1848 der deutschen Siedlungen am Schwarzen Meer*, M. Woltner

1. HISTORICAL BACKGROUND
- *The Mennonite Commonwealth in Russia*, D.G. Rempel, The Mennonite Quarterly Review, October 1973
- *None But Saints*, J. Urry
- *Mennonite Historical Atlas*, W. Schroeder, H. Huebert

2. MENNONITE BUILDINGS
- *The Origins of Modernism in Russian Architecture*, W.C. Brumfield
- *Kindertempel or Shack? The School Building in Late Imperial Russia*, B. Eklof, The Russian Review, Vol. 47, 1988

3. CHORTITZA COLONY
- *Mennonite Encyclopedia*

Burwalde
- *Mennonite Encyclopedia*
- *Die Gemeinde Berichte von 1848 der deutschen Siedlungen am Schwarzen Meer*, M. Woltner

2. Cemetery
- *S. Shmakin, Zaporoshye*

Chortitza-Rosental
- *Mennonite Historical Atlas*, W. Schroeder, H.T. Huebert

1. Chortitza Village School
- *Mennonitisches Jahrbuch, 1911-12*

2. A.J. Koop Factory
- *The Emergence of German Industry in the South Russian Colonies*, J.B. Toews, Editor, The Mennonite Quarterly Review

3. Hildebrand & Priess Factory
- *The Emergence of German Industry in the South Russian Colonies*, J.B. Toews, Editor, The Mennonite Quarterly Review

4. Niebuhr Bank
- *The Emergence of German Industry in the South Russian Colonies*, J.B. Toews, Editor, The Mennonite Quarterly Review

5. Lepp & Wallmann Factory
- *The Emergence of German Industry in the South Russian Colonies*, J.B. Toews, Editor, The Mennonite Quarterly Review

6. Volost
- *First Mennonite Villages in Russia*, N.J. Kroeker

7. Chortitza Mennonite Church
- *First Mennonite Villages in Russia*, N.J. Kroeker

8. Chortitza Zentralschule
- *First Mennonite Villages in Russia*, N.J. Kroeker

9. Müsterschule
- *First Mennonite Villages in Russia*, N.J. Kroeker

10. Chortitza Mädchenschule
- *Glückliche sonnige Schulzeit*, H. Toews

11. Wallmann House
- *Letter from F. Fröse, Der Bote, April 22, 1992*
- *Interview with Mrs. L. Dyck, Winnipeg*

12. Lehrerseminar
- *First Mennonite Villages in Russia*, N.J. Kroeker

14. Hospital
- *First Mennonite Villages in Russia*, N.J. Kroeker

17. Rosental Village School
- *First Mennonite Villages in Russia*, N.J. Kroeker

INFORMATION SOURCES

18. **Photo Atelier**
    ●Forever Summer, Forever Sunday: Peter Gerhard Rempel's Photographs of Mennonites in Russia, 1890-1917, edited by J. Rempel and P. Tiessen
    ●Notes from interview of Heinrich Peter Rempel by J. Urry, April 8, 1974
    ●Lexikon der Modernen Architektur, Knaur
    ●The Sources of Modern Architecture and Design, N. Pevsner

19. **Kroeger Factory**
    ●Clock & Motor Works D.D. Kroeger, A. Kroeger

20. **Johann D. Kroeger House**
    ●A. Kroeger, Winnipeg

21. **David Kroeger House**
    ●A. Kroeger, Winnipeg

Einlage
●Mennonite Encyclopedia
●Die Gemeinde Berichte von 1848 der deutschen Siedlungen am Schwarzen Meer, M. Woltner

1. **Mennonite Church**
   ●H. Bergen, Regina

2. **Alexandrabad**
   ●Das verschwundene Dorf, C. Martens - Berg, Der Bote, April 28 1993

Insel Chortitza
●Erinnerungen von Bernhard Heinrich Pauls

2. **Cemetery**
   ●S. Shmakin, Zaporoshye

Kronsweide
●Mennonite Encyclopedia
●Die Gemeinde Berichte von 1848 der Deutschen Siedlungen am Schwarzen Meer, M. Woltner

1. **Bethania Heilanstalt**
   ●Mennonitisches Jahrbuch, 1910-1913

2. **Cemetery**
   ●S. Shmakin, Zaporoshye

Neuenburg
●Die Gemeinde Berichte von 1848 der deutschen Siedlunger aun Schwarzen Meer, M. Woltner
●S. Shmakin, Zaporoshye

Neuendorf
●Neuendorf in Bild und Wort, F. Thiessen
●Letter from E. Wiebe, Kelowna, B.C.

1. **Neuendorf Mennonite Church**
   ●Neuendorf in Bild und Wort, F. Thiessen

3. **Mill**
   ●Neuendorf in Bild und Wort, F. Thiessen

5. **Tiessen House**
   ●H. Thiessen, Winnipeg

6. **Penner House**
   ●J. Thiessen, Espelkaup, Germany

7. **H. Braun House**
   ●J. Thiessen, Espelkaup, Germany

10. **P. Hildebrand House**
    ●H. Thiessen, Winnipeg

12. **Cemetery**
    ●S. Shmakin, Zaporoshye

Neuhorst
●Neuendorf in Bild und Wort, F. Thiessen

Neuosterwick-Kronstal
●Zur Jahrhundertfeier der Kolonie Neu-Osterwick, jetzt, Pawlovka, D.G. Rempel, Mennonitisches Jahrbuch, 1911-1912
●Osterwick 1812-1943, J.J. Neudorf
●Mennonite Encyclopedia

2. **Kronstal Cemetery**
   ●S. Shmakin, Zaporoshye

3. **Rempel Factory**
   ●Osterwick 1812-1943, J.J. Neudorf

4. **Konsum Store**
   ●Osterwick 1812-1943, J.J. Neudorf

5. **Neuosterwick Village School**
   ●Osterwick 1812-1943, J.J. Neudorf
   ●Mennonitisches Jahrbuch, 1911-1912

INFORMATION SOURCES

6. Neuosterwick Zentralschule
   - *Osterwick 1812-1943, J.J. Neudorf*
   - *Letter from J. Sawatsky, Mountain Lake, Minnesota, March 12, 1993*
   - *Letter from H. Wiebe to Der Bote, December 9, 1992*
7. Peter D. Schulz House
   - *Osterwick 1812-1943, J.J. Neudorf*
   - *A. Kroeger, Winnipeg*
8. Dietrich B. Schulz House
   - *A. Kroeger, Winnipeg*
9. Schulz Factory
   - *Osterwick 1812-1943, J.J. Neudorf*
   - *A. Kroeger, Winnipeg*
10. Neuosterwick Cemetery
   - *S. Shmakin, Zaporoshye*

Nieder-Chortitza
- *Mennonite Encyclopedia*
- *Die Gemeinde Berichte von 1848 der deutschen Siedlungen am Schwarzen Meer, M. Woltner*
1. Wiebe Mill
   - *I. Wiebe, Winnipeg*
2. Krause House
   - *I. Wiebe, Winnipeg*
3. Neustater House
   - *I. Wiebe, Winnipeg*
5. Cemetery
   - *S. Shmakin, Zaporoshye*

Rosengart
- *Die Gemeinde Berichte von 1848 der deutschen Siedlungen am Schwarzen Meer, M. Woltner*
3. Cemetery
   - *S. Shmakin, Zaporoshye*

Schöneberg
- *Die Gemeinde Berichte von 1848 der deutschen Siedlungen am Schwarzen Meer, M. Woltner*
- *Osterwick 1812-1943, J.J. Neudorf*
1. Cemetery
   - *S. Shmakin, Zaporoshye*

Schönhorst
- *Die Gemeinde Berichte von 1848 der deutschen Siedlungen am Schwarzen Meer, M. Woltner*

3. Cemetery
   - *S. Shmakin, Zaporoshye*

Schönwiese
- *Mennonite Historical Atlas, W. Schroeder, H.T. Huebert*
- *Die Gemeinde Berichte von 1848 der deutschen Siedlungen am Schwarzen Meer, M. Woltner*
1. Julius Siemens House
   - *Zaporoshye State Archives*
2. Heinrich K. Hübert House
   - *Zaporoshye State Archives*
4. Abraham A. Koop House
   - *Margarete Bergmann, Winnipeg*
5. H.A. Niebuhr Mill
   - *The Emergence of German Industry in the South Russian Colonies, J.B. Toews, Editor, The Mennonite Quarterly Review*
6. A.J. Koop Factory
   - *The Emergence of German Industry in the South Russian Colonies, J.B. Toews, Editor, The Mennonite Quarterly Review*
7. A.J. Koop & Hölker Factory
   - *The Emergence of German Industry in the South Russian Colonies, J.B. Toews, Editor, The Mennonite Quarterly Review*
8. Lepp & Wallmann Factory
   - *The Emergence of German Industry in the South Russian Colonies, J.B. Toews, Editor, The Mennonite Quarterly Review*
9. Hildebrand & Priess Factory
   - *The Emergence of German Industry in the South Russian Colonies, J.B. Toews, Editor, The Mennonite Quarterly Review*
12. Bär Hospital
   - *Zaporoshye State Archives*

4. YAZYKOVO COLONY
- *Zaporoshye State Archives*
- *Mennonite Encyclopedia*

Adelsheim
- *Zaporoshye State Archives*

INFORMATION SOURCES

● *Mennonite Encyclopedia*
1. **Village School**
   ● *Letter from J. Sawatzky, Mountain Lake, Minnesota, March 12, 1993*
2. **Cemetery**
   ● *S. Shmakin, Zaporoshye*

Hochfeld
● *Zaporoshye State Archives*
● *Mennonite Encyclopedia*
2. **A. Rempel House**
   ● *Letter from P. Epp, Bielefeld, Germany to Der Bote, January 13, 1993*
3. **Cemetery**
   ● *S. Shmakin, Zaporoshye*

Nikolaifeld-Franzfeld
● *Zaporoshye State Archives*
● *Mennonite Encyclopedia*
● *Jasykowo, Siedlungsschicksal am Dnjepr, J. Loewen*
1. **Nikolaifeld Mennonite Church**
   ● *Mennonitisches Jahrbuch, 1913*
   ● *Letter from P. Epp, Bielefeld, Germany to Der Bote, April 15, 1992*
2. **Nikolaifeld Zentralschule**
   ● *Jasykowo, Siedlungsschicksal am Dnjepr, J. Loewen*
7. **Nikolaifeld Cemetery**
   ● *S. Shmakin, Zaporoshye*
8. **Store Complex**
   ● *Jazykowo, Siedlungsschicksal am Dnjepr, J. Loewen*
   ● *Letter from P. Epp, Bielefeld, Germany to Der Bote, January 13, 1993*
10. **Franzfeld Cemetery**
    ● *S. Shmakin, Zaporoshye*
5. **BARATOW & SCHLACTIN COLONIES**
   ● *Against the Wind, J. Friesen*
   ## Gnadental
   ● *Against the Wind, J. Friesen*
   ## Gruenfeld
   ● *Against the Wind, J. Friesen*
   1. **Gruenfeld Mennonite Church**

● *Against the Wind, J. Friesen*
2. **Jakob Rempel House**
   ● *Against the Wind, J. Friesen*
3. **Johann Froese Factory**
   ● *Against the Wind, J. Friesen*
4. **Johann Froese House**
   ● *Against the Wind, J. Friesen*

Neu-Chortitza
● *Against the Wind, J. Friesen*

Steinfeld
● *Against the Wind, J. Friesen*
1. **D. Schapansky House/Barn**
   ● *Against the Wind, J. Friesen*
2. **A.P. Martens House/Barn**
   ● *Against the Wind, J. Friesen*
6. **MOLOTSCHNA COLONY**
   ● *The Molotschna Settlement, H. Goerz*
   ● *Mennonite Historical Atlas, W. Schroeder, H.T. Huebert*
   ## Alexanderkrone-Lichtefelde
   ● *Mennonite Encyclopedia*
   ● *The Molotschna Settlement, H. Goerz*
   ● *Die Gemeinde Berichte von 1848 der deutschen Siedlungen am Schwarzen Meer, M. Woltner*
   2. **Alexanderkrone Zentralschule**
      ● *For Everything a Season, T.D. Regehr*
   3. **Alexanderkrone Mennonite Church**
      ● *Mennonite Encyclopedia*
   6. **Windmill**
      ● *Letter from D. Wiebe, Winnipeg to Der Bote, January 27, 1993*
   ## Alexandertal
   ● *Mennonite Encyclopedia*
   ● *Die Gemeinde Berichte von 1848 der deutschen Siedlungen am Schwarzen Meer, M. Woltner*
   ● *The Molotschna Settlement, H. Goerz*
   2. **Alexandertal M.B. Church**
      ● *P. Toews, Fresno, California*
   ## Alexanderwohl
   ● *Mennonite Encyclopedia*
   ● *Die Gemeinde Berichte von 1848 der deutschen Siedlungen am Schwarzen*

INFORMATION SOURCES

Meer, M. Woltner
●*The Molotschna Settlement, H. Goerz*
1. **Alexanderwohl Mennonite Church**
    ●*Mennonite Life, March, 1986*
Altonau
●*Mennonite Encyclopedia*
●*Die Gemeinde Berichte von 1848 der deutschen Siedlungen am Schwarzen Meer, M. Woltner*
●*S. Shmakin, Zaporoshye*
Blumstein
●*Mennonite Encyclopedia*
●*Die Gemeinde Berichte von 1848 der deutschen Siedlungen am Schwarzen Meer, M. Woltner*
●*S. Shmakin, Zaporoshye*
Elisabethtal
●*Die Gemeinde Berichte von 1848 der deutschen Siedlungen am Schwarzen Meer, M. Woltner*
●*Mennonite Encyclopedia*
●*The Molotschna Settlement, H. Goerz*
Fischau
●*Die Gemeinde Berichte von 1848 der deutschen Siedlungen am Schwarzen Meer, M. Woltner*
●*Hierschau, H.T. Huebert*
●*S. Shmakin, Zaporoshye*
Friedensdorf
●*Die Gemeinde Berichte von 1848 der deutschen Siedlungen am Schwarzen Meer, M. Woltner*
●*The Molotschna Settlement, H. Goerz*
Friedensruh
●*The Molotschna Settlement, H. Goerz*
●*S. Shmakin, Zaporoshye*
Fürstenau
●*Die Gemeinde Berichte von 1848 der deutschen Siedlungen am Schwarzen Meer, M. Woltner*
●*The Molotschna Settlement, H. Goerz*
1. **Village School**
    ●*Mary Neufeld and the Repphun Story, H.A. Neufeld*
2. **Wilhelm Neufeld House**
    ●*Mary Neufeld and the Repphun Story, H.A. Neufeld*

Fürstenwerder
●*Die Gemeinde Berichte von 1848 der deutschen Siedlungen am Schwarzen Meer, M. Woltner*
●*The Molotschna Settlement, H. Goerz*
●*Letter from A. Reger, Weissenthurm, Germany to Der Bote, October 19, 1994*
Gnadenfeld
●*None But Saints, J. Urry*
●*Mennonite Historical Atlas, W. Schroeder, H.T. Huebert*
●*The Mennonite Brotherhood in Russia, P.M. Friesen*
1. **Gnadenfeld Mennonite Church**
    ●*1835-1943 Gnadenfeld, Molotschna, A. Schmidt*
2. **Gnadenfeld Zentralschule**
    ●*The Molotschna Settlement, H. Goerz*
    ●*Mennonitisches Jahrbuch, 1911-1913*
3. **Johann Rempel House**
    ●*A. Schmidt, Kitchener, Ontario*
4. **Volost**
    ●*Mennonitisches Jahrbuch, 1910*
5. **Post Office**
    ●*A. Schmidt, Kitchener, Ontario*
6. **Doctor's Clinic**
    ●*A. Schmidt, Kitchener, Ontario*
7. **Klaas Heide House**
    ●*A. Schmidt, Kitchener, Ontario*
Halbstadt-Muntau
●*Die Gemeinde Berichte von 1848 der deutschen Siedlungen am Schwarzen Meer, M. Woltner*
●*The Molotschna Settlement, H. Goerz*
1. **H.H. Willms Mill**
    ●*The Mennonite Brotherhood in Russia, P.M. Friesen*
    ●*The Molotschna Colony, A Heritage Remembered, H. Tiessen*
2. **Hermann Neufeld Brewery**
    ●*Letter from H. Enns, Buhler, Kansas, September 14, 1992*

INFORMATION SOURCES

6. **Halbstadt Zentralschule**
●*The Molotschna Settlement, H. Goerz*
●*The Molotschna Colony, A Heritage Remembered, H.B. Tiessen*
8. **Diakonissenheim "Morija"**
●*Mennonitisches Jahrbuch, 1909, 1910*
●*The Molotschna Settlement, H. Goerz*
●*Letter from A. Enns, Winnipeg, January 14, 1992*
9. **Diakonissenheim "Morija"**
●*Mennonitisches Jahrbuch, 1911-1913*
10. **Halbstadt Mädchenschule**
●*The Molotschna Settlement, H. Goerz*
12. **Franz & Schröder Factory**
●*The Mennonite Brotherhood in Russia, P.M. Friesen*
13. **Muntau Hospital**
●*Mennonitisches Jahrbuch, 1911-1913*

Hamberg
●*Mennonite Encyclopedia*
●*Die Gemeinde Berichte von 1848 der deutschen Siedlungen am Schwarzen Meer, M. Woltner*

Hierschau
●*Hierschau, H.T. Huebert*

Juschanlee
●*Johann Cornies, D.H. Epp*
●*None But Saints, J. Urry*

Kuruschan
●*The Molotschna Settlement, H. Goerz*
1. **Altenheim Kuruschan**
●*Mennonitisches Jahrbuch 1904-1913*
2. **Wilhelm Neufeld House/ Barn**
●*F. Wall, Winnipeg*

Ladekopp
●*Die Gemeinde Berichte von 1848 der deutschen Siedlungen am Schwarzen Meer, M. Woltner*
●*The Mennonite Settlement, H. Goerz*

1. **Village School**
●*The Molotschna Colony, A Heritage Remembered, H.B. Tiessen*

Landskrone
●*Die Gemeinde Berichte von 1848 der deutschen Siedlungen am Schwarzen Meer, M. Woltner*
●*The Molotschna Settlement, H. Goerz*

1. **Landskrone Mennonite Church**
●*Mennonitisches Jahrbuch, 1910*
●*State Archives of Simpferopol*

Lichtenau
●*Die Gemeinde Berichte von 1848 der deutschen Siedlungen am Schwarzen Meer, M. Woltner*
●*Mennonite Encyclopedia*

Liebenau
●*Die Gemeinde Berichte von 1848 der deutschen Siedlungen am Schwarzen Meer, M. Woltner*
●*The Molotschna Settlement, H. Goerz*

Münsterberg
●*Die Gemeinde Berichte von 1848 der deutschen Siedlungen am Schwarzen Meer, M. Woltner*
●*Mennonite Encyclopedia*
●*S. Shmakin, Zaporoshye*

Neukirch
●*Die Gemeinde Berichte von 1848 der deutschen Siedlungen am Schwarzen Meer, M. Woltner*
●*Mennonite Encyclopedia*
●*S. Shmakin, Zaporoshye*

Ohrloff-Tiege
●*Die Gemeinde Berichte von 1848 der deutschen Siedlungen am Schwarzen Meer, M. Woltner*
●*Mennonite Encyclopedia*
●*Mennonite Historical Atlas, W. Schroeder, H.T. Huebert*

1. **Ohrloff Mennonite Church**
●*The Mennonite Brotherhood in Russia, P.M. Friesen*
●*Mennonite Encyclopedia*

INFORMATION SOURCES

2. **Ohrloff Zentralschule**
   - *The Mennonite Brotherhood in Russia, P.M. Friesen*
   - *Braeul Geneology (1670-1983), J.P. Dyck*
   - *State Archives of Simpferopol*
3. **Ohrloff Hospital**
   - *Mennonitisches Jahrbuch, 1911-1913*
4. **Tiege M.B. Church**
   - *State Archives of Simpferopol*
5. **Marientaubstummenschule**
   - *The Molotschna Settlement, H. Goerz*
   - *Mennonitisches Jahrbuch, 1903-1913*
6. **Ohrloff Cemetery**
   - *S. Shmakin, Zaporoshye*

Petershagen
- *Die Gemeinde Berichte von 1848 der deutschen Siedlungen am Schwarzen Meer, M. Woltner*
- *The Mennonite Settlement, H. Goerz*
1. **Petershagen Mennonite Church**
   - *Mennonite Encyclopedia*

Rückenau
- *Die Gemeinde Berichte von 1848 der deutschen Siedlungen am Schwarzen Meer, M. Woltner*
- *The Molotschna Settlement, H. Goerz*
1. **Rückenau M.B. Church**
   - *Die Rueckenau Mennoniten-Brüder Kirche, W. Schroeder, Mennonitische Rundschau, December 14, 1977*
   - *Letter from A. Laser, Winnipeg, February 11, 1992*

Rudnerweide
- *Mennonitisches Jahrbuch, 1913*
- *Die Gemeinde Berichte von 1848 der deutschen Siedlungen am Schwarzen Meer, M. Woltner*
- *The Molotschna Settlement, H. Goerz*
1. **Rudnerweide Mennonite Church**
   - *Mennonitisches Jahrbuch, 1913*
   - *The History of the Rudnerweide*
     Church, V. Kliewer

Schönsee
- *Die Gemeinde Berichte von 1848 der deutschen Siedlungen am Schwarzen Meer, M. Woltner*
- *Mennonite Encyclopedia*
1. **Schönsee Mennonite Church**
   - *State Archives of Simpferopol*
   - *Mennonite Encyclopedia*

Steinbach
- *None But Saints, J. Urry*
- *I. Wiebe, Winnipeg*

Steinfeld
- *None But Saints, J. Urry*
- *The Molotschna Settlement, H. Goerz*

Waldheim
- *Die Gemeinde Berichte von 1848 der deutschen Siedlungen am Schwarzen Meer, M. Woltner*
- *Mennonite Historical Atlas, W. Schroeder, H.T. Huebert*
- *S. Shmakin, Zaporoshye*
1. **Waldheim Hospital**
   - *Mennonitisches Jahrbuch 1907, 1908*
2. **J.J. Neufeld Factory**
   - *State Archives of Simpferopol*

7. **ZAGRADOVKA COLONY**
   - *Mennonite Encyclopedia*
   - *Mennonite Historical Atlas, W. Schroeder, H. Huebert*

Nikolaifeld
- *Mennonite Encyclopedia*
- *Mennonite Historical Atlas, W. Schroeder, H.T. Huebert*
1. **Nikolaifeld Mennonite Church**
   - *Mennonite Encyclopedia*
   - *S. (Flaming) Sabadosh, Nikolskoye, Ukraine*

Orloff
- *Mennonite Encyclopedia*
1. **Allianz Church**
   - *Mennonite Encyclopedia*
   - *Russian Mennonites and Allianz, J.B. Toews, Journal of Mennonite Studies, Vol. 14, 1996*

INFORMATION SOURCES

Tiege
- *Mennonite Encyclopedia*
3. **Tiege Hospital**
   - *Mennonite Encyclopedia*

8. **CRIMEA**
   - *Mennonite Settlements in Crimea, H. Goerz*
   - *Mennonite Historical Atlas, W. Schroeder, H.T. Huebert*

Karassan
- *Mennonite Settlements in Crimea, H. Goerz*
1. **Karassan Mennonite Church**
   - *Mennonite Settlements in Crimea, H. Goerz*
2. **Karassan Zentralschule**
   - *Mennonite Settlements in Crimea, H. Goerz*

Spat
- *Mennonite Settlements in Crimea, H. Goerz*
1. **Spat Zentralschule**
   - *Mennonite Settlements in Crimea, H. Goerz*

Tchongraw
- *Mennonite Settlements in Crimea, H. Goerz*
1. **Gerhardt Wiens House**
   - *M. Unger, Toronto*

CREDITS

2. **MENNONITE BUILDINGS**
   Housing, *p.24*
   Photo: from Heritage Remembered, G. Lohrenz
   Drawings: from H. Sudermann, Winnipeg
   Churches, *p.27*
   Upper Photo: from Forever Summer, Forever Sunday, P.G. Rempel
   Lower Photo: from Christlicher Familienkalender, 1915
   Schools, *p.29*
   Photos: from Heritage Remembered, G. Lohrenz
   Industrial Buildings, *p.32*
   Upper Left Photo: from Heritage Remembered, G. Lohrenz
   Upper Right Photo: from In The Fullness of Time, W. Quiring
   Lower Photo: from Iwanowka, J. Epp
   Gateposts and Fences, *p.34*
   Photos: from In The Fullness of Time, W. Quiring

3. **CHORTITZA COLONY**
   Burwalde
   1. **Store**
      Photos: J. Urry
   2. **Cemetery**
      Photos: P. Reitsin
   Chortitza-Rosental
   1. **Chortitza Village School**
      Photo: from First Mennonite Villages in Russia, N.J. Kroeker
   2. **A.J. Koop Factory**
      Photo, p.45: S. Bizhko
      Photos, p.46: P. Reitsin
      Floor Plans: P. Turkovsky
   3. **Hildebrand & Priess Factory**
      Photos: P. Reitsin
      Advertisement: from Mennonitisches Jahrbuch, 1913
   4. **Niebuhr Bank**
      Photo: P. Reitsin
      Floor Plan: P. Turkovsky
      Advertisement: from Mennonitisches Jahrbuch, 1913

5. **Lepp & Wallmann Factory**
   Photos: P. Reitsin
   Floor Plans: P. Turkovsky
   Advertisement: from Mennonitisches Jahrbuch, 1913
6. **Volost**
   Floor Plan: P. Turkovsky
   Photo, p.51: from Heritage Remembered, G. Lohrenz
   Upper Photo, p.52: R. Friesen
   Lower Photo, p.52: P. Reitsin
7. **Chortitza Mennonite Church**
   Upper Photo, p.53: from H. Sudermann, Winnipeg
   Lower Photo, p.53: from Neuendorf in Bild und Wort, F. Thiessen
   Photo, p.54: from H. Sudermann
8. **Chortitza Zentralschule**
   Floor Plan: P. Turkovsky
   Photo, p.55: Mennonite Heritage Centre, Winnipeg
   Photos, p.56: R. Friesen
9. **Musterschule**
   Upper Photo: R. Friesen
   Lower Photo: P. Reitsin
   Floor Plan: P. Turkovsky
10. **Chortitza Mädchenschule**
    Photo, p.58: from Forever Summer, Forever Sunday, P.G. Rempel
    Other Photos: R. Friesen
    Floor Plans: P. Turkovsky
11. **Wallmann House**
    Upper Photo: P. Reitsin
    Lower Photo: from Bildband Zur Geschichte Der Mennoniten, H. Gerlach
    Floor Plan: P. Turkovsky
12. **Lehrerseminar**
    Upper Photo: from Mennonite Heritage Centre, Winnipeg
    Other Photos: R. Friesen
    Floor Plan: P. Turkovsky
13. **Factory Hospital**
    Photo: P. Reitsin

CREDITS

Floor Plan: P. Turkovsky
14. **Hospital**
Upper Photo: from First
Mennonite Villages in Russia, N.J.
Kroeker
Lower Photo: P. Reitsin
Floor Plan: P. Turkovsky
15. **Housing for Factory Workers**
Photos: P. Reitsin
Floor Plans: P. Turkovsky
16. **H. Dyck House and Mill**
Photos: R. Friesen
17. **Rosental Village School**
Lower Photo: from Forever
Summer, Forever Sunday, P.G.
Rempel
Other Photos: R. Friesen
18. **Photo Atelier**
Photo: from Forever Summer,
Forever Sunday, P.G. Rempel
19. **Kroeger Factory**
Advertisement: from Christlicher
Familienkalendar 1904
Upper Photo: from Heritage
Remembered, G. Lohrenz
Lower Photo: E. Kroeger
Floor Plan: R. Friesen from plans
by A. Kroeger
20. **Johann D. Kroeger House**
Photo: P. Reitsin
Floor Plan: P. Turkovsky
21. **David Kroeger House**
Floor Plan: R. Friesen from plan
by A. Kroeger
22. **Penner Brick Factory**
Photos: P. Reitsin
Floor Plans: P. Turkovsky

Einlage
1. **Mennonite Church**
Photos: from In The Fullness of
Time, W. Quiring
2. **Alexandrabad**
Photo: from Mennonite Heritage
Centre, Winnipeg
Advertisement: from
Mennonitisches Jahrbuch 1911/12

Insel Chortitza
1. **House-Barn**
Photo: R. Friesen
2. **Cemetery**
Photos: P. Reitsin
Kronsweide
1. **Bethania Heilanstalt**
Photos: from In The Fullness of
Time, W. Quiring
2. **Cemetery**
Photos: P. Reitsin
Neuenburg
Photo: P. Reitsin
Neuendorf
Photos: P. Reitsin
1. **Neuendorf Mennonite Church**
Photo: from Neuendorf in Bild und
Wort, F. Thiessen
2. **Village School**
Photos: R. Friesen
3. **Mill**
Photos: from Neuendorf in Bild
und Wort, F. Thiessen
4. **Granary**
Photos: P. Reitsin
5. **Tiessen House**
Photos: P. Reitsin
6. **Penner House**
Photo: I. Thiessen
7. **H. Braun House**
Photo: I. Thiessen
8. **Mennonite House**
Photo: P. Reitsin
Floor Plan: P. Turkovsky
9. **House/Barn**
Photos: P. Reitsin
Floor Plan: P. Turkovsky
10. **P. Hildebrand House**
Photo: P. Reitsin
Floor Plan: P. Turkovsky
11. **Barn/Shed**
Photos: P. Reitsin
Floor Plan: P. Turkovsky
12. **Cemetery**
Photos: P. Reitsin

CREDITS

Neuosterwick-Kronstal
Photos: P. Reitsin
1. **Kronstal Village School**
   Photo: R. Friesen
2. **Kronstal Cemetery**
   Photos: P. Reitsin
3. **Rempel Factory**
   Photos: R. Friesen
   Advertisement: from Christlicher
   Familienkalendar, 1905
4. **Store**
   Upper Photo: from Osterwick
   1812-1943, J.J. Neudorf
   Lower Photo: R. Friesen
5. **Neuosterwick Village School**
   Photo: from Osterwick 1812-1943,
   J.J. Neudorf
6. **Neuosterwick Zentralschule**
   Photo, p.110: R. Friesen
   Upper Photo, p.111: R. Friesen
   Lower Photo, p.111: from
   Osterwick 1812-1943, J.J. Neudorf
   Floor Plan: J. Peters from sketch
   by H. Wiebe
7. **Peter D. Schulz House**
   Upper Photos: R. Friesen
   Lower Photo: P. Reitsin
8. **Dietrich B. Schulz House**
   Upper Photo: R. Friesen
   Lower Photo: from A. Kroeger
9. **Schulz Factory**
   Site Plan: J. Peters from sketch by
   A. Kroeger
   Upper Left Photo: J. Urry
   Upper Right Photos: from A.
   Kroeger
   Lower Left Photo: R. Friesen
   Lower Right Photos: P. Reitsin
10. **Neuosterwick Cemetery**
    Photos: P. Reitsin
Nieder-Chortitza
Photo: P. Reitsin
1. **Wiebe Mill**
   Upper Photo: I. Wiebe
   Lower Photo: J. Urry

2. **Krause House**
   Photo: I. Wiebe
3. **Neustater House**
   Photo: I. Wiebe
4. **House**
   Photo: J. Urry
Rosengart
1. **Village School**
   Photos: R. Friesen
2. **House**
   Photo: R. Friesen
Schöneberg
Photos: P. Reitsin
Schönhorst
Photos: P. Reitsin
1. **Village School**
   Photo: R. Friesen
   Floor Plan: P. Turkovsky
2. **Granary**
   Photo: R. Friesen
Schönwiese
Photos: P. Reitsin
1. **Julius Siemens House**
   Photos: P. Reitsin
   Floor Plans: P. Turkovsky
2. **Heinrich K. Hübert House**
   Site Plan and Facade Drawing:
   from Zaporoshye State Archives
   Floor Plan: P. Turkovsky
   Photo: P. Reitsin
3. **Tavonuis Pharmacy**
   Upper Photo: from In the Fullness
   of Time, W. Quiring
   Lower Photo: P. Reitsin
   Floor Plan: P. Turkovsky
4. **Abraham A. Koop House**
   Upper Photo, p.141: from In The
   Fullness of Time, W. Quiring
   Lower Photo, p.141: P. Reitsin
   Upper Photos, p.142: P. Reitsin
   Lower Left Photo, p.142: P. Reitsin
   Lower Right Photo, p.142: R.
   Friesen
   Floor Plan: P. Turkovsky
5. **H.A. Niebuhr Mill**
   Photos: P. Reitsin

CREDITS

*Advertisement: from
Mennonitisches Jahrbuch, 1913*
6. **A.J. Koop Factory**
   *Photo, p.144: S. Bizhko
   Upper Photo, p.145: from You
   Have Not Vanished, Like
   Shadows ..., M. Sheveljov
   Lower Photos, p.145: P. Reitsin*
7. **A.J. Koop & Hölker Factory**
   *Site Plan: J. Peters from
   Zaporoshye State Archives
   documents
   Photo: S. Bizhko*
8. **Lepp & Wallmann Factory**
   *Site Plan: J. Peters from
   Zaporoshye State Archives
   documents
   Advertisement: from Christlicher
   Familienkalender 1915*
9. **Hildebrand & Priess Factory**
   *Advertisement: from Christlicher
   Familienkalender 1904*
10. **Johann G. Lepp House**
    *Upper Photo: P. Reitsin
    Lower Photo: S. Bizhko
    Floor Plan: P. Turkovsky*
11. **Abraham P. Lepp House**
    *Upper Photo: from In The Fullness
    of Time, W. Quiring
    Middle Photo: S. Bizhko
    Lower Photo: P. Reitsin
    Floor Plan: P. Turkovsky*
12. **Bär Hospital**
    *Photos: P. Reitsin
    Advertisement: from
    Mennonitisches Jahrbuch, 1911/12
    Floor Plan: P. Turkovsky*
4. **YAZYKOVO COLONY**
   <u>Adelsheim</u>
   Photo: J. Sawatzky
   1. **Village School**
      Photo: J. Sawatzky
   2. **Cemetery**
      Photos: P. Reitsin
   <u>Hochfeld</u>
   Photos: P. Reitsin

1. **Village School**
   Photos: P. Reitsin
2. **A. Rempel House**
   Photo: P. Reitsin
3. **Cemetery**
   Photo: P. Reitsin
<u>Nikolaifeld-Franzfeld</u>
Photos: P. Reitsin
1. **Nikolaifeld Mennonite Church**
   *Photo, p.165: P. Reitsin
   Upper Photo, p.166: from Heritage
   Remembered, G. Lohrenz
   Lower Photo, p.166: P. Reitsin
   Floor Plan: J. Peters from sketch
   by P. Epp and plan by P. Turkovsky*
2. **Nikolaifeld Zentralschule**
   *Photos: P. Reitsin
   Floor Plans: P. Turkovsky*
3. **Teacher's Residence**
   *Photos: P. Reitsin
   Floor Plan: P. Turkovsky*
4. **Teacher's Residence**
   *Photo: P. Reitsin
   Floor Plan: P. Turkovsky*
5. **Barn**
   *Photo: P. Reitsin
   Floor Plan: P. Turkovsky*
6. **Nikolaifeld Village School**
   *Photos: P. Reitsin
   Floor Plan: P. Turkovsky*
7. **Cemetery**
   Photos: P. Reitsin
8. **Store Complex**
   *Photos: P. Reitsin
   Floor Plans: P. Turkovsky*
9. **Franzfeld Village School**
   *Photos: P. Reitsin
   Floor Plan: P. Turkovsky*
10. **Franzfeld Cemetery**
    Photos: P. Reitsin
5. **BARATOW/SCHLACTIN
   COLONIES**
   <u>Gruenfeld</u>
   1. **Gruenfeld Mennonite Church**
      *Upper Photo: from In The Fullness
      of Time, W. Quiring
      Lower Photo: J. Friesen*

CREDITS

2. **Jakob Rempel House**
   Photo: J. Friesen
3. **Johann Froese Factory**
   Photos: J. Friesen
4. **Johann Froese House**
   Photo: J. Friesen

Neu-Chortitza
Photos: J. Friesen

Steinfeld
1. **D. Schapansky House/Barn**
   Photo: J. Friesen
   Plan: J. Peters from plan by J. Friesen
2. **A.P. Martens House/Barn**
   Photos: J. Friesen
   Plan: J. Peters from plan by J. Friesen

6. **MOLOTSCHNA COLONY**
   Alexanderkrone-Lichtefelde
   Photo: R. Friesen
   1. **Alexanderkrone Village School**
      Photo: R. Friesen
   2. **Alexanderkrone Zentralschule**
      Upper Photos: R. Friesen
      Lower Photo: from In The Fullness of Time, W. Quiring
      Floor Plan: J. Peters from plan in For Everything a Season, T.D. Regehr
   3. **Alexanderkrone Mennonite Church**
      Photo: F. Wall
   4. **Doctor's Office/Pharmacy**
      Photos: R. Friesen
   5. **House/Barn**
      Photo: R. Friesen
   6. **Windmill**
      Photos: R. Friesen

Alexandertal
Photo: P. Reitsin
1. **Village School**
   Photo: P. Reitsin
2. **Alexandertal Mennonite Brethren Church**
   Photo: P. Toews

Alexanderwohl
1. **Alexanderwohl Mennonite**

Church
Photo, p.208: R. Friesen
Upper Photo, p.209: J. Schroeder
Lower Photo, p.209: from Mennonite Life, April, 1955
2. **Village School**
   Photos: R. Friesen

Altonau
Photos: R. Friesen
Advertisement: from Christlicher Familienkalendar, 1905

Blumstein
Photos: P. Reitsin

Elisabethtal
Photo: J. Schroeder

Fischau
Photo: P. Reitsin
1. **Village School**
   Photos: R. Friesen

Friedensdorf
Photo: P. Reitsin

Fürstenau
1. **Village School**
   Photos: P. Reitsin
2. **Wilhelm Neufeld House**
   Photo, p.221: P. Reitsin
   Upper Photos, p.222: from H.A. Neufeld
   Lower Photo, p.222: R. Friesen
   Floor Plan: P. Turkovsky

Fürstenwerder
1. **Village School**
   Photo: A. Reger

Gnadenfeld
Left Advertisement: from Christlicher Familienkalendar 1904
Right Advertisement: from Christlicher Familienkalendar 1905
1. **Gnadenfeld Mennonite Church**
   Photo, p.226: from Heritage Remembered, G. Lohrenz
   Upper Photo, p.227: from A. Schmidt
   Lower Photo, p.227: from Heritage Remembered, G. Lohrenz
   Floor Plan: R. Friesen from sketch

CREDITS

by A. Schmidt
2. **Zentralschule**
   Photo, p.228: R. Friesen
   Upper Photo, p.229: from
   Heritage Remembered, G. Lohrenz
   Middle Photo, p.229: from In The
   Fullness of Time, W. Quiring
   Lower Photo, p.229: A. Schmidt
   Floor Plan: J. Peters from sketch
   by A. Schmidt
3. **Johann Rempel House**
   Upper Photos: R. Friesen
   Lower Photo: A. Schmidt
4. **Volost**
   Upper Photo: from Heritage
   Remembered, G. Lohrenz
   Lower Photo: R. Friesen
5. **Post Office**
   Upper Photo: R. Friesen
   Lower Photo: I. Wiebe
6. **Doctor's Clinic**
   Upper Photo: I. Wiebe
   Lower Photo: from A. Schmidt
7. **Klaas Heide House**
   Photo: A. Schmidt

Halbstadt-Muntau
Photos: P. Reitsin
Left Advertisement, p.236: from
Christlicher Familienkalender 1915
Right Advertisement, p.236: from
Christlicher Familienkalender 1905
Advertisement, p.237: from
Christlicher Familienkalender 1915
1. **H.H. Willms Mill**
   Upper Photo: from Heritage
   Remembered, G. Lohrenz
   Lower Photo: R. Friesen
2. **Hermann Neufeld Brewery**
   Upper Photo: R. Friesen
   Lower Photo: from H. Enns
   Advertisement: from Christlicher
   Familienkalender 1904
3. **David Willms House**
   Upper Photo: J. Urry
   Lower Left Photo: P. Reitsin
   Lower Right Photo: R. Friesen

Floor Plan: P. Turkovsky
4. **Heinrich Schroeder Enterprise**
   Photo: R. Friesen
   Advertisements: from Christlicher
   Familienkalender 1905
5. **Kreditanstalt**
   Upper Photo: R. Friesen
   Middle Photo: from In The
   Fullness of Time, W. Quiring
   Lower Photos: R. Friesen
   Floor Plan: P. Turkovsky
6. **Halbstadt Zentralschule**
   Floor Plan: P. Turkovsky
   Photo, p.243: from Heritage
   Remembered, G. Lohrenz
   Upper Photo, p.244: P. Reitsin
   Lower Photos, p.244: R. Friesen
7. **Volost**
   Upper Photo: from Heritage
   Remembered, G. Lohrenz
   Lower Photo: P. Reitsin
   Floor Plan: P. Turkovsky
8. **Diakonissenheim "Morija"**
   Upper Photo: from In The Fullness
   of Time, W. Quiring
   Lower Photo: R. Friesen
9. **Diakonissenheim "Morija"**
   Upper Photo: from In The Fullness
   of Time, W. Quiring
   Lower Photo: P. Reitsin
10. **Halbstadt Mädchenschule**
    Upper Left Photo: from In The
    Fullness of Time, W. Quiring
    Other Photos: R. Friesen
11. **Heinrich Willms House**
    Upper Photo, p.249: R. Friesen
    Lower Photo, p.249: from H.
    Quiring
    Photos, p.250: R. Friesen
    Floor Plans: P. Turkovsky
12. **Franz & Schröder Factory**
    Photo: J. Urry
    Advertisement: from
    Mennonitisches Jahrbuch, 1903
13. **Muntau Hospital**
    Photo, p.252: from In The Fullness

CREDITS

of Time, W. Quiring
  Upper Photo, p.253: from In The
  Fullness of Time, W. Quiring
  Middle Photo, p.253: from
  Heritage Remembered, G. Lohrenz
  Lower Photo, p.253: P. Reitsin

Hamberg
1. **Village School**
  Photo: R. Friesen

Juschanlee
Photos, p.256: J. Urry
Photos, p.257: J. Urry
Site Plan: J. Peters from sketch by J. Urry

Kuruschan
1. **Altenheim Kuruschan**
  Photos: from Heritage Remembered, G. Lohrenz
2. **Wilhelm Neufeld House/Barn**
  Photo: F. Wall

Ladekopp
1. **Village School**
  Photos: P. Reitsin

Landskrone
Photo: P. Reitsin
1. **Landskrone Mennonite Church**
  Photos: R. Friesen
  Floor Plan: J. Peters from State Archives of Simpferopol documents
  Drawings: from State Archives of Simpferopol

Lichtenau
Photos: P. Reitsin
1. **Lichtenau Train Station**
  Photo: W. Unger

Liebenau
Photos: P. Reitsin
1. **Jakob Franz Factory**
  Photos: P. Reitsin
  Advertisement: from Christlicher Familienkalendar, 1915

Münsterberg
Photos: P. Reitsin

Ohrloff-Tiege
1. **Ohrloff Church Building**
  Upper Photo: from In The Fullness of Time, W. Quiring
  Lower Photo: R. Friesen
2. **Ohrloff Zentralschule**
  Photo: from Mennonite Heritage Centre Archives
  Drawings: from State Archives of Simpferopol
3. **Ohrloff Hospital**
  Photo: from Heritage Remembered, G. Lohrenz
4. **Tiege M.B. Church**
  Photo: from In The Fullness of Time, W. Quiring
  Drawings: from State Archives of Simpferopol
  Floor Plan: J. Peters from State Archives of Simpferopol documents
5. **Marientaubstummenschule**
  Upper Photo, p.280: from Heritage Remembered, G. Lohrenz
  Lower Photo, p.280: J. Urry
  Upper Photo, p.281: from In The Fullness of Time, W. Quiring
  Middle Photo, p.281: from Heritage Remembered, G. Lohrenz
  Lower Photo, p.281: R. Friesen
6. **Ohrloff Cemetery**
  Photos: P. Reitsin

Petershagen
1. **Petershagen Mennonite Church**
  Upper Left Photo: from In The Fullness of Time, W. Quiring
  Other Photos: R. Friesen

Rückenau
1. **Rückenau M.B. Church**
  Upper Left Photo: from Heritage Remembered, G. Lohrenz
  Other Photos: R. Friesen

Rudnerweide
  Left Photo, p.287: P. Reitsin
  Right Photo, p.287: R. Friesen
  Photo, p.288: R. Friesen
1. **Rudernweide Mennonite Church**
  Photo: from Heritage Remembered, G. Lohrenz
  Floor Plans: R. Friesen from conversations with H.J. Friesen and

CREDITS

plans prepared by V. Kliewer
Schönsee
Photo: P. Reitsin
1. **Schönsee Mennonite Church**
   Upper Photo, p.292: R. Friesen
   Lower Photo, p.292: from In The
   Fullness of Time, W. Quiring
   Upper Photo, p.293: R. Friesen
   Lower Photo, p.293: from In The
   Fullness of Time, W. Quiring
   Floor Plan: J. Peters from State
   Archives of Simpferopol documents
   Drawings: from State Archives of
   Simpferopol
Steinbach
Upper Photo, p.294: P. Reitsin
Lower Photo, p.294: from I. Wiebe
Site Plan: R. Friesen from sketch by I.
Wiebe
   Jakob Dick House
   Photo, p.295: from In The Fullness
   of Time, W. Quiring
   Photos, p.296: P. Reitsin
   Jakob Dick Barn
   Photo, p.296: P. Reitsin
   Upper Photo, p.297: from
   Heritage Remembered, G. Lohrenz
   Lower Photo, p.297: P. Reitsin
   Nikolai Schmidt House
   Upper Photo: from I. Wiebe
   Lower Photo: P. Reitsin
   Garage
   Upper Photo: from I. Wiebe
   Lower Photo: P. Reitsin
Waldheim
Photo: P. Reitsin
1. **Waldheim Hospital**
   Photo: R. Friesen
2. **J.J. Neufeld Factory**
   Photo: from Heritage
   Remembered, G. Lohrenz
   Site Plan: J. Peters from State
   Archives of Simpferopol documents
   Advertisement: from Christlicher
   Familienkalendar, 1915

7. **ZAGRADOVKA COLONY**
Nikolaifeld
Photos: R. Friesen
1. **Nikolaifeld Mennonite Church**
   Photo, p.310: R. Friesen
   Upper Photo, p.311: R. Friesen
   Lower Photo, p.311: from Heritage
   Remembered, G. Lohrenz
Orloff
Photos: R. Friesen
1. **Allianz Church**
   Upper Left Photo: R. Friesen
   Upper Right Photo: K. Boldt
   Lower Photo: from Heritage
   Remembered, G. Lohrenz
Tiege
Photo: R. Friesen
1. **Village School**
   Photos: R. Friesen
2. **Store**
   Photos: R. Friesen
3. **Tiege Hospital**
   Photo: R. Friesen
8. **CRIMEA**
Karassan
Photos: F. Wall
1. **Karassan Mennonite Church**
   Photos: F. Wall
2. **Karassan Zentralschule**
   Upper Photo, p.324: F. Wall
   Lower Photo, p.324: from In The
   Fullness of Time, W. Quiring
   Photos, p.325: G. Dyck
3. **Karassan Hospital**
   Photos: F. Wall
Spat
Photo: R. Friesen
1. **Spat Zentralschule**
   Upper Photo: R. Friesen
   Lower Photo: from In The Fullness
   of Time, W. Quiring
Tchongraw
Photo: W. Unger
1. **Gerhardt Wiens House**
   Photos: W. Unger

INDEX

INDEX

350

INDEX

INDEX

INDEX